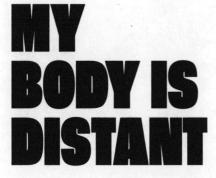

MY
BODY IS
DISTANT

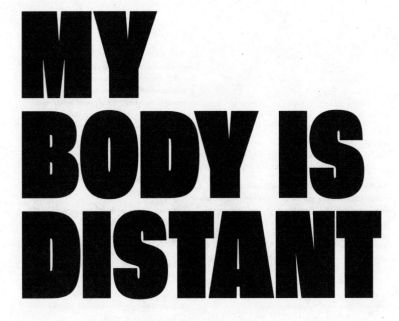

MY BODY IS DISTANT

A MEMOIR

PAIGE MAYLOTT_

Editor for the Press: Jen Sookfong Lee
Copy editor: Rachel Ironstone
Cover design and artwork: Ian Sullivan

This book is memoir. It reflects the author's present
recollections of experiences over time. Some names
and characteristics have been changed, some events
have been compressed, and some dialogue has been
recreated. All name usage of private individuals is
used with permission, and where permission was not
sought, all names have been changed.

LIBRARY AND ARCHIVES CANADA CATALOGUING
IN PUBLICATION

Title: My body is distant : a memoir / Paige Maylott.

Names: Maylott, Paige, author.

Identifiers: Canadiana (print) 20230237207 |
Canadiana (ebook) 2023023724X

ISBN 978-1-77041-691-8 (softcover)
ISBN 978-1-77852-188-1 (ePub)
ISBN 978-1-77852-189-8 (PDF)
ISBN 978-1-77852-190-4 (Kindle)

Subjects: LCSH: Maylott, Paige. | LCSH:
Transgender people—Canada—Biography. |
LCGFT: Autobiographies.

Classification: LCC HQ77.8.M385 A3 2023 | DDC
306.76/8092—dc23

This book is funded in part by the Government of Canada. *Ce livre est financé en partie par le gouvernement du Canada.*
We acknowledge the support of the Canada Council for the Arts. *Nous remercions le Conseil des arts du Canada de son*
soutien. We acknowledge the funding support of the Ontario Arts Council (OAC), an agency of the Government of
Ontario. We also acknowledge the support of the Government of Ontario through the Ontario Book Publishing Tax
Credit, and through Ontario Creates.

PRINTED AND BOUND IN CANADA   PRINTING: MARQUIS   5   4   3   2   1

MIX
Paper from
responsible sources
FSC® C103567
www.fsc.org

This book is dedicated to Sarah Brophy,
whose wisdom, compassion, and endless supply of
tissues equipped me with the tools to create
something beautiful in a time of despair.

Contents

Press  to Skip
Introduction

Memory is a slippery and selective thing. To provide an example, think back to your earliest memory. One of mine was a hot summer day in 1979 — I would have been four years old, and my sister, Lana, only two. The memory begins with us running barefoot across cool, shaded grass behind the turn-of-the-century schoolhouse our father skillfully converted into our childhood home. As I ran and Lana chased after me, grasshoppers sprang from the grass, cicadas screeched in the trees, and the neighbour's cows grazed in fields on the other side of the electrified fences which surrounded our property.

Already, I have fabricated details to draw you into my story. While I know there were often cows in the fields which surrounded our house, and that cicadas often screeched in the trees, I don't remember how warm it really was, and I can't recall whether cicadas were out or if there were cows nearby that day. I have only included these pseudo-facts to pave the way to a moment that stuck with and still shapes who I am forty-something years later.

I remember we found ourselves in the sun-warmed, wood-scented back shed, where we discovered my father's tackle box.

We pried open squeaky metal clasps, and inside we found the most incredible fishing lures. To our inexperienced eyes they looked uncannily like actual fish, with shining scales drawn with metallic paints, and gleaming bright eyes — some were hinged in the middle to mimic realistic swimming, I assume. Lana grabbed as many fish as she could, somehow avoiding hooking herself. She looked up at me, her body vibrating with excitement as she said, "Let's see them swim."

I agreed and gathered the rest.

We ran out of the shed and across the lawn holding handfuls of jingling fish. I followed Lana to a deep circular pond, ringed with flagstones, which my father had dug in the middle of our yard. Lana wasted no time as she climbed the stones and threw her handfuls into the water.

When they struck the surface, years of dust splashed away, and the lures came to life. The tiny fishes twisted and flipped just below the surface. Their chromatic scales flashed in a dizzying rainbow of colours before they sank. Each twinkled in the sunlight one last time, as if giving thanks, before they disappeared into the murky depths of the pond.

"Did you see that?" Lana asked. "Throw yours."

I recognized the potential consequences of tossing away my father's prized lures, but I couldn't help myself. I wanted to see those colours.

I needed to see if they truly could come to life again.

I tossed mine, alone and in twos, at Lana's impatient urging. We watched with amazement as they rolled and flashed in the murky water as they sank, leaving us with vivid memories and regret.

For me, memory is a lot like my fish story.

I seem to remember only moments which particularly delight or trouble me, and sometimes the ones that flash brightest are the ones that do both. I like to think my brightest memories are also the ones which have taught me valuable lessons, like how throwing away antique heirloom fishing lures can make your father cry.

This memoir is, therefore, imperfect. It will contain details as true as I can remember them, and I am certain some recollections will be incorrect or incomplete. All I can promise is that the memories in these pages are, to the best of my knowledge, influential moments of my life which have shaped me into the woman I am today.

I hope you graciously accept that possibility as I recall these stories with you. By reading them, you cause these memories to flash and sparkle once more. While not every recollection in this memoir shines, I believe it is important to include the difficult parts, and the ones that beacon on regrettable decisions, because if we don't record these multicoloured memories as accurately as possible, they might sink into the darkness and be lost forever.

What Isn't This Book About?

If you are coming to *My Body Is Distant* in search of a book that thoroughly explores gender or cancer, you are looking in the wrong place. While there are depictions of both elements, I prefer to think of this story as a tribute to those who seek love when they feel unlovable, the things we do to accept the parts of us we cannot change, and the complicated, selfish choices we sometimes make to protect our bodies and hearts.

As is the way of things when we make selfish decisions, too often others are hurt. However, when the threat has passed and the smoke clears, we count the bodies and discover we have become an unintentional casualty too.

Content Warning

Spoilers Ahead.

This memoir contains true events of homophobia and transphobia (both microaggressions and overt threats), though I am certain some individuals may perceive other unintentional examples. There are also graphic scenes of cancer, suicidal fixation, infidelity, surgery, and abuse of power by medical professionals, mental health professionals, and authority figures.

Finally, there are sexual situations that can be perceived as quite graphic. While all sexual acts described were consensual by all parties, some are awkward, and distracted, and dysphoric, and sometimes just uncomfortable, as non-fictitious sex can sometimes be.

On Language

In my effort to be honest and truthful, I have tried not to revise the language of my memories. Except for a few *them*s, *they*s, and *their*s, I have therefore maintained the flawed and sometimes regrettable language I used. Some included terms are not contemporary, and certainly more will be exposed as problematic in years to come. That said, I have avoided using the terms FTM and MTF when possible, as I loathe the context and imagery they evoke, no matter the date I am recalling, and it is my book, after all.

On Who Is Named, and Why

Both my given deadname and current legal name are accurate. I realize critics might weaponize my old name. However, after writing this memoir, I can't foresee anything more damning they could unearth than the confessions I disclose in these pages. And, as evidenced by websites which attack trans women online, such information can be easily obtained by those who seek it out.

While I won't confide which other names are real or not, I will say that every real name used in this book was included with permission. Each person I contacted was given the choice to either keep their name or choose a pseudonym. I have changed the names of those with whom I could not connect, or those whom I chose not to — to protect the (not so) innocent.

On "Flow"

In my vision for this memoir, I wanted the concept of flow to feature prominently.

The scientific definition of flow, as shown in the *Oxford English Dictionary*, gives us a hint of how the word developed etymologically:

> flow (n.) A gradual deformation of a solid (as rock or a metal) under stress in which it suffers a per- manent change in shape without fracture or loss of cohesion between its parts.

While using this to define the process of gender transition holds metaphorical merit, it isn't accurate for my purpose. For that, we must refer to Hungarian-American psychologist Mihaly Robert Csikszentmihalyi's concept of the "psychology of optimal experience"; I'll paraphrase his definition of flow as:

> The mental state where a person performing an activity is fully immersed in a feeling of energized focus, full involvement, and enjoyment in the activity's process. *Being so involved in said activity that nothing else seems to matter.*

That last sentence is integral to understanding what flow means. Flow isn't distraction, or being empty-headed, but a type of Zen state where one is wholly entirely focused on the enjoyment of an activity.

Imagine a record needle impossibly balancing on the peak above musical grooves. Then imagine that needle falling into one of those grooves, finding its home, and your favorite song plays all around you.

Flow feels just like that.

In your groove, even if nowhere else, you belong. You would rather be here, doing this thing you love, than be anywhere and doing anything else in the world.

Flow is life at its most fulfilling.

Flow is love at its deepest.

Flow is home at its safest.

Perhaps, like me, you have found your flow in virtual worlds. Or maybe, one day, you can tell me what flow means to you.

0

Dreams

I was born a second time in a supply closet that glowed electric blue. My first birth, the regular kind, happened nine and a half years before this and isn't worth mentioning other than to say both times I was swaddled in the same colour.

Three days earlier, the principal assembled our class to unveil a machine he called "educational and efficient." I pushed through the crowd and wedged myself against the doorframe for a better look. As blue radiation bathed my face, I knew that computer was something greater than circuits and floppy disks. I needed it more than Michael Jackson's iconic red jacket, a Nintendo, or even an Omnibot — it wasn't just a distraction. It was my ticket out of here.

The principal invited students to give the computer a try. The school bully, Todd, and some red-headed kid with a moustache forced their way into the only two seats. While the principal was distracted teaching us how to load up the approved educational games, the red-headed kid withdrew a thin black disk from the desk and slid it into the drive. He expertly tapped commands onto the screen and soon the two bullies were no longer with us as they disappeared into an invisible world within the computer monitor.

The boys' body language spoke volumes. Their eyes widened, their shoulders relaxed, and as one they leaned toward the screen. They stopped answering questions from the crowd and even ignored the principal when he asked what game they were playing. They were swept away by something I couldn't yet comprehend. I jostled against the other kids to position myself for a better look, but on the screen were only slowly scrolling words.

Todd said, "But if I put the candle in the basket and lower it, the light goes out."

"Then light a match," said his friend.

"I only have two left, and my lantern ran out of oil in the maze. I'll take my chances."

Todd typed a short line and clacked the return key. A block of neon words appeared. The boys threw their hands in the air and shouted furiously at the screen.

As I looked over Todd's shoulder, I wondered, How did they know what to do? There were no blocks to break and no animated characters. How could they be so invested? So excited about simple words? It was as if they were interacting with a world beyond our sight and reality, and since then I haven't been able to stop thinking about it.

On this, the day of my second birth, bulky Scotch tape holds my glasses together and scratches my cheek, so I pull them off and flatten the sharper edges. Mrs. Lampman taps the last digits of a math problem on the chalkboard. Across the room, Kevin stares. He grips his pencil in a meaty fist and shakes his head at me. It's not enough that he tripped me on the ice and broke my glasses, but now rumour has it that both he and his older brother Todd are planning to kill me for telling.

My stomach twists into knots thinking about my no-win situation. If I say I'm sick, Mom will pick me up, but they'll just get me tomorrow. And if I stay, I'm dead next recess. My only alternative is to attempt my plan, and it better work.

I open my notebook and write out the equation. Mrs. Lampman points her chalk at the class and says, "Once you complete these problems, you are welcome to do whatever you like until lunchtime. You may begin."

Pencil scratches echo through the class, accented with confused groans. Mrs. Lampman circles the room, glancing at notebooks as she passes. "You can draw, review your answers, or —"

I slap my pencil onto the desk and thrust my hand into the air so fast I skew my glasses and the broken arm falls into my lap. When I pull the rest of the frames off my face, the room smears into obscurity. I replace the arm and pinch the surrounding tape. It will probably be another month before Dad can buy me a replacement pair. That also means less for Christmas.

Kevin is such an asshole.

Mrs. Lampman clops over on brilliant white heels, a perfumed cloud of flowers washing over me a moment after she arrives. She crouches, knees clicking, and supports herself with a hand on my desk. Her painted nails are as white as her shoes. "Did you have a question, Paul?"

The question I want to ask is, How do I talk you into letting me skip recess from now until forever so I don't get my glasses all the way smashed in, but I say, "No, Mrs. Lampman, I'm finished."

"Done?" Mrs. Lampman scoffs and spins my notebook. She traces through math problems with the tip of a manicured nail. "This is excellent. You can draw, or rest your head if you like?"

Before she escapes to her desk, I hurriedly ask, "Can I study on the school computer?"

She leans in conspiratorially. "Are you allowed to?"

"We're allowed to play math games. Nobody uses it right now."

Mrs. Lampman eyes the clock, then her desk and her waiting novel. "I don't see any reason to say no, you seem to have all the right —"

But I'm already hurrying toward the door, ignoring Kevin's confused glare, past inquisitive faces glancing up from half-finished work with surprised but unspoken *why are you allowed to leave* expressions.

"— answers." Mrs. Lampman calls after me, "Just until lunchtime!"

I flash a bucktoothed smile. "Thank you, Mrs. Lampman." I close the door and speed walk, rubber sneaker soles squeaking down the empty hall.

Just until lunch. Thirty minutes isn't enough. I pump my arms, stride around the corner, and duck into the supply room beside the principal's office. The room is stocked with metal-edged rulers, chalk erasers, reams of paper, and reeks of ammonia from the hand-cranked photocopy press. But, tucked against the back wall dwells, in all its glory, the school's Commodore 64.

Encased in grey, brown, and black to show it means business, the computer rests upon a repurposed wooden teacher's desk and is lit from above by a dim hanging bulb. Word on the playground is that the C64 was a donation from some kid's rich farmer parents when their family upgraded to the new Macintosh. According to the clock, this badass machine is mine for the next twenty-six minutes and forty-three seconds.

Someone left the monitor on, and its intoxicating light floods the room with electrifying promise. I pass through the doorway — the hum of the machine resonates within the small room. Wiping sweaty palms against my pants, I approach the desk with reverence and drag back the heavy wooden chair to sit. The cursor on the screen flashes, waiting for me to interact, to allow it to take me somewhere else — hopefully somewhere things make sense and bullies can't find me.

Laminated instructions for starting *Math Blaster!* rest in front of the tape drive, but I have no intention of playing that. I tug open drawers and find instruction manuals and old pens, a wayward key, some gum wrappers, and several heavy data cassettes. Near the back, hidden inside the Commodore manual, is the slender black floppy disk I saw the boys insert. Decorated upon the sleeve are swords, an egg, and a single word: *ZORK*.

I slide the paper-thin diskette into my shaking hand, insert it into the disk drive, and lock it in place. The screen reads

`READY.`

After a few failed commands, I type

`LOAD "$",8`

I press RETURN and the computer rewards my success with crunches and whirs.

`SEARCHING FOR $`

`LOADING`

`READY.`

I refer to the laminated sheet and type

`LIST`

The machine crunches again, and a directory of the disk's contents appears. I spot what I'm searching for.

`84 "ZORK" PRG`

I hunt and peck one letter at a time with my fingertips.

`LOAD "ZORK",8,1`

The screen flashes, goes dark, and for a moment I think I've somehow broken the computer. Then the disk hums to life, vibrating the desk, and deep within the Commodore's unknowable guts, something buzzes, whirs, and text appears on the screen. The game begins with no fanfare, no accreditation, only two sentences written in the second person imperative.

`You are standing in an open field west of a white house, with a boarded front door.`

`There is a small mailbox here.`

A point of light expands from the centre of the screen and explodes in a blinding flash of blue. I find myself standing in a vast open field. My eyes widen, my shoulders relax. Gooseflesh pimples my skin. I lean forward and allow *Zork* to take me away.

Sunlight dapples through fluffy grey clouds and beams warmly upon my face. Other than the repeated throaty cry of some unknown tropical bird, the only sound comes from the hiss of wind blowing through hip-high grass. Wheat-tipped and fragrant, it sways in hypnotizing waves across the valley like a yellow-green ocean. Jutting from this swaying sea are massive grey flagstones that were, perhaps once, part of long-forgotten buildings.

Ringing the field are unnaturally tall and densely packed red-wood trees. Impossible to miss, however, is a once-impressive two-storey home left in this field to rot. There are no roads, no gate, and no driveway. It's as if something plucked this house out of another world and placed it here. Placed here, like me.

From deep within the forest, something inhuman screeches. As the shrill cry echoes across the field, it changes to a ringing bell. Startled birds of the forest take flight, amassing into a dark cloud overhead, which throws the valley into shadow. The birds' squawk-ing resembles laughter and their beating wings like thundering footsteps. As the last echoes of the birds fade into the distance, I rise from the safety of the grass and turn my attention to the house.

I remove a pamphlet poking out of the mailbox. On the cover *ZORK* is written in an ominous bricked font, and within the folds are drawings of lean, hungry thieves, ancient maps, and something with glowing eyes and sharp teeth lurking in the dark.

Leaving the boarded-up house behind, I enter the mysterious forest and fill my lungs with scents of cedar and damp earth. High above, a bird sings — and, while beautiful, buried in its song are notes of melancholy. In my search for the bird, I glimpse some-thing glimmering within an empty nest.

I climb the tree until I reach the thin swaying branches near the canopy to discover an egg decorated in mother-of-pearl, inlaid with fine gold, and encrusted with green and turquoise gemstones. Unlike normal eggs, this one has a hinge and a lock. As I stare at it, overwhelmed by the tantalizing promise of treasure within, I hear a muffled voice from inside. I press the egg to my ear and a girl whispers, "I only open when you break yourself."

I decide it's better to bury it in my backpack until I'm better equipped to decipher it, and yet the egg's riddle reverberates like a dreaded prophecy.

I shimmy down the tree and continue along the path. It dips into a valley and the trees crowd close, forming a shadowy tunnel. I forge into the darkness and the chorus of forest life fades away, as if the world drew a breath and held it.

A woman steps out of the darkness — her face obscured by long, stringy hair.

In a smoky, deep voice, she says, "Go no further, child, or I will eat you." Through the mass of hair, a dark void of a mouth opens, and she unleashes a terrifying shriek that somehow morphs to a ringing school bell. The same terrible sound from the field, but so close now that I cower and cup my ears.

When I recover, I find the woman crouched over me — her face an inch from mine. Deep within the core of my being I know I am doomed, yet I gather the courage to ask one question before she kills me. "Who are you?"

Her shoulders shake with silent laughter. As she looms over me, I notice that under the hair she wears glasses, like me, but her lips are curled into a cruel crimson smile, teeth filed sharp. I recognize the eyes and teeth from the pamphlet — this monster is a grue.

She asks, "Don't you recognize me?"

"Hey, kid," someone shouts behind me. "Are you even supposed to be in here?"

I turn to find Kevin and his older brother Todd in the doorway. I strain my distracted brain to think of a way to escape the room intact. "The teacher said I could play until after lunch," I lie.

Todd asks, "Hey, Kev, is this the tattletale? The one who makes those stupid paper dolls?"

I stare at his feet. "They're not stupid. They're video game characters."

"Yeah, that's him," Kevin says.

Todd says, "Lunch was hours ago, faggot. Get lost."

The clock confirms it. Two fifteen? I somehow played not only through the lunch bell but into last recess.

Glowing text flashes upon the screen:

```
Oh, no! You walked into the slavering fangs of a
lurking grue.

As you take your last breath, you feel relieved
of your burdens. The feeling passes as you find
yourself before the gates of Hell, where the spirits
jeer at you and deny you entry.
```

I died?

"You're playing *Zork*? You better not have saved over my game!" Todd lunges for me, but I throw myself out of the chair and land on the floor.

I clamber to my feet and shove Kevin against the doorframe to escape. I sprint down the hallway and slam my hands on the door's release bar, stumbling into the crowded schoolyard and the frigid chill of mid-December. I take a few hesitant steps toward the shark-like teacher patrolling the basketball court with a dozen pilotfish children trailing behind her for safety.

Kevin and Todd hang in the doorway for a moment before Todd disappears into the school. Kevin lingers, waving and smiling in a creepy way that reminds me of the Grue before he follows his brother. I take slow, deep breaths, puffing clouds into the chilly air.

Crouching against the trunk of a tree nearby, I push my hands out of my sweater sleeves and dig into my pocket. I unfold a creased and crinkled paper cut-out of Q*bert. Holding him at arm's length, I pretend his birdlike legs leap from branch to swaying, skeletal, leafless branch — but the magic is no longer there. I created these paper dolls as a compromise until my parents bought me an Atari or a Nintendo, but now I can't stop thinking about the fantastical world I had just glimpsed hidden inside that magical box within the supply closet.

I let Q*bert go, and the wind catches him, tugging him from my fingers, and he flips end over end, catching here and there in the brittle brown grass before landing in a puddle of melted snow. I watch as he floats — the paper turning translucent before sinking below the surface. A squealing winter gale blows against the back of my ears. I hug my knees and wait out the last minutes of recess.

Part 1

Connect

◣ i ◢

Kind of a Girl

2009 — Twenty-three years, a medical crisis, and a bankruptcy later

"You can't make me dance," I shout at Sapphire over pounding club music.

Saph tries to pull me onto my feet — but there's no contest between my fat ass and her scrawny arms. I'm nowhere near as adventurous as Saph, despite my outfit, and much happier after she gives up. I retreat into the cave-like corner of the booth, close my eyes, and enjoy the thumping bass buzzing the leather straps and jingling chrome buckles that barely qualify as my clothing.

"You're just going to sit there?" Saph asks. She's one of those enviable wasp-waisted women who appears perpetually eighteen, though her deep smoker's voice makes me think she's much older — not that she'd ever admit it. Tonight, she's pulled her thick blonde hair through the cowl of her electric blue catsuit and into a dommy topknot, which admittedly looks damn hot.

It's not that I'm shy. You don't win a blue ribbon for "Best Ass" at a dance club for sitting and drinking beer. The thing is, others only tolerate people like me as a fetish — and while this might be a BDSM club, what I am teeters on the edge of acceptable tolerance.

Toff is the tamest of our group and often our voice of reason. She's also probably the most conservatively dressed in her sequined club dress. But even she decisively puts down her drink and grabs my free hand. Together, she and Saph pull me onto my feet and drag me toward the stage.

"No, Toff, don't," I plead as I abandon my drink on a passing table before it spills. I drop my weight, digging in my heels, and hope they'll give up.

Toff shouts, "You're the one who said you're bored."

They drag me relentlessly toward the stage. The scene draws the attention of two voyeurs who stop swiping at their phones and move closer for the impending show. I give up and obediently clop along on platform boots, allowing them to lead me.

Saph leaves me with Toff, and I lose her in the glare of blinding stage lights.

Toff leans close, and her curly red hair tickles my face. "Listen, girl," she says, "what's the point of showing up in that cute outfit and shoving your tail in our faces if you're not willing to shake it?"

I rarely enjoy being held accountable for my playful nature, but I'm warming to the thought of dancing.

The track abruptly cuts, exposing scattered conversations which quickly fade to whispers. From the DJ booth, Saph waves to draw our attention and holds her hands in the shape of a heart.

Over the speakers, a breathy female DJ says, "This one goes out to our sexy bunny girl, Lydia, on her birthday. Show us what you got, girl."

A powerful techno beat thumps the stage, buzzes through my thigh-high platform boots, and vibrates my bare ass cheeks around my leather G-string. With each bass thump, the buckles that secure the six strategically placed belts on my outfit jingle.

The soft leather buzzes against my skin. One belt is clasped around my throat as a choker, one encircles my chest and barely hides my nipples, one is wrapped under my heavy breasts for added support, and another ties my waist. Two bind my thighs like garters, and two skinny straps tenuously hold the whole outfit together.

This close to the speakers the music is both deafening and orgasmic. Woofers throb to the beat, and the waves of sound flutter my hair and buffet my long white ears. Above my award-winning ass, my pointed fluff of a tail unconsciously twitches in time with the beat. Then over the speakers, Benny Benassi's robotic voice sings the titular line, "Who's Your Daddy?"

As the song blasts around me, I grin despite myself, flashing a hint of bucked front teeth. Toff smiles and clops down the steps to join Saph. I close my eyes and allow the pounding, deafening music to soak into my body. My heartbeat syncs, and I allow myself to forget the eyes upon me.

I strut toward centre stage and wrap my fingers around the pole. Catwalk stepping around it, I curl a leg around the cool metal and tug myself off the ground, twirling to shrill whistles from the crowd. I dance around the pole then bend and swing my ass to the audience, dipping my head low until my hair sweeps the stage. I drag a handful of hair and lop ears out of my face and body roll.

Before I know it, the song is fading into a new track. I blow kisses to the audience and clop my way toward the stage stairs before I'm drawn into an unintentional encore.

Saph jams her fingers in her mouth and wolf whistles above the dying tune. "Take it off!"

I shake my head and mouth "No way." My body buzzes with a cocktail of alcohol, adrenaline, and dopamine, and my face hurts from smiling. As I navigate the shadowy stairs, a Neo-looking guy in a trench coat stuffs a ten into my tip jar.

Neo raises his scotch. "I'm not usually into furries, but you're gorgeous."

"Hey, thanks," I say.

"And you've got a cute voice."

My smile melts as I spiral into panic. My voice? Why is it cute? Too high? Does it not sound normal? I grab the jar and hurry back to the safety of our booth. As I dive into my chair and grab the waiting fresh drink, I peripherally register Saph and Toff piling praise on me for my performance. I smile and nod in distracted appreciation. None of that matters right now.

People are either into furries like me, or they aren't. But, if my voice gets clocked, that's a more complicated issue. "Cute voice," he said. *Cute.* My pitch is definitely too high. I knew I shouldn't have fucked with the settings.

Saph stares expectantly at me.

I ask, "Did you say something?"

Saph asks, "Is that your phone ringing?"

I glance at the lit cellphone buzzing on my desk. The realization of an incoming call tears me out of the club, out of my head, back to my office chair and the real world. I am left dizzy, disoriented, and unsure how to negotiate reality.

I wonder how long it rang before I noticed. It's probably Karen.

In my rush to answer, my knuckles crack against a half-drunk mug of yesterday's cold tea, and it tumbles over my keyboard and into my lap.

"Shit!" I shout and leap out of the chair, but I forget how short my headset cord is, and it violently yanks at the side of my head, painfully tugging my headphones onto my face and skewing my glasses.

I wrestle the headset off as tea drips down my legs. I fumble with the mute switch and grab the phone. A wave of guilt and shame floods over me as I recognize the number. I reassure myself that Karen can't see my computer screen or know that I'm secretly a hyper-sexualized anthropomorphic rabbit wearing a bondage outfit in a virtual BDSM club.

I unlock the phone. "Hi Kitty," I say as calmly as someone can who has tea dripping into their slippers.

"Did I wake you?" Karen sounds tired. She coordinates cranky contractors with big pickup trucks and even bigger egos.

"No, I'm just playing a game," I lie as I turn my keyboard upside down, shaking droplets of tea onto the floor and hoping it doesn't short-circuit.

There is a drawn-out moment of silence before she answers. "Okay, I'm going to be late. There's a shipment coming, and they need me. I know you had your chemo treatment this morning, but can you fend for yourself?"

"Yeah, of course," I say, but I'm distracted by a musical *ding* and lines of text appearing in the club chat.

Toff says: Is that Lydia talking? She sounds weird.

My heart sinks as a wave of nausea chokes me.

Saph says: It sounds like she's using voice software. Hear that reverberation when she shuffles around? I think I heard a cat. It sounded . . . wrong.

I realize that maybe I didn't push the mute switch all the way over.

"Paul, are you there?"

I feed the headset cord toward me and thumb the mute switch, though the damage is already done. "I'm here. Sorry, my brain is still cloudy from the chemo." Which probably is true, and the reason why I just fucked up.

Karen feigns a chuckle, the edge of annoyance in her tone softening. "Okay, could you take the chicken out of the freezer to thaw? What's that music?"

I turn down the volume before someone speaks on the club's open voice channel and Karen asks questions I'm not prepared to answer. I say, "Oh, dance music. It cheers me up."

Toff says: I guess we know why it took "her" so long to voice chat now.

"I didn't know you were into stuff like that," Karen says.

Instead of suggesting she has no idea what I'm into, I ask, "Huh?"

"It doesn't matter. You should turn off that game and rest."

Of course, leaving the club now would be social suicide and only confirm the suspicions that Toff already has. I ask, "How can I rest? I'm too excited about that cake you promised."

Karen goes quiet — a pencil scratches on paper.

Last year she bought me dollar store toys and gave me a sweet, but ultimately unfulfilled, series of IOU notes. I've never figured out what busies her head so completely to make her the serial procrastinator that she is, but if you love Karen, you simply need to accept she forgets about you sometimes.

It's been five years since I met her at a medieval LARP. Someone told a joke, and I laughed at the same time she threw a spell packet. Against all odds, the tiny birdseed-stuffed packet sailed across the room, into my mouth, and lodged in my throat. I had already been aware of the dark-haired, olive-skinned girl who was part firefighter, part dancer, and geeky enough to spend her weekends with the rest of us sweaty fantasy nuts. So, when this basically perfect woman pinned me down, dug the packet out of my mouth, cradled me as I coughed, then laughed with me as our eyes met, we both just knew.

"About the cake . . ." Karen says. "They screwed up the one I ordered. I'll pick up a cupcake for now. Is that okay?"

"That's fine. I love you."

"Love you too. Go rest."

I hang up but double-check to ensure the phone is off before slipping the cushioned headphones back over my ears. The club music thumps, but the chatter has stopped. Toff and Saph sit in silence next to each other, probably whispering privately.

I tab to my voice-changing program and dial the pitch down a few levels then say, "Sorry everyone, I had to take that call."

It takes too long for an answer, and I'm sure they are privately scrutinizing the way I sound.

Toff says, "That's okay, Lyds. I'll be back. Kids are acting up."

"No problem," I say. "I'm going to turn off my mic. I spilled tea on the connector." There might be a way to salvage this if I have a convincing enough story. Telling the truth would be significantly worse. I mute my mic, cup my hands over my mouth, and rock in my chair.

"Sure, sweetie," Toff says.

Sweetie? I hunt through my bank of life experience, trying to recall if girls call each other sweetie. It is a term of affection, or feigned affection at least, but my instincts suggest this is usually a term women reserve for speaking to men or children. However, I vaguely recall a drive-thru server calling Karen sweetie once. Ambiguous for sure, and nothing Toff has called me before.

Saph remains quiet, then her avatar sparkles and disappears.

-Sapphire has disconnected-

I've done that before. Real Life comes first, but the timing is suspicious.

You say: Is Saph okay?

Toff whispers to you: She said she was tired. I should go as well to make the little bits dinner.

Well, there it is. I've fucked it up again. Most people are already uncomfortable having a furry girl in their club, but most overlook that if you're nice enough. But if they think you're a guy masquerading as a girl, that is a crime too heinous.

I knew when I started using voice chat I was upping my risk, but typing doesn't cut it with today's technology. Text is impersonal, formal, and distracting. In action games or social settings like this, if you don't use voice, people become suspicious, make assumptions about your identity, ask too many questions.

Besides, if technology can somehow get me a little closer to being "one of the girls," how can it not be worth the risk? Just moments ago, as everyone cheered me on stage, I was one of the girls, and I know they believed it as much as I did.

You whisper to Toff: Why are you whispering? Sorry if I screwed anything up. Thanks for hanging with me on my birthday. See you soon! <3

Toff: Don't worry about it. Happy birthday, Lydia.

- Toff has disconnected -

As Toff's avatar disappears, mine is left alone on the couch.

I slump back into my chair, away from the monitor, and allow my eyes to rest and unfocus. As my chemo-weakened eyes cross, the club separates into two copies, spreads apart, and blurs into obscurity. Bile rises in my throat, and I swallow it down. It's impossible to tell if I'm sick from medication or humiliation.

No matter how many times I'm exposed as an impostor or how often I convince myself I'll stop, I always come back. Sometimes I lie awake beside Karen, struggling with the morality of this charade, and wonder how I can ethically expect others to see me as a woman when I'm too afraid to be one.

I'm tempted to put a disclaimer on my character profile that tells people I'm a guy. If I did, I'm sure people wouldn't be as cruel, but probably would treat me like a pervert playing a female character to get himself off. Sure, some might not care and would play along, but that's not what I need.

It's never been only about the sex. I *need* this escape because it's becoming harder to live in this shitty world as the guy I'm supposed to be. It used to be easier, living as Paul, logging in once or twice a month to get my female fix — but that's no longer enough. I am now a frequent-flier tourist in the world of digital womanhood. I live my alter ego through video games, chat rooms, and now primarily in the sim world of *Second Life*.

Sometimes I believe everyone deserves to be angry with me. This masquerade is a deception, and no one enjoys being lied to. But I either lie to Karen and explore my womanhood here, or I lie to myself by repressing these urges and living an inauthentic life. On top of it all, the inevitability of being caught, being exposed, and being shunned is depressing.

For those who only come to places like this for sex, who can know who they are in Real Life? They log in, pick up, jerk off, and log out — no one has time to know who they are. But for people like me, the ones who want more, who seek deeper connections and authentic interactions with others, it's only a matter of time before we're caught. Lasting friendships and romances require trust, disclosure, and honesty. At some point, these half lies I weave expose me, and I hate myself for it.

I regret sneaking around behind the backs of people I love, but I no longer think it's possible to repress *her*. I don't want to think about what I would do if I didn't have a digital outlet to explore this side of myself — privately wearing Karen's clothes could never deliver this experience.

Karen is right, I should rest, but every moment I'm logged into the online world is one minute fewer I have to pretend to be me — no, *him* — in this physical world. I'm no longer sure which is worse: surviving and living the rest of my life as a lie, or wasting away in this apartment and dying from this cancer.

2

Disturbia

"Paul, wait up!" Karen opens a glass door before I walk into it. She hugs the handle to her chest.

I step into thick, moist air. It's one of those unusually warm spring mornings, but I feel it only peripherally through my numbed, air conditioned skin. Or am I in shock?

Pausing on the clinic stoop, I let my eyes adjust. In the bustling parking lot, people rush to their cars, probably returning to work. I pre-emptively took the day off, but I wonder if it's better to go in anyway. I would look so productive if I walked back into the office saying, "Yeah, it's cancer. So, what's on the agenda today?" I bet it'd earn me a lot of brownie points, and they'd probably insist I go home anyway.

Karen's expression is almost comically compassionate, like the one she uses to manipulate me, but this time there are actual tears. I wonder if she's overreacting, or if I'm really in danger.

Across the damp, snow-thawed asphalt, a mother argues with a fussy child in a car seat. She's struggling with the kid's seatbelt as a squirrel races across the fence behind her car. The squirrel's tail flips back and forth, a high-speed balancing act, before scrambling up a tree and leaping onto a nearby garage roof. The sky is the bluest and clearest I can ever remember, and the morning stinks of fresh spring mud and oily road snow. There's a stillness to the world that I hadn't noticed before. I stand speechless, watching the world around me with new eyes — like I have forgotten my next line, and existence itself waits in anticipation. I stare at clouds crawling across the sky until I feel dizzy.

Karen touches my arm and strokes her fingers to my elbow. "You're really pale." I fumble for my keys, and she cradles my cheek with her soft, warm hand. "Do you want me to drive?"

For a moment, I consider it. But then I realize that if I do, she'll think I'm upset. Are men allowed to cry for things like this? Do I get a free pass for having cancer?

No, if I cry, she'll tell people I'm upset, then it'll get back to Mom and that will make *her* upset, and then Karen's parents and my sister, and then all of them being upset will probably make me upset too, and none of it will help me. There's no need to panic and start feeling sorry for myself. It could all be nothing. People survive cancer all the time — right?

I take her hand from my face and lace my fingers with hers. "I'll drive, but can you call my mom and put her on speakerphone?"

Karen buckles herself in. "Are you sure you don't want a few minutes?"

"No, she'd want me to call right away, even if the news is bad."

"We can't know if it is."

"I'm sure that in a year from now, we'll look back and laugh about how worried we were. It's probably just day surgery, you watch." I internally grin at my flawless execution of confidence.

Karen rubs my leg, and her assurance and kindness go a long way. She's not usually this touchy — she comes from one of those icy European families who sneer at familial affection. She slides her hand to my knee and holds it as her thumb nail clicks on the screen. The phone rings and Karen taps up the volume.

When Mom answers, I say, "Before I tell you something, remember that it isn't as bad as it sounds. Do you promise not to freak out?"

The line hangs in silence for a long moment before my mother replies in monotone, "No. Tell me right now."

～～～

I didn't know there were consultation rooms in hospitals.

This one is small, and already cramped with my tiny five-foot-nothing mother, Karen, a nurse, and, from what I've just been told, soon to be three cancer specialists. It's exactly like a normal family doctor's office and even has one of those sanitary metal counters covered in jars of tongue depressors and cotton balls and boxes of rubber gloves. There are even unsettling plastic diagrams hanging on the wall detailing the inside of your throat and what testicles look like without skin. What's odd, though, is that there are two doors in this tiny room — one for us to enter, and the other, currently closed, presumably reserved for doctors.

While Mom and Karen grill the uninformed nurse about potential outcomes, I sit and wait beside the inspection bed, wondering how much those things cost. There are bolts holding it to the floor, and it must be incredibly heavy, near immovable — and everyone knows that heavy means expensive in tech, so someone must make a fortune building these somewhere. Why am I waiting so long? Do they have a full schedule of telling other people how bad their cancer is? I wonder what number I am today.

Karen came straight from a belly dancing lesson and still wears her garish, coin-covered costume, which exposes a scandalous amount of sun-kissed cleavage. She holds my sobbing mother, and they console each other on the far side of the room. I sit alone, disconnected, like a disembodied spirit hovering over a deathbed, watching them grieve. I want to reach out, to comfort them, to tell them everything will be all right, but an ugly wave of revulsion rises in me that questions their right to be more upset about this than I am. After all, they are only making this more difficult — this isn't about them.

I wonder if this is how poltergeists get made.

With a metallic *shir-kik* the doctor's door slides open, and I'm taken aback by how much nicer it is, not even using hinges like our pleb door. Into the room steps a tall man wearing a light grey lab coat. He's young, maybe mid-thirties, well-groomed, and tanned. I stare at the line on his cheek from the sunglasses he must have been wearing on the weekend and wonder if a tanned cancer doctor is an ill omen.

"Hi . . ." The doctor draws a blank, then reviews his clipboard. He smiles and continues, "Paul." He shakes my hand. "I'm Doctor McLean, your oncologist."

"Tell it to me straight, Doc." I wink at my support group.

"Of course." Dr. McLean furrows his brow and flips up the top paper on the clipboard. He takes far too much time reading for someone who is about to tell me I have nothing to worry about. He flips the paper back down. "We believe your cancer is stage two or three, but we can't be sure without further testing."

More tests? While I'm relatively certain stage four is the worst, three is still bad — however, I vaguely remember hearing that someone recovered from stage three. Anyway, doctors have to give you a worst-case scenario. It's probably stage two. I've already had more CT scans and X-rays in the past two weeks than I have in my entire life — but if they need more, they'll get them. What's that saying, measure twice, cut once?

Dr. McLean continues, "I've spoken with your surgeon. Have you met Doctor Teller yet? No? He is one of the most famous colorectal specialists in Canada. He believes that the best plan of attack is . . ." He glances at his clipboard again.

A deathly silence has settled over the previously noisy room. My arms tingle and prick with tiny electric shocks that sneak to my fingertips. My thoughts fight their way through icy slush, alerting me that my previous assessment of the situation is dangerously incorrect, or he's got the wrong chart.

I stare at his mouth and think about how young he is. His stubble is growing back. He must have started work early, I bet. Maybe I'll have to take some time off work — that wouldn't be too bad. The doctor says, "Since you are so young, we want to start you on an aggressive plan. Typically, in situations like yours —"

I have a "situation like" mine?

"— we advise immediate surgery with twelve months of chemotherapy and targeted radiation. However, Doctor Teller wants you on fluorouracil right away, which should help the radiation target the cancer and make things easier for surgery. I believe he will prescribe a stronger cocktail of chemotherapy to boost its efficacy between cycles, but you'll mostly be on a drip for twenty-four hours a day for about six months before your operation, and the other six months after. Do you have any ques—"

"I have questions," my mother interrupts. "How long before —"

Shir-kik.

My mother cuts herself off as the doctor's door opens and in walks a small, balding, frowning man.

Two chairs and six people now. I don't enjoy staring at everyone's bellies, but I can't find the strength to join them on their feet.

"Hello." The small man speaks to no one and avoids eye contact with me. "I thought Doctor Teller would be here."

The nurse interjects, "Doctor Teller said he might run late. He is performing follow-up consultations today."

The small man groans. "Should I come back?"

"No," Dr. McLean says, smiling too much, "why don't you introduce yourself to Paul?"

Like Max Schreck in *Nosferatu*, the small man spins in place and gazes down his nose at me. He hesitantly offers a soft, chilly hand, and I take it. I squeeze the lifeless fish and give it a single shake before he slithers it out of my grip. He says, "I am Doctor Bakker, your radiologist. Has anyone discussed your care pre or post ostomy?"

Did he just say colostomy? No, he said ostomy. Is that the same thing? I force myself to say, "No . . . what?" The small doctor doesn't acknowledge me and instead says something about weekly radiation schedules and sunburns on my intestines, but my brain has locked onto the word *ostomy*.

Ostomy like colostomy? The bag-thing that old people wear that fills with their shit? A literal bag of shit against my stomach? Will it stink? Doesn't that mean intestines come out of your stomach?

Dr. Bakker looks down at me. "Do you have questions about the radiation process?"

"Wait . . ." I croak. My throat is dry, and the word sticks in my mouth, so I force myself to swallow some spit and try again. "Did you say something about a colostomy?"

Dr. Bakker narrows his brow and flexes the muscles in his jaw. "Most likely a colostomy, yes. You have colorectal cancer, right? This is all very standard. It's possible that the surgeon will opt for an ileostomy, however."

My mother shrieks, but I'm stunned, wondering if ileostomies are for pee and if I'm going to have both, but reason that it can't possibly be that bad.

Shir-kik.

As my mother wails, the nurse insistently encourages her into the hallway, whispering into her ear. I realize that at some point, another man, this one with orange hair, has come into the room through the doctor's door.

I say, "No one said anything about a colostomy. I thought you'd just . . . remove the lump or whatever."

Dr. Bakker sighs. "It is important to concentrate on fighting the cancer right now."

"But do you have to give me one?"

The smiling ginger man interjects, "We can talk about options —" before Dr. Bakker cuts him off.

"Listen, if this is about you living or dying, having an ostomy is better than dying, wouldn't you say?"

My mother shouts from the hall, shakes off the nurse's grip, and stampedes into the room, but the nurse protectively positions herself in front of Dr. Bakker, who is wisely retreating toward the safety of his fancy door.

My mother stabs her finger in the direction of the recoiling radiologist. "You insensitive, horrific man. I'll have you know this is the first time any of us have heard that he might have to have a . . . a *bag*. If your mother had to get one, would you tell her like this?"

As my brain struggles to register how I'm being likened to this middle-aged radiologist's mother, I try to answer the doctor's initial question. I say, "Yeah, I suppose it's better than dying."

The smiling ginger man touches the radiologist's arm, and they exit through the doctors door while Dr. Bakker complains about "being realistic" and "shouldn't be so irrational" as the door clicks shut behind them.

The ginger man returns momentarily without the radiologist. He offers me his hand. "Good day, Paul, I'm Doctor Teller." His voice is deep but outrageously enthusiastic, with a nasally pitch that reminds me of Kermit the Frog.

My mother's voice carries from the hall. She is debating loudly with the nurse now, and all I catch is "shouldn't be talking like that."

"So, young man," Dr. Teller continues, "typically in these situations, we suggest operating immediately. However, as this is a rare case for someone your age, we want to give you every opportunity to have a full life."

"What do you suggest?"

"With your permission, we will start you on a regimen of chemo-therapy and radiation for six months on a daily drip of fluorouracil, also known as five-eff-you."

I involuntarily chuckle.

He flashes a polite smile and continues, "We will also give you weekly boosts with a stronger solution. You may or may not lose hair, but most do not. Once a week, when you come in for that boost, you will also visit Doctor Bakker for targeted radiation treatment. Paul, do you have children?"

"No children." Karen is hovering close to my shoulder, her face pale.

"If you plan on having children, you might consider sperm banking, or there are other ways we can protect your fertility. There is a lead box that you can . . . well, it isn't comfortable, but you might avoid sterility."

As I weigh how important kids really are to me, I ask, "Do you do sperm banking here?"

"No. There are local facilities who provide that service. It is quite expensive, however."

That settles that. Lead box on my balls and roll the dice, I guess.

"I'll look into it," I lie.

"Good," Dr. Teller says, too upbeat to be genuine. "After your cycle of chemotherapy, we will have you come in for surgery. We will create a temporary stoma, about the size of my thumb, and it will divert output into a pouch. This allows your insides time to heal. We will need to either give you an ileostomy on the right side of your abdomen, or a colostomy on your left."

He touches his fingertips to my belly, and my stomach muscles involuntarily spasm. "Colostomy output is closer to normal con-sistency, and ileostomies tend toward being more liquid. This will be temporary or permanent, depending on what we discover on the day of the surgery. If temporary, once you have healed, we will reverse the procedure, and you'll carry on with a surgical scar."

I ask, "If it isn't temporary?"

Dr. Teller sits on the examining bed, the sanitary paper crinkling in protest. "If that happens, we will make sure you are well-informed on how to care for your ostomy. People continue to lead normal lives with their prosthesis. I can see you are nervous about this."

No shit. I make myself nod.

"I might know more if you let me examine you. I will have a better idea how close the growth is to your anus."

"Sure . . . Yes please."

"In that case, I'll ask everyone to give Paul and me some privacy."

Karen squeezes my hand, her fingers pale and white when I release them. She kisses me on the cheek and whispers, "It'll be fine, you'll see."

Tears well and everything goes blurry. I say, "I hope so."

Karen leaves and closes the door. The little room feels much larger with only Dr. Teller and me in it.

He pats the examination table. "Hop up, lie on your side, and face the wall. Pull your pants and underwear down and draw your knees up as close to your chest as you can. You don't have to put a gown on, this will only take a minute."

Mechanically, I obey, and there is a squelch of lube a second before he rests a hand on my hip and is pushing two thick fingers into my ass. I unsuccessfully stifle a grunt and grip the bed rail as I resist crying out — whatever is inside me lances an electric bolt of pain into my belly. Fingers stretching my asshole isn't a foreign sensation, but the way his fingertips poke and explore over something lodged inside me certainly is.

"Try to relax, you're quite swollen from all the attention." He pushes on the hard lump just inside my anus and firmly explores around. He traces his fingertip over the surface of my tumour firmly enough that I can tell it has a rough or ridged side that makes me think of a meatball.

Dr. Teller corkscrews his fingers and draws them back. I groan in anticipation of it being over, but his fingertips linger inside, and I swear I'm seconds away from shitting on his inspection bed. He swiftly pushes back in and probes deeper — way deeper.

I groan and clench my jaw and grip a handful of the crinkly sanitary paper. I whimper as the thing inside me fires spikes of pain into my belly. Without warning, he tugs his fingers out, leaving my asshole burning and throbbing and probably gaping like some ass-play porno. The now-inflamed tumour seethes and swells in protest, leaving me feeling full and struggling to clench myself together in hopes of preserving my underwear.

"All done," he says. "I apologize if that hurt. I will give you a moment to clean up." He places a box of tissues beside me and leaves the room.

Shir-kik.

When he leaves, I lay back on the table, knees spread frog style, holding my dick and balls so I can reach under to wipe. Back to front — I've heard that's not a good thing to do if you have a vagina. On the paper towel is a little brown but mostly dark red blood swirled with what must be a half bottle of lube . . . and thank the gods for all that lube. It's the same crimson I saw in the toilet bowl a year ago, the blood my doctor should have seen as a warning sign instead of dismissing it as a hemorrhoid or irritable bowel syndrome because of my age.

Dr. Teller knocks. "Coming in."

I pull up my pants.

The doctor wheels a chair close. "Good news."

My shoulders involuntarily relax muscles I didn't realize had tensed.

"To reverse an ostomy, I need at least one centimetre to work with between your anus and the tumour. You are very close, about two centimetres, but I believe I can do it. The chemotherapy should shrink the tumour and make it easier to manage, so I am optimistic your ostomy will be reversible."

"You really think you can do it?"

"I have performed this procedure many times, and in cases worse than yours," he says warmly.

I feel optimism returning, and foolish for doubting my luck. "Thank you," I say, sitting on my swollen, throbbing asshole.

"I'll call them back in now, shall I?"

◖ 3 ◗

Feel Good Drag

.

2009 — Back in the club

My rabbit avatar sits on the couch and stares from the monitor into my eyes. In the club, virtual strangers pass between us.

Every so often, a scripted algorithm initializes, selects a random fidget from a preprogrammed list, and my avatar emulates being a living person. She might fix her hair, slump into her chair, stretch, scratch her neck, or rest her hands on her knees. As I watch, still stewing in self-loathing for being so careless, my avatar buries her face in her hands. I've never seen her do that before — I sit up to get a better look, but she's already checking her nails.

I'm overtired, or maybe the chemo is getting to me. Side effects weren't a big deal for the first few weeks. I knew it was powerful after my first infusion when my skin became so sensitive to the cold that I burned my mouth eating ice cream. But I didn't notice any other changes at first — no nausea, no hair loss, nothing like the movies teach you; all those things snuck up on me. After a month, my energy drained away, and then after two my mouth and throat filled with ulcers. Soon my hair fried to brittle straw, yet did not conveniently fall out. Instead, I found it on my pillow, and broke as I brushed it — and when my head resembled a three-year-old's Barbie, post-haircut, I walked across the street into a barbershop and told them to shave it all off.

These days I'll hit an invisible wall just from walking across my apartment. My energy plummets randomly, and I stagger and pass out on the nearest piece of furniture for an hour. I haven't hallucinated yet, but after over four months of infusions, this poison is so thick in my veins that if my cat drank out of the toilet after I pissed, it would literally die — so I can't rule out the possibility.

I click off the desk lamp and remove my glasses. Leaning back in my chair, I close my eyes and rub the ball of my hand into my eye socket until the pressure creates a pixelated kaleidoscope behind my eyelids. I keep rubbing as the rolling disco ball flashes of yellow lights give me vertigo, and I wonder how hard I need to push before I permanently ruin my eyes, if such a thing were possible.

The soft *pling* from the computer speakers alerts me that someone is whispering. I slip my glasses back on and scrunch my nose to reposition them. My vision is clouded and black and still sparking with yellow flashes as I lean forward and focus on the screen, only to realize there is another furry behind my avatar. A white-furred cat girl leans over the back of the couch and looks down my top.

Kali whispers to you: Mew.

Fucking hell, not one of those weirdos who plays up the whole "cute me" crap. She's probably prowling for doms to take advantage of her. I guess I resemble one in this outfit. And I guess I am in a BDSM club. Probably a guy, I bet. I should log out and save myself the drama.

I drag the pointer to the system menu and navigate the process of logging out. I may be in a shitty mood, but she shouldn't have to suffer.

I type.

You whisper to Kali: I'm actually logging out shortly.

. . .

Kali: Too bad. You're cute. I hope I see you again someday.

I shouldn't feel bad, she'll probably move on to the next target the moment I log out. I hover the pointer over the door icon and a pop-up appears over the couch.

Do you want to QUIT? [YES / NO]

Kali: You're an amazing dancer.

Sliding the pointer away from yes, I click no and scoot my chair closer to the desk and write back.

You: Listen, you're sweet, but I'm not interested. I only date men and I really do need to leave soon.

Kali: I don't have to be.

You: You don't have to be what?

Kali: I don't have to be a girl. You're cute, and you seem fun. I don't care what I am. I would love to hang out with you, even if you have to go soon.

I could use the company — especially with someone who is eager to cheer me up. But there's something unsettling about being with a guy who pretends to be a girl. The dramatic irony of that prejudice isn't lost on me.

A flurry of space dust swirls around the cat. Their shape changes, grows taller, muscular, and lithe. In the place of the petite cutesy kitten girl is now an undeniably sexy cheetah man. His lips spread in a predatory grin. He's sporting a fifties vibe with a white t-shirt and leather jacket and only those two pieces of clothing. He offers a clawed hand, and through my headset his warm caramel voice purrs, "Spend that little time with me? We can stop whenever you like."

I switch applications, check that my voice altering program hasn't timed out, and I unmute my mic. "Just for a little." I take his hand.

I follow his teleport prompt, and we arrive on the shore of a secluded beach far from the club. The crash of waves and crying of seagulls catches me off guard. Usually when I'm summoned, I typically appear in some dude's underlit bedroom.

A nearby sign reads, CLOTHING OPTIONAL BEYOND THIS POINT.

Kali motions to the sign. "You don't have to —"

"I don't mind."

I unfasten my belted outfit, leather creaking and buckles gleaming in the summer sun. As each piece of clothing falls from my fingertips, it dematerializes in midair, returning to my inventory before it touches the sand.

Kali watches, as I hoped he would. I make sure that my character has her high-definition polygon nipples showing, not the cheapo skinned breast texture which comes stock when you buy the avatar. They cost extra, but the little details make all the difference here. As I undress before him, Kali's avatar freezes.

I wave my hand in front of his face. "Is everything okay?"

Kali's avatar returns to life, and through my headset comes laughter. "I was . . . distracted. I'm more than okay. You're beautiful, and your voice is so cute."

Dammit.

I can't deepen it now — he'll clock me for sure — however, that probably means he didn't catch my mistake in the club.

Kali shrugs off his jacket and wrestles his shirt over his head, revealing pierced nipples — a sexy touch. As he steps forward to take my hands, I notice his sheath has swollen and the tip of his cock pokes out. He obviously pays attention to the little things.

I fully expect him to pounce me immediately onto the sand, but he leads me toward the water, sand squishing between my avatar's toes as we walk together across the deserted beach. While late in the season, one would think a place this beautiful must be a hotspot, but today Linden Lab has rendered the beach just for us.

Lounge chairs wait under umbrellas, tiny crabs scuttle over washed up seashells, and the water is icy blue. Across the sand, waves crest, roll thunderously, crash, then hiss watery fingers onto the shore.

"Last one in . . ." Kali releases my hand and sprints for the water.

Laughing, I try to keep up. I leap into the waves, and they burst against my thighs, splashing up my chest and into my face. "No fair! You're asking me to outrun a cheetah?"

I fight past the waves to Kali, who waits for me in waist deep water. His short hair hangs wet and stringy over his grinning face while waves crash against his back. I take his hands, and he drags me through the water. He pulls me until my breasts crush against him.

Kali stops playing and holds me, gazing into my eyes. "Is this okay?"

Who the hell is this guy? Panting, I say, "Yes."

He pulls me tighter, and I drape my arms around his neck. He asks, "If you could have a perfect date, what would it be?"

"You're doing pretty good so far."

"No, seriously . . ."

I rest my nose against his as I think. "I guess some food at an authentic fifties style diner and maybe go dancing? But I am loving this."

"A diner? Like, a *greasy diner*?" Kali laughs.

I pull away, unsure if he's teasing. "They don't have them where I live. You must be from the States."

"They're everywhere here." He turns, lifting and spinning me slowly, dragging my legs through the water. "It has been noted."

I slip my pointed tongue over his nose. "What's *your* perfect date?"

Kali grooms his rough feline tongue against my cheek as he thinks. "I'm boring. I think any date is perfect as long as it ends with a beautiful bunny sitting in my lap or pressed against me like this."

"You're so cheesy. That answer is a total copout."

"I'm only being honest." He cups my ass and grips, claws digging into my cheeks. "Is this okay?"

"It's more than okay."

Kali grins, displaying predatory fangs. His chest rumbles, and through those teeth vibrates a deep and throaty purr. His sharp-clawed fingertips slide up the back of my neck and into my hair. Goosebumps prick my flesh as he cradles my head.

Then he leans in, my heart races, and his lips find mine. We exchange soft, unhurried kisses. His mouth opens against mine and soon his rough tongue pushes inside. He picks me up and I wrap my legs around him and he strides purposefully through the waves, carrying me back to shore. Our tongues spar, and I involuntarily muffle a moan of contentment into his mouth as he lowers me into the sun-melted plastic of a lounge chair.

The sun is bright and warm against the side of my face. He crawls over me, pressing me down with his weight, and I let him spread my legs with his knees.

My heart pounds in excitement as I slide my hand down his furry stomach, my fingers wrapping around him, feeling his excitement pulsing in my hand.

"You're fun, Lydia," Kali pants into my ear, "and you're incredibly hot."

I say, "I like you too," but all I can think about is how fucking badly I want him right now. I guide him between my legs and pant, "Now fuck m—"

I'm whiplashed back to reality by the thud of the apartment door against the wall followed by the muffled crash of grocery bags. I reflexively check, and it's impossibly eight o'clock.

There's a clatter of spilled cans. "Shit," Karen mutters. Across the room Karen shuffles in the door with her coat hanging open, her loose bun falling apart, and she blows stray hairs from her face. She shuts the door with her foot. I wrestle off the headset and realize I am poking out against the front of my pajamas, and I'm suddenly thankful we have a desk between us.

"Oh, you're awake. Happy birthday! How are you feeling?" Karen stoops and picks up cans.

On the screen, Kali's hips lower and my avatar's back arches in pleasure. He moans through my headset.

I fight through the embarrassment, and the guilty realization that Kali will soon hate me, but I mute my sound and tell the computer to shut down.

If you shut down now, you may lose any unsaved progress. Shut down anyway? [YES / NO]

I click yes. My avatar, the beach, and Kali all flick away to a black screen that reflects a bald man in glasses. I imagine the man controlling Kali out there, somewhere, waiting for me to respond, and realizing, eventually, that I have bailed on him.

I know I would take it personally.

"Thank you. I'm okay," I call across the apartment, wrestling with the ache of guilt that sours my stomach. Mercifully, the shock has already calmed me. My body hasn't responded that strongly in a long time, and it has only gotten worse since the chemo treatments, but that wasn't a problem a few moments ago.

As Karen noisily drags split grocery bags to the kitchen, I disentangle myself from cables and meet her, wrapping a blanket around myself, just in case. I shuffle across the floor to her, moving slowly so the bottle of chemo belted to my hip and hooked into my arm doesn't catch on anything.

"Where's the chicken?" Karen asks. Judging by her knitted brows and pursed lips, I'm sure she's already guessed.

"I must have fallen asleep," I lie.

Karen sighs but lets it go as I help her unload groceries onto the counter.

I never used to be so careless with these excursions into digital spaces. There have never been so many close calls before, and I suppose I should be more careful, but I just can't stop myself.

Even though I boot up daily to distract myself from the way the cancer treatments are poisoning me, or how it's becoming more difficult to look at myself in the mirror, the six to ten hours a day I'm spending online isn't enough. I know this addiction is getting worse, and if Karen ever found out, it would crush her. Back when I was a teenager, being a woman online for even an hour would keep me happy for a month or more. Cancer changed all that when it made existing in this body even more unbearable, so I no longer restrict my screen time.

I know I'll be back tomorrow. Like a junkie, I'll anxiously wait until Karen leaves for work, then I'll plug in and ride my euphoria fix, even though that satisfaction now only lasts until the screen goes dark.

4

Going Backwards

Ice-glazed grass crunches under our shoes as we cross the lawn in darkness. Mom watches from the porch, her coat hugged tightly around her bathrobe as she sips from a steaming mug. I load my suitcases into the trunk and take Sarah's out of her hands.

My stepfather emerges from the house, kisses Mom, and says, "Traffic's light at the border. Getting him over should be easy."

"It's *her*." Though she whispers, Mom's voice carries across the stillness of pre-dawn.

Wayne glances to us across the lawn. I try not to react as I load Sarah's cases beside mine.

"He can't hear us," Wayne says. "Got to go, hun."

"Drive safe."

I resist confronting Wayne when he gets in and starts the car. Years of Trump-related arguments have worn me down. And while it's possible the only reason Wayne agreed to drive me is to prove to my mother that he and I can get along, the main reason I don't argue is because I need his help.

Besides, I have more pressing issues on my mind. I forget his callous remark by the time a sign slides by on the highway: Last exit before Rainbow Bridge to U.S.A.

Soon we're in line at a customs booth.

"I don't think I know this guy," Wayne says. My stepfather presses a button, and his window sucks into the door with a mechanical hum. December vacuums heat from the car. Wayne maneuvers behind an SUV being inspected by a booth guard. "Got your passports?" Wayne asks.

My teeth involuntarily chatter, but I'm unsure if it's from the cold or my nerves. At almost ten degrees Celsius, in Ontario, in December, it's unusually warm — ideal for shuffling suitcases into an airport. While the promise of California palm trees and warm breezes is mere hours away, it does nothing to stop the gut-twisting anxiety I feel from staring at the Aryan-looking border guard.

"Yes," Sarah says from the back seat.

I pry open the stiff, week-old passport and take comfort in the recently revised sex marker. The indisputable *F* helps settle my stomach, even though the Cro-Magnon ridge shadowing my eyes undermines that reassurance without my face-concealing oversized glasses.

Wayne opens his hand over his shoulder. "Right, give them here." Wayne's recent money-making scheme is driving successful business executives across the border to fly out of Buffalo. There are extra fees for people flying internationally out of Toronto, even if that's only to the U.S., so people who live close to the border cut costs by doing this. The venture ended up so successful that he's now somewhat of an expert at border-crossing.

I add my passport and a printed flight itinerary to Sarah's and ask, "If the guard wants to know why I'm going to California, what should I say?"

"The truth."

I let my head fall against the seat and stare up at fuzzy fabric — I was hoping for more of an insider tip, not something that has previously blown up in my face.

Our car lurches forward. The SUV, now inspected, merges into American traffic just beyond the border. As we approach the booth, the guard could be any forgettable blond-haired white guy you've ever seen in your life. Clean-shaven, square jawed, and probably goes to the gym a couple times a week. He has that practised bored deadpan expression every customs officer wears. "Citizenship and destination?" he asks.

We all announce Canadian, and I tell him Sarah and I are headed for California.

The guard puts down all the passports but one and turns to me. "How long are you staying in California?"

A pinprick tingling begins in my face and spreads down my neck, and if I wasn't speaking out of an open window, I would have sworn someone cranked the heat. Flexing my larynx, I aim for a medium pitch — I need to be ambiguous, androgynous — and not my falsetto telephone voice because then he might grow suspicious. He has the paper right in front of him that says F in government ink. All I need to do is not screw up this time.

I say, "We're going for nine days."

"What are you doing there? Going to Disneyland?" The border guard smiles at me.

I've never seen a border guard smile before. For a moment I stare, trying to figure out if he's flirting with me. If so, it's the perfect opportunity to sideswipe him with the truth.

"No, I'm getting GCS," I say.

The guard's smile plummets into a scowl. Not anger — confusion.

I realize my miscalculation. I may have just placed myself in a situation where I need to explain to this stranger exactly what GCS means. The rest of the world fades and darkens in my periphery. Wayne and Sarah melt away as well. The only thing that remains is the inky tunnel of anxiety which ties me to the border guard.

Sarah grips my shoulder, squeezing it, though it's more distracting than comforting, and I need to focus. More than a few moments have passed since I've been staring at the guard and willing time to reverse.

"What is that?" the guard asks. He scrutinizes a passport.

I know he would understand "sex change," but it's neither an accurate nor a current term. My palms sweat, the muscles in my neck tense, and I start to shake. I can't bring myself to say it. In my panicked state, I can't even remember what GCS stands for, or if I'm using the most up-to-date language.

I decide to just open my mouth and hope it remembers.

"Genital reconfig— . . . reassignment surgery?" Then I realize the word is confirmation. With a *c*.

Our border guard's expression doesn't budge. He stares blankly at me and closes the passport. I realize this is a crucial time to explain myself, because I'm familiar with what happens to people who confuse border guards.

I try again. "I'm going for trans—"

"All right." The guard cuts me off and hands Wayne our passports, then motions for us to drive on.

Wayne, tight-lipped, says, "Thank you." He raises the windows and drives. The now red-faced guard waves the next car forward.

I fall back into my seat as warm electric currents of relief buzz through my body, returning sensation to my fingertips. Wayne merges onto a highway.

I may have discovered a new transsexual superpower to add to my character sheet: the power to embarrass a guard enough to bypass border security.

We pass through the frozen, gritty industry of Buffalo. As my anxious blush fades from my cheeks, I recognize how chilly the car is and appreciate the heat blasting through the vents. I rest my forehead against the window, enjoying the way the cooler glass allows me to refocus, as I let the familiar sights of Buffalo soothe me: helicopter rides this way, boarded-up houses, cheap smokes, factory outlet sales.

Sarah massages my shoulder and whispers against the back of my ear. "You did great, baby."

"You're free to leave, ma'am." A blue-gloved customs agent opens the door, and I leave the inspection booth to the cacophony of carry-on inspection lines and tinny PA announcements.

Sarah leaps from her chair and rushes over, her suitcase's tiny wheels struggling to keep up as it swings precariously behind her. Bow-lipped, freckled, and red-haired, she has the face of a fairy and curves dramatic enough to make any burlesque dancer jealous. However, those curves don't do the degenerative disease in her joints any favours.

"Are you okay?" Sarah asks as she abandons her suitcase and throws her arms around my neck. She eyes the shoes I'm holding. "Your clothes . . . did they?"

I sit on a planter and slip on my shoes. "Security saw my appliance in the X-ray. They had me run a swab over it and analyzed it in a machine."

Sarah says, "Probably to check it for drugs."

"I bet they're glad they didn't have to search it." I laugh at my joke, but Sarah just taps and slides her finger against her phone.

We find our gate unstaffed and grab a beer at a nearby sports bar even though airport restaurants are still serving breakfast.

Sarah rests her bottle on a coaster. "Aren't you scared?"

I wash away mouth-slime with bitter IPA. "About surgery? Nah, if she screws up, I won't feel anything . . . ever again."

"Don't say that."

"I'm kidding," I half lie. "I doubt that will happen. Doctor Bowers is one of the best *and* a trans woman. She'll make my pussy prettier since she understands the importance of aesthetic. If she's good enough for Jazz Jennings, she's good enough for me."

"I guess it's a good thing you had to choose a doctor. You could be in Quebec right now, getting surgery from that asshole."

"Let's not think about that. To new adventures." We raise our drinks and down the dregs.

As we're gathering our things, Sarah grabs my face and kisses me. A wave of panic rolls through my body. From the next table, an elderly couple grimace in disgust.

Sarah says, "You earned this."

As we wheel our luggage toward the gate, Sarah asks, "Did you notice that old couple giving us the stink-eye? The best."

I chuckle. "Yeah, the best." It's a common enough joke between us in the relative safety of Canada, but ever since Trump won the election, things have changed here South of the border.

Sarah groans as she sinks into a chair at the gate.

I say, "I'll get our seats fixed. Wait here." Sarah closes her eyes and nods, relaxing further. She puckers her lips. I kiss her and try not to care who is watching, but the entire time I'm imagining people are amazed to catch a true sighting of lesbians in the wild.

A hand-talking businesswoman in a form-fitting grey blazer and matching pencil skirt argues with the gate's service agents. As I approach, the taller agent says, "Of course you shouldn't have to worry about that. I see here that you are a preferred flier." After noisily clacking on a keyboard, she adds, "I shuffled things around and would like to offer you an upgrade to business class."

The businesswoman says, "I hoped you would say that."

The gate guard prints new tickets. "We board in approximately one hour. We'll call you for advanced seating."

The businesswoman wordlessly takes the tickets and leads her suitcase to the bar.

"Can I help you, miss?" the agent asks me.

I hand her our tickets. "I got these from the machine and hoped you could help seat my partner and I together?"

The gate agent reviews my tickets and clacks on the keyboard. "Sarah is your partner?"

I expect that tone from older people and anyone in a red ball cap, but not young people representing an international company. I try not to jump to conclusions, but I suddenly wish I were wearing a pencil skirt instead of jeans. I say, "Yes, she is. Is it possible for us to sit together?"

The gate agent clicks. "We have a full flight today. There is nothing I can do unless there are cancellations." She slides the tickets forward.

I leave the tickets on the podium and fidget with the tag on my suitcase. In situations like this, I try to consider what my mother would say. She once took me out to lunch, and our waiter was rude, and instead of a tip, he got a lecture. While it made me want to crawl under the table and die, I have never doubted my mom's ability to stand up for herself. Though I can't morally bring myself to berate anyone in a service position to get what I want, I do sometimes channel my inner Mom when I know I'm being discriminated against.

"When I booked this flight months ago, your online service asked me if we needed to be seated together. It's a long flight to be separated and among strangers."

"Please . . . ma'am. There is no need to get upset."

"I'm not upset." I try to ignore the hesitation in her statement and take a deep breath. There are probably too many people eager to publish a headline of an angry transgender woman attacking an innocent airline agent, so I need to calm down.

The tight-lipped service agent says, "I'll do my best to seat you together for your flight." The patient restraint in her voice hints at an imminent verbal beat down if I push the subject. "If you wait until everyone has boarded, I'll check again." She pushes the tickets further toward me until they nearly fall off the podium.

"Thanks." I take the tickets, recognizing a fight I can't win.

The gate fills past capacity like an over-inflated balloon and splutters down the tunnel. We watch the passengers' distorted shapes pass by the accordion bridge's flexible rubber windows. They fill a plane whose engines whine in anticipation just outside our vibrating window.

I approach the kiosk where three attendants are now smiling brightly at the two of us.

"Thank you for your patience," says the same agent from before. "I have your new tickets, and I hope you like these seats better. I also adjusted your transfer tickets for your layover."

"Okay, thanks," I mumble, and hand Sarah her ticket — cautiously relieved it worked out.

We enter the plane to the inevitable mayhem one can expect from boarding last. Almost everyone is standing and removing outerwear, others attempt to stuff the few remaining carry-on luggage spots with jackets, presents, or lunches. Despite the chaos, it's surprising to see so many empty seats after the fuss the agents made.

Sarah squeezes around a guy with a dark sweat stain sticking his grey t-shirt to his body, and I follow her all the way back near the bathrooms. Sarah motions to some seats with her ticket. "We're here."

My ticket doesn't match any seats beside her. After a moment of confusion, I find my seat a row in front and across the aisle. I visualize that if she reached forward, and I reached back, we could try for an awkward, diagonal, supportive handhold during the long flight ahead.

A flight attendant loudly states, "Please take your seats. If you need help with luggage, raise your hand and someone will assist you."

Sarah double-checks her ticket but is pushed into her seat as the man in the sweaty shirt forces past her to sit by the window. Her voice wavers as she asks me, "Can we see if we can switch with someone?"

"I don't know if they do that."

"Ma'am," a flight attendant wearing a smart vest and short black hair says, "please sit down. Oh, let me help you with that."

He takes my suitcase and carries it past a crowd of people to the front of the plane where I see him slide it into someone else's overhead storage.

My phone buzzes in my back pocket. I tug it out but almost drop it when someone crashes their suitcase wheel into my elbow. I cringe as hot electricity surges to my fingertips — I give up and sit to open the message.

Sarah: I swear that service rep did this to us on purpose. Did you see the way they looked at each other?

Paige: I thought they were being apologetic. Do you think they could have made a mistake?

"Please turn off all handheld devices," the flight attendant says to my general area from a few seats up.

I ignore him.

Sarah: This would have had to have been a HUGE mistake! We're in separate rows. The letters don't match! I can't even hold your hand. 🖐

Turbines spin up and whine, and the plane jostles. As we back away from the terminal and taxi down the runway, someone over the speakers is trying not to sound bored as they explain which strings to pull when we're screaming and begging for our lives in the event of a crash.

When I look to Sarah, she points at a flight attendant and questions with her hands.

Paige: They said they tried to seat us. I guess they didn't say together, just better.

Sarah: Do you think they'll let us find seats together after we're in the air?

The engines scream, and the plane rumbles forward, faster, then faster still. A child screams in terror. G-force pins me to my hideously patterned seat, cleverly engineered to hide past vomit stains. The front of the plane lifts, the fuselage shudders ominously, and for a moment I fear we've failed to take flight, possibly because my cellphone shorted out the airplane, but Buffalo falls away outside the window. The buildings and streets below looking conspicuously like model-train scenery.

Soon I'll be in California, and this thing will finally be over.

It doesn't feel that long ago that Kali held me in his virtual arms, and I wished I could trade my male-presenting body with that of the woman on my screen. I wanted, more than anything, to mirror those intimate moments with him in Real Life.

Now, years later, I sit in this airplane, and that male body I once owned has softened and grown curves. While I'm deeply thankful to have Sarah in my life, a part of me still wishes Kali could witness this woman I've become.

When I glance down the airplane aisle, I find Sarah's face creased in concern. I force myself to give a reassuring smile, though I'm doubtful of how convincing it might have been. The truth is, as much as I love Sarah, it feels wrong that the man I made those wishes with can't be here with me as I fulfill this last step.

My phone lights up and buzzes.

Sarah: Baby, are you crying? I'm right behind you. I wish I could hold your hand.

I begin to type: I feel|

The flight attendant leans into my row, smiles with a perfect set of ivory veneers, and points at the phone. "Ma'am, I asked you to turn off all devices."

The woman beside me accentuates a sigh so loud that her accompanying eye roll is audible.

I hold down the power button until an annoyed woman glares at me from the black mirror in my hand.

Part 2

Log In

⬛ 5 ⬛

Fire with Fire

2010 — Seven years earlier, deep behind enemy lines

Upon the tip of my staff, a metal claw grasps a gleaming onyx orb. I stare into its reflective surface and comb my long black hair with sharpened fingernails, inwardly marvelling at my dark elven perfection.

A puff of air hisses behind me. An untrained ear would dismiss this slight disturbance, but it's the accompanying scent of decomposing corpses that betrays the assassin's presence.

"Here to report?" I ask.

Behind me a cruel squeak of a voice scratches like dagger tip on slate. "I bring news, my lord."

I regard the messenger — her face decorated with fierce jewellery and partially obscured within a mane of white hair that would put a glam metal groupie to shame. Her armour is purely ornamental, constructed of spikes and chains and designed to distract, leaving exposed ample curves of corpse-white flesh decorated by dried blood splatters.

She continues, "The forces of Order muster on yonder hill." She points to rising dust clouds on the western horizon, the kind armies kick up during a forced march.

```
- Your friend Kali has logged in -
Kali whispers: Good morning, my gorgeous bunny.
Happy anniversary! I hoped you'd be around to
receive your surprise. <3
```

"Just a sec, RL is interrupting," I say to the Witch Elf assassin.

"No problem, dude," the Witch says. "Take your time. I need a bio anyhow." The witch freezes in place and inspects her dagger at arm's length.

```
You whisper to Kali: Happy anniversary, baby. I
love surprises! *^.^* And good morning? It's 2pm.
Kali: That's morning to me. Are you busy right
now?
You: I think we're about to get rolled by
Order, but I want to see how it plays out.
Kali: Playing WAR? I still have some finishing
touches I want to make, anyway. Message when
you're done?
You: Of course! I can't wait for my surprise.
Love you! <3
Kali: You're going to love it. See you soon,
baby. MWAH!
You: MWAH!
```

My character unfreezes. "Sorry about that."

Smacks of chewing sounds come from the Witch's microphone. "No worries."

I say, "Fool of a Witch. Our forces rode for Cinderfall. Order would never leave their castle undefended."

The witch elf sneers, teeth filed sharp. "Cinderfall's defenders were crushed. The victors ride on this keep."

"Khlar!" I bang the tip of my staff against the flagstone in frustration. Including the Witch, we have maybe ten to twelve battle-ready souls at the keep: a few orcs brawling in the dirt, two Goblins peeing off battlements, and others overseeing repairs. We don't have enough to win a battle. "Very well, leave before we're besieged and gather reinforcements. We'll hold as best we can."

"Die well, Vhiron." The Witch bows, and in a puff of acrid smoke, she's gone.

Clanking metal draws my attention to the wall walk where I see approaching our army's most formidable Chaos Knight. At seven feet tall, he wields a heavy axe larger than most of his foes. His cast iron helmet resembles a steam engine's cowcatcher, and within dwells the stuff of nightmares — tentacles and teeth and dull red infernal eyes.

The beast of a knight looms over me as he leans on his axe, and in a booming voice says, "Hey, man, I'm bored waiting. I might throw a steak in the oven." He stretches his back and swings his arms back and forth.

I ask, "In the oven?"

"Yeah, you never baked a steak?"

The peak of a trebuchet rises above the hill. "No . . . ? Listen, Kris —"

Kris interrupts. "You totally should. Smear on a bit of butter, throw some salt and pepper on there, maybe some Montreal steak spice. Chuck it in the oven on low, and it just falls apart in your mouth."

Someone yells from the courtyard below. I point over the wall with my staff. "Kris, we're about to be attacked."

"Why didn't you say so? Cool, you going to shoot them from the wall here? Pew pew?" He makes finger guns toward the army cresting the hill.

"I was thinking of doing that, yes."

"Sounds good. I think I'll go prepare the defenses at —"

One of our Goblins emerges from around the bailey wall, flailing its arms as it sprints across the courtyard. "Run!" it squeals. "Krieb is in —" His last words are cut off as the crack of a flintlock pistol echoes throughout the keep. The goblin's back arches and its body crumbles in a heap, revealing a smoking hole in its back.

From around the corner emerges one of the most feared characters on the server. Wearing skin-tight leather, tall boots, and a wide-brimmed hat — the only thing more distinctive than Krieb's handlebar moustache is his near flawless kill streak.

A grin tugs at the corner of Krieb's mouth as he spots the two of us.

We have hunted each other over countless battlefields, but every time I face him without backup, I die. His level is too high, his reflexes flawless, and he has a knack for avoiding my attacks. They say he and his brother were the first ones in the game and tirelessly ground out levels to ensure they remained the most powerful players.

Kris leaps from the battlement, hurtling twenty feet into the courtyard. Krieb takes a single step backwards when, with a thunderous *FOOM*, Kris's giant sabatons impact with the cracking earth. As Kris lands, he swings a shield the size of a door from his back and points. "Krieb, you're mine!"

Krieb nods, accepting the challenge. An honour few receive.

Knowing how dangerous this enemy is, Kris doesn't hesitate. He swings his axe to decapitate his foe, but Krieb rolls to the side, pulls a boot knife, and buries the blade in a vulnerable patch of leather in the armpit of Kris's armour. In a splash of blood, Kris stumbles, and the two crash to the ground.

But only Krieb stands. He spits a mouthful of blood, gathers his hat and dusts it off.

Kris groans, the wound not a mortal one, but there are only a few precious moments before Krieb realizes he hasn't quite killed my friend.

With sharp-taloned fingers I coax smoky darkness out of the onyx in my staff, form a magical pulsing ball of death, draw back my arm, and cry, "Kynth kar!" I lob the magical orb toward my foe and it screams through the air. However, just before it strikes,

Krieb slashes the magical missile in half with his sword. My spell puffs into harmless smoke and passes around him.

I say, "Come on, dude. Haxors?"

Krieb says, "Git gud, noob. Get ready to be owned." Though his voice sounds like it comes from a twelve-year-old, he's no less intimidating. He twists his moustache and tosses a smoke bomb that fills the courtyard. I know that at any moment he'll leap out and slice my throat. Unlike Kris, I don't have protective armour.

Accompanied by a musical *ding*, a chat window expands across my screen and blocks my game.

Kali whispers to you: Hey baby, still busy?

"Dammit, not now!"

Krieb says, "Yeah now."

"Not you." My shaking hand makes it hard to click the tiny minus sign, but I succeed on the third try. I'm still alive, and the smoke has spread onto the keep wall where I'm standing.

"Arha . . . Arha menlu," I chant forbidden magic that vibrates my bones and painfully expands within me. Blood trickles from my ears as oily darkness spills from my eyes, my mouth, my fingertips. I gurgle and laugh as ichor spills down my body, splashes on the flagstones, and streams down the walkway.

Predictably, Krieb springs from the smoke, but not from the stairs like I thought. He dives from my left. I shriek and trip over myself in panic as my magical trap activates and glistening tentacles explode from the ichor to coil around the Witch Hunter, binding him in place. Krieb struggles, but his fury makes the tentacles wrap tighter, and he drops his sword with a clatter.

"You got lucky, noob." Krieb spits blood onto my robe.

"Maybe." I touch the orb to Krieb's forehead and chant, "Kheir-khlar . . ." Krieb's face relaxes and turns ashen, the colour drains from his eyes, and his body hollows out. His misty spirit pours from his mouth, his eyes, his ears until he becomes a dried husk that quickly disintegrates.

```
KILLING BLOW!
VICTIM: KRIEB
You: 6, Krieb: 5
```

The kill count hovers above the pile of dust in glowing medieval font. I hadn't realized the kill would put me ahead, and I know that means he'll be looking for revenge as soon as he respawns.

As arrows and catapult stones sail over the walls from the now assembled enemy army, I help Kris stand and offer a glowing potion from my satchel. "On your feet, solder."

"Is he dead?" Kris takes the potion and squeaks open his visor to drink it.

"You softened him up for me."

I open Kali's chat window.

```
You whisper to Kali: Hey baby, sorry. Give me
like 5 or 10 more minutes?
Kali: I'll go make breakfast. Don't wait too
long, you'll want time to enjoy this.
You whisper: I'll hurry.
```

Perched atop the gatehouse, two Goblins cackle and high-five each other before tipping a brimming pot of boiling oil upon the heads of the battering ram crew. A moment later, the battlefield echoes with the horrified screams of the burned and surely dying below.

I wonder if Kali bought us something sexy, or if he's taking me on another date.

A Goblin falls to its death with a piercing scream behind the melee, and the tide of battle seems to be turning. Kris and the orcs are pushed back through the keep doors as spells and arrows batter their shields. If they're pushed into the courtyard, we'll be surrounded and wiped out.

Typically, I'd hide on the walls and kill enemies from a safe distance, but I only have a few hours before Karen is home, so I try something risky. I summon darkness from every corner of the castle — the unpredictable winds of Dhar are difficult for even Dark Elves to master, though we're its undisputed experts. The chaotic power lashes out, whipping tendrils of dark magic through the gate and into the valley.

An Order Knight yells, "How did Vhiron get in there? Hax!"

A Bright Wizard shouts, "Told you I saw him!"

The darkness turns inward and claws at my soul. The more I restrain it, the more it saps my life and lashes friend and foe alike.

"Yes, Vhiron is here," I say.

I outstretch my hands and a roaring tidal wave of noxious darkness washes enemies out of the gates. Those who don't die are cut down or pushed back by our troops. As the wave subsides, I stride onto the battlefield behind Kris's charge. The few remaining enemies soon fall victim to my curses and shadowy bolts.

A terrifying war horn echoes across the smoke- and blood-choked battlefield, and a stampede of mounted Dark Elves, Orcs, Goblins, and the mutated forces of Chaos charge their twisted and monstrous steeds into the scattering forces of Order. The Witch Elf leaps on the back of a fleeing Archmage and repeatedly digs her knives into his back until he drops. Kris splits the back of a fallen Knight with his axe. I rest my hands on my knees, my health bar flashing as the darkness fades from my eyes.

Kris smacks me on the back so hard that I nearly collapse. "That was fucking outstanding! Easily the most intense fight I've had in this game. And we killed Krieb!"

"Yeah, amazing," I say. "I should go. I'm not feeling well."

"Chemo kicking your ass?"

"Yeah, I'm having a tough day."

Kris rubs my shoulder with a massive gauntlet. "Damn, you'd think that after surgery they'd be done with all that stuff. Okay, go get well, man."

I switch to my chat window.

```
You whisper to Kali: Hi, handsome, I'm on my
way.

   Kali: Great! I'll switch over. See you soon!
```

- Your friend Kali has logged out -

Kris taps two fingers to the side of his helmet. "Bye, dude."

I drag the mouse pointer over and click the camp icon.

`You are in a combat area. You will log out in`

`5 . . . 4 . . . 3 . . . 2 . . 1 . . .`

My stomach sours as the game freezes and the screen goes dark. While I dislike lying to Kris, I can't imagine a world, virtual or otherwise, where Kris and Lydia could coexist. We've been through too much together to let our friendship end this way.

6

Live Like
We're Dying

2010 - One minute later

The screen shifts from battlefield to character selection, then shuts down, leaving me staring at a desktop cluttered with folders, short-cut links, and unorganized photos.

There are pictures of me, Kris, and Karen wearing Medieval Times crowns and holding roasted turkey legs. There's a picture of me as Edward Scissorhands back in my goth days. Me and Kris are at some bar in this one, drinking beer and wearing tough-guy dude faces for the camera. The most recent is a picture of me as a zombie in a blood-soaked dress shirt and tie. I made the perfect zombie since I was so pale from chemo, and my shaved head seemed to help too. That was taken just before my bosses pushed me to go on disability leave.

That Halloween was the day I proposed to Karen. Both of us in costume, which now feels uncomfortably appropriate. The engagement picture is on my desktop as well: Karen at the steakhouse, biting the menu with happy tears in her eyes. Even though that was fewer than six months ago, it feels like a lifetime.

I push myself away from my desk and sweep the blanket from my legs. Supporting my weight, I struggle to my feet. Even though it has been months since my operation, the sloshing chemo bottle at my hip still feeds me a steady supply of poison. They had me plugged back in the moment they felt I was strong enough after surgery. It's supposed to ensure cancer doesn't return, but it also slows post-surgical healing.

Karen's cat scratches in the litter two rooms away.

Every day is the same.

I wake as Karen closes the apartment door. Then it's tea and choking food down while checking my email. Dishes go in the sink, and I'm back to the computer. I'll get up to use the bathroom or refill my tea, but otherwise I'm here. I'm too sick to walk very far, and the chemicals have made my brain too foggy and eyesight too blurry for me to be creative.

I'll sometimes sit on the doorstep and watch normal, living people go by. It's hard to remember being like them, the not-sick. If I catch them staring, they either look away or smile with painful sympathy. It's getting easier to spot the ones who know someone with cancer — painful recognition followed by the remembrance of loss.

But as I sit, dark thoughts wiggle in; they tell me I'm going to die accomplishing nothing. What's worse, they tell me I'll die a coward, having never listened to the little voice that laughed every time I tried to tell myself I was a boy. It sometimes whispers that the cancer will come back and kill me properly this time.

Sometimes I think that dying might be easier than being authentic.

I adjust the chemo bottle for walking. Its plastic tube disappears under the hem of my t-shirt, up my chest, and then plunges in the flesh of my inner bicep and into a vein. Recently, a nurse fed this rubbery plastic into my body until the end of the six-foot tube pushed into my beating heart. It's still there, every few seconds dripping poison so that it can spread throughout my body.

It's impossible, but sometimes I think I know it has dripped by the tiny convulsions my heart makes. At this dosage, either the chemo or cancer could kill me now, or ten years from now. Place your bets.

I shuffle to the kitchen in oversized rabbit slippers. I carry a glass of water to the bathroom, sit, and groan as my bladder empties. The familiar acrid retch of chemo piss fills the air, and I flush it away before the smell makes me vomit.

During my retreat to the computer, I glimpse my reflection in the mirror and stop before it. Maybe it's because I've been online so much, but I feel betrayed when I see this unexpected person. Like the Dark Elf I play with Kris, I expect the beautiful, androgynous person I was in my teens and early twenties. I was feminine *enough* back then to hide from my growing dysphoria with long hair and goth makeup. Another secret part of me hopes for a hint of femininity, leeched perhaps from the soy in tofu or by osmosis from the female characters I play through my computer screen. I'll wake to discover breast growth, narrow shoulders, or anything to justify all these days of unspoken wish-making. I long to return to the magical days of childhood, where anything felt possible.

Instead, in the mirror is a hunched bald man with hollowed features and dark rings around his eyes. I have never less resembled the feminine person I am in my mind. I run fingers over the white peach fuzz on my head. Even before cancer, my body betrayed me. It's been doing so ever since puberty. Over the years, testosterone has altered me by imperceptible degrees like a boiled frog, until one day I realized that I was irretrievably separated from the feminine ideal I hoped to resemble.

Surely, I would have done something if I knew I would end up like this.

"Fuck you," I say at my reflection in a deep, unmistakably masculine voice. Hearing that voice triggers a cold panic. I feel an instinctive need to escape, but escape what, my body? I choke on a sob, and tears drip down my cheeks. My knees wobble. I sit back down on the toilet before I fall.

Acknowledging the lost opportunity of transitioning when I was younger can only be described as bereavement. The *what ifs* haunt me. If I had transitioned younger, I could have held onto my teenage beauty, like the flawless teenage trans women of today. It would be easy to blame the transphobic assholes of the nineties and the way they beat any notion of transition out of me with their man-in-a-dress jokes and violent "really a man" reactions. The sadder truth is, without the internet and avenues of support, I had internalized those toxic concepts and imprisoned my authentic self within a trap of my own design.

I rest my head in my hands, snot dripping through my fingers as I sob. I tug too much toilet paper and then roll it back up because I can't afford to waste it, count off three squares, and blow my nose on that.

Then I remember Kali has a surprise for me.

After a few deep, calming breaths and a half glass of water, I scrape my slippers back to my computer and sit down. I wheel myself closer, pull on my headphones, power up my voice changer, and listen to my pitch rise.

I clear my throat. "Testing." A fraction of a second later, a nasal voice repeats my words into my ear.

"Testing?" Barry White asks. I flinch and dial it back up.

"Hi, I'm Lydia. Nice to meet you." I can still hear a hint of bass, but it's close.

"Hi baby, I missed you." Satisfied with my voice, I boot up *Second Life* and log in.

Server: Verifying identity.
Server: Identity Found. Welcome back, Lydia!
Server: Returning to your last visited location.

The virtual world blooms into vibrant existence. It doesn't take long for the dazzle of flashing lights and steady, thumping electric beats to trigger an association with the scents of stale beer, vinegar cleaning spray, and pumped-in air conditioning. It's early with few people online, and the club is empty. I open the menu to check my friend list, but then I'm alerted with a musical chime to a message.

`System: You have received a teleport summons from Kali.`

I click ACCEPT.

A warm white light surrounds me and lifts me into the air. The floor falls away like crumbling Lego blocks, and the bar shatters into a shower of pixels only to re-form as a swirling vortex that sucks me in. I tumble and twist, hurtling across the world, a cacophony of conversations babbling in the periphery. Then suddenly it's over as my feet find solid ground.

I stand in a grassy field east of a quaint thatch-roofed cottage. Nestled against the foundation grow colourful flower bushes, and window boxes spill with fresh herbs. It is hard to know whether this is a recreation of a hamlet in Northern England, or a scene from a Tolkien book. Behind the cottage, down winding sandy paths, distant buoy bells echo over the crash of waves.

The front door opens and out walks Kali, wearing leather pants and a biker jacket. The tall cheetah strides confidently, nearly concealing a knowing grin. "Welcome home, beautiful."

I pad up the cobblestone path to meet him. "Are you saying this place is yours?"

"Ours."

I cup a hand over my mouth.

"I listen sometimes." He grabs my hips. "Is anything missing?"

I struggle to find imperfection and say, "If we own the place, we need a red door. Maybe a willow tree in our yard?"

"I can do that. But first, another surprise."

"Another . . ." My words trail off as Kali sinks to one knee.

From behind his back, Kali presents a jewellery box.

"Lydia, I know we've only known each other for a year, but I feel more connected to you than anyone I've ever met. You've helped me more than you know." His avatar engages the second part of the animation as he opens the box and holds it out. Within gleams a green ring. "I love you. Will you marry me?"

My heart pistons a staccato and I fumble my headset off and mute the mic. I stare at the screen, at my avatar cupping her mouth, at Kali kneeling at her feet. While I've known *Kali* for a year, I still know nothing about the person controlling Kali.

Until now, I've resisted sharing Real Life details with Kali. However, this isn't the first time I've pushed an online relationship too far when I've enjoyed myself. One of my rules is to never let an online romance spill into reality. I don't know what would happen if a relationship ever transcended the digital world, but I have an ominous feeling that, like Pandora's Box, once I let my secrets fly out, the lid can never be replaced. For that reason, I don't allow my peas to touch my carrots, and I diligently watch for signs that my online partner wants to push our relationship in a Real Life direction. It usually starts with asking for my phone number, or a photo, or my real name. When they do, I disappear. If they persist, I block them, or delete my character, or change server, or move to a new game. Heck, I've ghosted online partners only for wanting to be exclusive.

So why am I hesitating now?

And what if Kali is more emotionally detached than I thought, and this is only another roleplaying scene to him? A more frightening option is that he might be delusional and is proposing to Real Life me through the game.

I realize the difference is that I've somehow allowed myself to develop authentic feelings for Kali. Every morning my heart leaps when he logs in and his name flashes upon my screen. When he says that he loves me, my fingers fly to the keyboard to repeat the words faster than my lips could speak them. When we're together, it's so easy to forget the outside world and the cancer devouring my body.

I know we're playing pretend, but I want this and him like nothing before. A part of me wants even more of him — the real him, but I know that's impossible. He would never feel the same way if he knew the real me. And if I ever told him, he would crush my heart when he discovered what I am.

Maybe it's for the best if he rejects me. I'll confirm my suspicions, and it will hurt, but then I can move on like I always do.

But first I'll accept his proposal. I at least deserve a moment of joy to commemorate our relationship. I'll take a screenshot of our last moments together, then after he breaks up with me, I'll archive our love in the secret folder locked away under password protection in my file system.

Kali waits, still offering the ring, his arms shaking.

I say, "Yes. I'll marry you."

Kali's face lights up.

I take my screenshot.

Kali springs to his feet and tugs the ring from its box. He holds it out, waiting for me to accept the item swap prompt.

I title the screenshot "I do" and save it.

I say, "Before I put on that ring, I need to tell you more about the real me."

"I was hoping you might want to." Kali takes my left hand, then drops it. "You're not a mobster or anything?"

While I can't stop myself from laughing, delaying wasn't my intention. "You might not want to know. It's a lot." I lead him to the stoop of the cottage. I sit, the cool ocean breeze swishes the grass and flutters my hair.

Kali takes the hint and sits beside me.

What I planned to say is "Hey, you should know something. I'm a guy," like I have done a few disastrous times in the past, but I'm no longer sure that's the truth.

Instead, I tell him *everything*.

I tell him I'm a guy in Real Life, that I have a girlfriend — no, a fiancée — that I'm almost forty years old, that I use a voice-changing app to make myself sound feminine, that I've never had a boyfriend before, not in Real Life, but I've dated many online.

I tell him I've always been secretive about how I really feel, about who I really am, but that in my heart I'm the woman he knows. That somewhere in this poisoned puppet of a man is a woman who loves him dearly, that hopes he understands and doesn't want to run screaming for the breathtakingly rendered hills in the distance.

By the time I'm done, I have difficulty distinguishing the shapes on the computer screen through my tears. Lifting my glasses, I wipe my face and see that his avatar is still there. Like Saph, I expect him to disappear — that he actually logged out halfway through my disclosure, but the system hasn't caught up yet.

I wait for him to disappear — to never see his face again.

It's what I would have done.

Instead, he takes my hands and says, "I've dated a trans girl before. I'm fine with it."

I mute my mic. I had been steeling myself for rejection so completely that I didn't realize acceptance was a possibility. Not only that, but he's dated trans women?

Then I realize he's referring to *me* as a trans woman.

And I realize he's right.

Cool relief washes over me, and I breathe in air that tastes twice as fresh. I now recognize the monster in the darkness that has been trying to claw its way out of me all my life. I realize that admitting my feelings to Kali accomplished something much more important than companionship — something potentially bigger and more dangerous to my life than cancer.

But it's all too much to wrap my head around, and I explode into a sobbing mess as I unmute. "I love you so much, Kali." I fling my arms around his neck and kiss him.

"Are you okay? Does that mean that you'll marry me?"

"Yes, of course I will, you goof!"

I click ACCEPT, and the ring materializes on my finger.

7

Intercourse with the Vampyre

1995 – Fifteen years earlier, in a small country town in Southern Ontario

Connect tapestries.fur.com:2069

An intro page scrolls onto my screen.

```
    __
 -  ---___-                              ,
  (' ||      _                    || '
  (( ||     < \, -_-_    _-_  _-_, =||= ,._-_ \\ __-_    _-_,
  (( ||     /-|| || \\  || \\ ||_.  ||    ||    || || \\ ||_.
  (( //    (( || || || ||/   ~ ||   ||    ||    || ||/   ~ ||
  -___-  \/\\ ||-' \\,/  ,-_-  \\,  \\,  \\ \\,/  ,-_-
            |/
           '         http://www.fur.com/tapestries/
```

Tapestries MUCK is a cross between a real life BDSM play party, a free form roleplaying environment, and a social gathering place all within a furry theme. It strives to provide a place for safe and free exploration of dominance and submission

roleplay, as well as other forms of sexual
expression in public and in private. Tapestries
facilitates this by providing an environment that
is populated exclusively by adult players and
furry characters, as well as by setting guidelines
that encourage tolerance and respect of others'
fantasies and beliefs.

I wake to drops of water plunking in a clear dark pond. There is a musky scent, like snake moulting and sweat. It's too dim to see properly, but the looming shape of something the size of a small horse rests on the far side of the pond. Next to a smouldering fire, its back rhythmically rises and falls with each breath. Dark scales shimmer golden in the firelight, its long tail is wrapped protectively around itself as it slumbers.

Two, maybe three weeks have passed since I've been here, but seeing that sleeping dragon triggers a flood of memories. I recall his kind words that lured me out of the plaza, then how he told me to run as he bared his teeth. I ran through the forest only to stumble over a conveniently exposed root. He was on top of me immediately and clasped a collar around my neck while I made my requisite half-hearted protests. Then of course came the messy but mutually enjoyable mating.

I touch the soft ruff of ivory fur on my neck, but his collar is gone — no doubt already on another woman's neck, maybe even in this cave. I make a note of the dragon's name for a potential encore and leave the cave mouth to a warm summer breeze. Sun-dappled forest spreads before me, and I walk the soft woodchip-covered path back to civilization.

Ahead, trills of laughter and guttural moans drift through the trees. I emerge into a large plaza near a mixed group of Digimon characters, lizards, and furries of various species who brag about which subbed Tenchi Muyo! and Ranma ½ cassettes they recently imported from Japan.

They appraise my body with inquiring eyes, and some lean in to smell me as I pass.

Beyond this group, upon a massive pile of pillows, a naked female Pikachu, a rooster, and a vixen are intertwined. They writhe, grope, thrust, and lick each other as they perform for a crowd. Drowning out the exaggerated moans of the fox, a non-morphic floating dolphin argues that a rooster's cloaca could never impregnate a non-avian. A nearby kitten wearing an oversized bell collar scoffs in agreement, then adds that a beak could never be pleasurable for cunnilingus. Regardless, the vixen arches her back and wails in orgasm as she rides the rooster's face. It's inevitable that a vixen is involved in every encounter, because there're always twelve foxes, two kitsune, both with nine tails, one dragon, and a chakat in every public room.

I additionally fulfill one-third of the bunny quota.

Sharp claws trail down my back. "Nice tits," says a seven-foot bear named OldSmokey. His breath is hot against my long ears. He buries his nose in my neck and smells my hair. "Fertile too."

Looking down, I see my own light pink nipples and in an icy rush of panic I realize I've forgotten to wear clothes. I activate my inventory, and a white blouse bearing the crest of St. Mary's springs onto my body along with a kilt much higher up my thigh than school regulation allows. It's disappointing that so many might have seen me naked as I enjoy making people unwrap their present.

OldSmokey asks, "Why'd you do that?"

I candidly search the bear's preferences, and a shocking list of violent and undesirable kinks scroll. I sniff him back, as one does, and discover he's described his scent as gasoline and semen. Involuntarily gagging, I push past OldSmokey.

"Bitch," OldSmokey says.

I bury myself into the crowd to avoid the bear, but he's already playing with the kitten's oversized bell. Around me others sniff, and I sniff back. Eventually, a muscular wolf tugs my uniform's tie.

While Ace isn't a very sexy name, he and I seem to have complementary sexual preferences, so when he beckons and disappears in a flourish of sparkles, I follow along.

Ace the wolf's bedroom appears around me. Another cave, but this time filled with animal skins, an iron brazier filled with burning coals, and a naked and extremely aroused wolf. He's stroking his fingers along his shaft as I appear, but when I notice him, he growls and pounces me to the floor, claws gripping my shoulders, fangs bared as he eagerly forces his knees between mine to pry my legs apart.

Good boy.

The phone rings, and I realize it's somehow already dark outside. Call display says it's Dylan, this socialite club kid I met at a local LARP. Lately, he's been trying to lure me out to clubs. I debate ignoring the call, eager to finish this big, and not so bad, wolf, but I realize it's been a long time since I've talked to Dylan. If I don't answer now, I'll have to answer for ignoring him when we're in character, fighting for our lives together in the forest next month, so I pick up.

"Oh, you're home," Dylan sounds startled. "I'll pick you up at eight?"

Call display usually saves me from having to commit to Real Life responsibilities. I'm sure he thinks I have a rich social life, but really, other than an occasional nighttime walk to remind myself that a world exists outside of role-playing games and my internet line, I'm always home. And while I technically have enough dark clothing for his club, the concept of socializing with strangers at a bar is not only foreign to me, but also uncomfortable. I say, "I don't have a coat. Mine ripped."

"You can wear one of mine."

"I don't have any cool boots."

"Your Docs are fine, dude."

On the computer screen, a block of text appears. In a descriptive pose, the wolf describes how he grips the back of my neck in his powerful jaws, holding me in place as he hilts himself against my upturned ass, bucking as he unloads himself into my womb. Over the past few hours, we have written descriptive poses back and forth, weaving our perspectives into a single X-rated story. While lovers often compliment me on my prose, they just as often reply with uninspired responses such as "I came." But not Ace — while it's obvious he hasn't had much experience recognizing the subtleties of actual female anatomy, I'm still distracted by his deliciously lewd replies.

His skilled use of fluid descriptors is particularly noteworthy.

"Uh," I say into my phone.

Dylan says, "I'll take that as a yes. See you in two hours." He hangs up.

"Shit."

I politely write out a brief but descriptive orgasm pose for the wolf. It would be rude to leave him thinking he didn't satisfy, even if I'm no longer into it. Then I make up an excuse that my roommate came home and log out.

Over the last year, I've started replacing my wardrobe with anything tight and black. Another reinvention of myself, as I've done many times already.

These social chameleon shifts began as a reaction to being teased at school. Instead of hiding with the other bullied kids, I instead observed my tormentors. I concluded that the only difference between them and me was that they all wore similar clothes, and I wore whatever my mother bought me — from Kmart. Since clothes were inconsequential to me and mattered a great deal to the cool prep kids, I began emulating them.

I pinned my jeans close to my legs with a row of shiny safety pins, and whenever kids mocked what I lacked, I adapted. I conveniently tore my velcro shoes on a rock and told my parents I needed better ones than Kmart discounts, and I begged them to buy me a Swatch and overpriced Vuarnet t-shirts. Then, one day at school, I saw one of the unpopular kids had copied me by wearing the same Ralph Lauren shirt and Tretorn shoes, and I knew that I had succeeded.

When I entered high school, I allowed myself to remain fluid and spent a couple of years as a mod, wearing Doc Martens and parkas. When I graduated, I languished at home in plaid flannel and blasted Nirvana on my boombox. Neither fashion was truly *me*, but that hardly mattered when it ensured I was never alone.

Then I discovered the inky world of goth society. Last month I went to Siren in Toronto and bought a shirt with frilled cuffs, and wore it with my old boot-cut black jeans since I couldn't afford anything else. Last week, I stole some of my sister's Halloween nail polish, which I applied while waiting for Dylan to arrive. Maybe it's only the thrill of societal rebellion, but wearing polish, growing my hair long, and wearing beautiful clothes is fulfilling in ways other fashion never was.

Dylan's parents are rich, and he appears in front of my house in a scream of screeching tires that prompts three of my neighbours to pull aside curtains to investigate. Out front, Dylan impatiently revs the engine of the new black sedan his parents bought him. I'd never heard of a Chrysler Cirrus before, or how fast they could drive, until we roared out of Caledonia and toward the city. We weave through highway traffic at uncomfortable speeds and arrive in St. Catharines far sooner than we have any right to.

From outside the club, the place looks like a regular sports bar. And while a bar named the Frat House doesn't exactly scream goth, according to Dylan, once a month it belongs to us.

When I walk through the door, I immediately regret not staying home with my new wolf friend. Dylan flamboyantly introduces me to two different guys named Morpheus, a girl named Raven, and a freaky girl named Lucy with white contacts and pigtails. One of the Morpheuses eyes my outstretched hand as if I had just pulled it out of a toilet. My perception of goths being flexible and accepting shatters as these pale, willowy creatures float around me, eyeing my jeans unenthusiastically and laughing as I pass.

Surrounded by people with pierced tongues, lips, and eyebrows, I now realize how vanilla my presentation truly is. I try to make excuses to leave, but then Dylan introduces me to Fester, the club owner, who has a fiery red mohawk.

Fester has tree trunk–like legs trapped inside tattered cargo shorts adorned with thick chains. Most of his skin is covered in horror-themed tattoos, but most of those are covered with a shirt that reads Nitzer Ebb, "Down on Your Knees." He wears a dog collar with three-inch spikes, and through his nose is a large ring that makes his already beefy head look even more like that of a pissed-off bull.

"Hey," Fester says and offers me a meaty hand. He shakes gentler than I expected, considering how unimpressed he looks.

And why should he be impressed? He is fully committed to this lifestyle, and I feel like a tourist. I turn to discover that Dylan has disappeared, which he assured me he wouldn't do.

I scan the club for him with increasing anxiety, but I'm met with cold, uncaring stares and judgmental eyes. Fester grabs my shirt and tugs me to him. My heart freezes, and I'm expecting a fist, but he asks, "What are you drinking?" His breath reeks of Jägermeister.

"A beer, I guess?"

Fester cocks an eyebrow, still unimpressed.

I try to think of the gothest drink available. A Black Russian? Bloody Mary?

But instead, I say, "A Black Label . . . ?"

Fester waves the bartender over and orders one. Then he stumbles and nearly pulls me off my feet. "You look scared. You okay, man?"

"Yeah," I lie.

"Anyone messes with you, you come see me. You're one of us now. Okay?"

I laugh nervously and nod. "Yes, okay, thank you."

Fester hands me the Black Label and cracks the neck of my bottle with his. I swallow a mouthful, feeling more at ease, even when he staggers away to the DJ booth.

While I recognize Bauhaus when they come on, I've never heard most of the songs they're playing here, but the beats are familiar in a primal way that carries me with them into dark and dangerous places. The bands sing about social misfits, and private perversions, and things polite society never dares voice aloud. The lyrics speak to my heart and understand my place in this world. While I nurse my beer, I try to remember the songs and make mental notes for future purchases of boots and jackets, and I wonder if there are potential future girlfriends in the crowd.

I rest the empty bottle on the bar and head outside for a smoke.

Outside is brighter than I remember, even by streetlamp. Smoker goths huddle in a clique near the doors. Someone in a Mustang roars past and honks their horn. A jock hangs out the window and yells, "Freaks!"

Immediately, more than half of the goths look at their feet. A few flip the finger, and one girl runs after the car at least halfway down the block, the chains on her dress jingling as she screams after them.

When I look up, I realize how silly I must look standing here, away from the crowd. I'm clearly not allowed to be one of them, as Fester suggested. I'm just as much of a pariah to these people as the rest of the world that clearly dislikes people like me. I consider pretending I don't have a lighter in the hope one of them invites me into their circle, but I know my jeans won't win me any friends. Then I notice a goth girl down the street, sitting alone, reading a book under a streetlight.

I approach her and ask, "Mind if I sit with you?" The book has old, yellowed pages and has been re-covered in black cloth. I spot an illustration that reminds me of medieval woodcuts.

She looks up from her book to reveal a corpse-white face smeared with black makeup resembling The Crow. Her hair is dark and stringy and shines under the streetlight as if she hasn't washed it in a couple of weeks. She's wearing a frilly shirt, and over that a guy's coat at least two sizes too big. Other than the makeup, she has this tortured Alanis Morissette vibe that seems to linger under the growing smile she gives me.

She says, "You're cute. Come sit."

My heart leaps at the compliment. I sit and hold out my cigarette pack, "Want one?"

"I don't smoke."

"Oh." I stick out my arm, "Hey, look, we're twins." I twist my wrist, flaring my frilled cuff. I immediately regret it, thinking about how idiotic I probably look.

She holds her arm against mine. I realize that while my frilled pirate shirt is made of cheap white broadcloth, hers is antique off-white linen with crocheted frills. She snorts. "Hey, yeah."

I push my luck. "What are you reading?"

She considers the tattered book in her lap. "This? It's a primary school reader from the eighteen-hundreds."

I draw on my cigarette. The searing smoke fills my aching lungs and irons out my anxiety. I blow a spout of smoke away from her and ask, "You read kids' books?"

"It's the oldest book I own. Check this out." She shuffles closer as we sit together on the street curb, and she flutters the pages to the inside back cover. On the tattered onion-skin-thin page are pencil scribbles and a stick figure. "Isn't it interesting to think that the little kid who drew this probably grew old and died before we were even alive?"

I'm left speechless at her insight and feel brutish for not considering that books can signify more than just their story and decorative cover. As she shows me the tightly laced black thread that someone had used to secure the protective cloth cover, and the undeniably gothy list of long-deceased previous owners who wrote their names inside the cover, I remember there are other reasons to cherish a physical book. I am reminded of the undefinable satisfaction I receive when hugging a beloved story to my chest after I have finished reading. And as she continues to share her discoveries, I also realize that through time and interaction with others, a book's meaning can change entirely. A book can become a history lesson, and a time capsule, and a mystery. Only by physically interacting with a book can we discover these secrets. Whether left by violence or love, the marks upon a book can sometimes outshine its original intention with a unique magnificence.

I had too swiftly judged the book, and her, on appearances alone, and knew I was no better than any of the Morpheuses inside the club.

"It's very interesting," I say.

"Check out page seventy-one." The girl flicks through and fans open the book to reveal two pressed four-leaf clovers, brown now, but entirely intact. "I try not to open these pages too often. Two hundred-year-old clovers. I can't think of anything luckier than that."

She stands and drapes her hand toward me in a strangely formal way, which compliments the mannerisms of her whole being. She says, "Call me Anatole. It's nice to meet another child of the night."

Taking her hand in my fingertips, I allow her to help me stand, and I grind out my cigarette with the toe of my Doc. "That's a cool name. I'm Paul."

"I like the name Paul."

"It's okay, I guess."

Anatole stuffs her book into the large pocket of her trench coat. "Paul, do you want to walk with me?"

I glance at the club and the cliquey goths filing back in — the thumping music that awaits them. I wonder how safe it is to stray too far, but I feel an unusual kinship to this weird Alanis-Crow girl, so I say, "Sure."

We walk for a block in silence, and then two more exchanging all the usual all-about-you information — I learn she lives on the other side of the city, that she doesn't have a phone number for some reason, and that she somehow loves *The Crow* and Brandon Lee more than I do, which I didn't think possible. When she asks how long I've been goth, I say, "I've been into horror a long time, and I've always enjoyed the darker side of things, but I've only started dressing this way recently."

Anatole grins and grabs a loop of my jean and tugs me hard enough to stumble against her.

"Hey," I say, though I can't repress my grin.

"I can tell, but that's fine. Nice clothes are expensive."

"Yeah."

We walk another block, and I'm feeling better about my jeans and more at ease until Anatole asks, "Are you gay?"

"What? No."

While the question was unexpected, it wasn't surprising. It's one I've been asked again and again in various ways, some curious, some accusatorily, most of my life. Despite many efforts to shake any feminine cues from my presentation, my persistent inner self inevitably emerges and betrays me.

Anatole asks, "You sure?"

However, no one has ever double-checked. Instead of confirming, I say, "Why do you ask?"

Anatole stuffs her hands in her pockets. "Well, do you like guys?"

Maybe it's because I barely know her, and likely will never meet her again, but I feel light-headed as I admit the truth. "I'm not sure if I like guys that way."

"How do you not know?"

"I've never done anything with a guy in Real Life."

"What does that mean?"

"I think I like girls better." I pivot to avoid outing myself for feeling female, and dodging a conversation about furry porn. "I understand women. While I've thought about guys that way, I don't know if I want to . . . you know."

Anatole bumps my bony hip with her soft one. "Don't worry about it."

I exhale the breath I didn't realize I'd held.

We walk another block, turn, and make our way back toward the club. Both of us watch the sidewalk pass under our boots. Someone drives by in a car and whistles, then yells something indecipherable but undeniably lewd. He hangs out the window and licks the gap between two fingers.

Anatole says, "Fucking assholes." Her forehead is creased, and she's pulling her shoulders together as if trying to envelop herself in her coat. While I'm sure such catcalls are more traumatizing for women, being mistaken for one, especially from behind, isn't something new for me — and part of me secretly enjoys it.

I say, "They're just jerks, don't —"

"I think I might be a guy," Anatole says.

I expect her to follow that up with a grin — that she's going to tell me she loves guys so much that she's gay for them, in the exhausting way straight guys joke about being lesbian. However, her smile has vanished, and her previous elegance has somehow morphed her posture into a huddled, vulnerable creature who shuffles beside me. I realize I don't have a preprogrammed script for how to respond to a comment like that.

The only comparables my brain associates are the near infinite variations on sex and gender I see represented on Tapestries. The longer we walk in silence, the more tension I feel, so I say, "I've known a few people who don't conform to gender norms. Are you planning to do anything about it?" Then I remember the gender disclaimers I've seen in people's bios and ask, "Anatole, did you want me to call you a guy?"

"I don't know yet. I know I enjoy being called sir. For now, just call me Anatole."

I hip bump Anatole back. They stumble and I say, "Okay, sir."

Anatole's shoulders unfold, their smile spreads. "I'm talking to dealers about getting my hands on some T."

"I love tea, I guess we have that in common as well."

Anatole snorts, the corners of their mouth exaggerated by sharp, black-painted points. "You're pretty sweet for a not-gay guy.

I don't mean the drink. I want to start on a cycle of testosterone. Doctors around here don't take me seriously, so I might have to get black-market stuff."

The thought of taking testosterone with the intention of making myself more hairy, bald, brawny, and aggressive sends a shudder through my body. Why anyone would want to intentionally lock themselves in a meat prison like mine is beyond my understanding. I do, however, relate with Anatole's desire to make their body appear to be something it isn't — so I focus on that.

Of course, I should have reciprocated and confessed my own inner struggles, but instead I say, "Black market sounds dangerous. You be careful, okay?"

"I'll take my chances."

We emerge from an alley across the street from the Frat House. In front of the club a brown K-Car splutters, and, behind its rusted bumper, plumes of exhaust rise into the increasingly chill night air. Some guy in the driver's seat yells Anatole's name and waves at us.

"That's my ride," Anatole says. "And yes, I mean both my boyfriend and the car. It was nice to meet you." When they step away, I feel as if a part of myself moves with them.

"You're leaving already?" I want to know more, to discover how they came to recognize that hidden side of themself. I need to know how someone can be both gay and transgender simultaneously, and why they would even want to be. Dozens of other questions flower in my mind.

Anatole smiles again, then rushes back and hugs baggy sleeves around me, pulling me tight into their hidden soft curves. I hug back, and we hold each other until the car honks. When they lean away, we're both smiling into each other's faces. Anatole asks, "You're coming back, right?"

"Oh yes, definitely."

"Hey, you should have this." Anatole digs the old book out of their pocket and hands it to me. Their fingertips brush mine.

"Are you sure?" I take the book, still warmed by their body.

"Keep it safe for me." Anatole crosses the street and immediately begins to loudly argue with the guy in the car.

I hold the book and watch them bicker. While I can't hear what they're saying, I hope he's jealous over me and Anatole breaks up with him for being overprotective. I imagine walking with Anatole in the future and kissing them in one of the alleys we explored tonight. Or maybe they'll kiss me. But then I realize if that happened, and if it got serious, I'd have to tell my friends that I'm dating . . . what would that make me?

My heart sinks as Anatole kisses their boyfriend. The car pulls away and disappears down a darkened side street.

From the doorway, a song I've never heard mixes into one by Alien Sex Fiend, and the windows of the Frat House buzz.

I sit under a streetlight and read from Anatole's book.

⸮ 8 ⸮

Help! I'm Alive

2009 — Fourteen years later,
at Juravinski Cancer Centre in
Hamilton, Ontario

"Come in, Paul." Dr. Teller waves me into a makeshift hospital office the size of a closet and goes back to reviewing a file. "I am afraid this room is a little cramped. Pull up a chair and close the door."

It's hard to believe that six months of daily chemotherapy and weekly radiation could simultaneously feel like an eternity yet pass so swiftly. Stacked upon the desk are several folders under one marked with my name. Dr. Teller is a colorectal cancer specialist, and therefore each one of those folders must signify a person with cancer like mine. It makes me wonder how many of those people will receive surgery only to succumb to the disease anyway.

When I was younger, I believed that illness only happened to other people — the supporting actors in my life. The nameless, faceless *them* who existed solely as a teachable moment for me to eat better or exercise more. In that adolescent age of perceived invulnerability, I assumed if I were to catch a disease, it would be because of my negligence. If I had continued smoking, had unprotected sex, if I ate too much fast food, if I did any of those, I could acknowledge that I knowingly took a risk and that the world is cruel, but fair. Even thinking about how we *catch* disease seems to signify voluntary participation.

While I've heard of otherwise healthy people falling ill or dying, of athletes clutching their heart and collapsing mid-stride, I never imagined it would be me. Sometimes I wonder if the religious nutjobs waving their signs are right — that maybe it's God judging me for entertaining queer ideas. Or maybe it's God judging me for acknowledging the woman I am, yet not acting on it — a punishment for leading an unproductive, inauthentic life.

How strange would it be if this surgery doesn't work and cancer kills me? I'll die and stand before God, the grand game master, and they'll say, "Well, *Paul*, it's a shame that you hid from your true self. I sent you plenty of hints. No matter, let's reset your game and you can roll a new character."

I like that idea. It feels like mercy.

But I no longer believe I'm getting out of this lucky. All signs suggest I'll end up as a statistic — a warning to other people approaching middle age. People I went to school with will learn that I died and say, "He was so young, but he ate a lot of fast food," and they'll quietly give up McDonald's for a month. I'll linger in people's memory only as a teachable moment.

Dr. Teller slides the folders into his briefcase. He clasps my hand in his much larger one. A steady, confident, dry hand with manicured nails. I wonder if he's practised this handshake. Tight grip, one shake, on to work. He asks, "How are you feeling?"

I'm convinced that it's impossible to feel "good" with this much chemo in my system, even if he's weaned me off for tomorrow's surgery. I shift uncomfortably as the inflamed orb bleeds in retaliation for the radiation treatments and soaks into the toilet paper I've stuffed into my underwear. It's so swollen now I'm afraid to use the toilet, and afraid not to, and afraid of the pain, the blood in the water, and mostly that shitting over a cancerous lump every day is making my cancer worse. While my strength is creeping back, I don't yet have enough to feel human.

Still, complaining won't accomplish much. I say, "I'm okay, but a little sore."

"Good, good. The treatment can do that," he says in his cheery Kermit voice. "After we're done here, I will ask an ostomy nurse to prepare you for tomorrow, but first I need you to sign a liability waiver so I can act in your best interest."

"Best interest?" I try to read the form, but I can't make the words stick to my brain. The letters are small, crowded together, legal jargon.

"The form is standard, but in your case, it's possible we may decide during the surgery that a permanent colostomy might be a safer option for you."

"But that's not happening, right?"

Dr. Teller considers me. "We hope not. But —"

"You said I wouldn't need one," I interrupt. "Remember in the consultation room when you —" I twist two fingers into the air.

"We won't know for sure until you are in surgery." He seems to read my apprehension. "We can take another look now if you like?"

Within moments I am bent over beside him, gripping his desk, my pants and underwear around my ankles. Dr. Teller squelches lube over two meaty fingers that he recently shook my hand with. Before I remember to worry about the girth of those sausage fingers, he's pushing them inside me.

My forearm gives out and my elbow cracks against the desk. His fingers stretch and twist inside. He probes deep, pulling out to the tip and scraping around the inside of my anus. He prods the painful orb. I cry out and close my eyes and go inside my head.

I imagine grassy fields, breezy willow trees, lapping waves, anything to take me away from here.

"Sorry — you are very swollen. I will be careful. Hmm . . ."

The waves disappear. "Is it bad?"

"Like I said, you're very swollen." Dr. Teller twists his fingers, and I whimper, but he ignores my complaints and continues exploring.

"You said that the chemo would shrink the tumour, and you had enough to reconnect. There's still enough, right?"

"There's a little space." He pokes inside me. I ball my hands and grit my teeth. "About a centimetre, but there may only be a half. I think I still have enough to reconnect."

"You do?"

"Yes, there should be enough." He swiftly pulls his fingers out, and the tumour throbs and burns and lube drips down my inner thigh. "I'll be back in a moment." He hands me a box of tissues and opens the door. In the hall, nurses gossip as they pass, and I try to shuffle behind the door for privacy, my belt clanking on the wall tile.

"Oops," Dr. Teller says. He pulls the door closed behind him.

I crouch and frog-leg my knees apart and wipe until the paper no longer comes up looking greasy or red. Then I draw another clean tissue from the box to hide the soiled ones and bunch the filth together before dropping and hiding the balled-up tissue in his waste bin under similar tissue balls and discarded rubber gloves.

Dr. Teller opens the door while knocking. "All cleaned up?"

"Yes."

"Great!" he says with the enthusiasm of a cartoon tiger. He squeezes past me and sits in the squeaky chair. "I spoke with a surgical colleague, and he will pop in during your surgery so we can provide you with the best care. Is that okay with you?"

I wonder who, but quickly realize that asking wouldn't matter. I don't have a working knowledge of prominent cancer surgeons, and I don't plan on looking him up, anyway.

"Is that normal?" I ask.

Dr. Teller nods as he writes an addendum at the bottom of the waiver. "It is normal to have other people in the operating room."

He brightens and says, "I would also like to have some medical interns observe as well. Are you okay with that?"

I imagine myself naked on an operating table. My legs are spread, and my feet strapped into stirrups as if I were giving birth — in a way I suppose I am. As the crowd of medical students and professionals gather close, Dr. Teller will slice me open, exposing glistening pink intestines. He'll dig further and then hold up the tumour I've been nurturing inside me for everyone to see.

Maybe they'll clap.

I guess I really am a teachable moment.

I say, "Sure, if you think so."

"Read this over and sign at the bottom." Dr. Teller slides the form back to me and points at a line. "When you are comfortable, sign on these additional lines to consent to others being present in the operating room."

I take the cheap plastic pen and attempt to read again, but I can't make the letters stay still. I decide to trust my surgeon. I've come this far, and I feel as if I've already agreed to this when I accepted treatment. I hesitate and ask, "You're sure you'll be able to reverse the ostomy?"

"I'm confident that I can, but like I said, we'll have to review what we're dealing with in the operating room."

I tap the pen on the paper, wondering if this is like a contract, if I can make my own changes. I could put in, "I agree to this document as long as the ostomy surgery is reversible," but I don't. As soon as the thought crosses my mind, I realize how silly the idea is — that the surgeon certainly would be considerate of my preferences. He is a smart guy.

I sign the paper.

Dr. Teller gathers my chart and the signed form and secures them in his briefcase. "We will see you bright and early tomorrow. Stay here for the nurse." He shakes my hand and is gone. I realize I won't see him again until after surgery — if I wake up.

By the time I gather my belongings, two nurses wait in the doorway. "Paul?" the shorter one asks.

"Yes?"

"Come with us, honey, we need to mark you up."

I follow them down the hall. "Mark me up?"

"To show the surgeon where to place your ostomy."

"Oh."

The shorter nurse scouts ahead, peeking into rooms, and then excitedly waves us into one. We follow her into a small medical supply closet with chalk-white walls and that familiar hospital reek of latex and antiseptic.

"Did you bring markers?" the smaller nurse asks.

"No," says the taller. She proceeds to dig through unlabeled boxes until she triumphantly produces some.

I envision mismanaged paperwork, the doctor looking down at a pirate-like *X* on my belly and thinking, *I thought this patient was supposed to have a reversed colostomy, but I can't argue with this marker!*

The smaller nurse crouches in front of me and scrutinizes my midsection. I pull my hands out of my pockets and stand straight, hoping it helps. "What do you think?" The small nurse asks as she pokes just above my belt line with the cap of the marker.

The taller nurse asks me, "Is that how you normally wear your pants?"

"I just wear pants. I don't understand what you mean."

She reaches for my belt. "Can I show you?"

When I nod, she hikes up my shirt, exposing my belly, and mentally calculates something.

The shorter nurse asks, "Do you want it above or below your belt?"

"For the ostomy?" I ask.

"Do you want it to be here," she touches her fingertips to my belly above my belt line, "or down here," she touches low enough that it sends a confusing twinge of curiosity through my pelvis.

I allow myself to visualize having an ostomy and where the scar will be when it heals after the surgeon reverses it. I say, "I guess place it lower so I can hide it in my pants."

"Good idea," the small nurse says. I feel clever for having thought of it and consider writing a pamphlet to help future patients making life-changing medical closet decisions. She says, "Would you mind pulling your pants down a little?" She bites the cap off the marker and grips it in her teeth.

I jingle my belt open and pull my jeans down to my thighs, exposing my boxer briefs to the cool room. The small nurse tickles fingertips over my belly, and I try not to laugh or flinch. "Ahh ooo geyyin a iyyeossomi or—" She muffles a laugh and pulls the cap from her mouth. She smiles. "Sorry, are you getting an ileostomy or colostomy, dear?"

I fold my arms, suddenly unsure where I should put my hands. I ask, "Which one is temporary? Isn't it on your chart?"

The taller nurse points to something on my chart and turns the clipboard to show the shorter nurse. The small nurse looks annoyed, then says, "It's blank, so we should prepare for both. If it's a colostomy, I would mark an X on the left side of your stomach. If you're getting a temporary stoma, or an ileostomy, the X would go on the right. That's where the doctor will create your stoma."

I imagine a surgeon with elbow-length gloves snipping off my glistening pink colon with a pair of scissors. He fishes about inside my belly and pushes the tube through the meat-hole he cut out of the magic-markered *X*. I wonder if Dr. Teller ever jokes with medical residents during surgery and wiggles it like a Xenomorph emerging from someone's guts.

I dispel the mental image and decide I'm better off not knowing how the sausage gets made.

"I'm having an ileostomy," I say.

The smaller nurse lines up the marker and her fingertip brushes the elastic of my boxer briefs, and I wonder how embarrassing it would be to get an erection right now. Could I even get an erection while being drawn on by nurses?

I really need to stop thinking about erections.

"There looks good," the taller nurse says. "But I'm not sure. The last person I marked was a girl."

"This is different for girls?" I ask.

The smaller nurse says, "Completely different. Girls wear their pants higher or lower than guys, their waists are higher, so we usually mark the ostomy higher. We don't want the edge of your pants to chafe against your stoma."

I say, "If someone asked for it lower, they could hide it in their pants either way, right?"

"Some people like it higher so it doesn't pinch when you sit. Your first choice was excellent. I'll draw one on both sides, and your surgeon can choose the one he needs."

The cold tip of the marker touches my belly.

⌁⌁⌁

I'm swimming through Jell-O and struggling to keep my head above the muck, but I'm not alone.

A lurking monster rises through the darkness beneath me, hunting. I try to swim away, to play dead, to hide, but it always finds me. It grabs my leg, its claws bite into soft flesh. I scoop at the jelly and pull myself away, but then the monster pulls me down. I struggle, but my body is so heavy . . . no, it's my head that's heavy. It is taking all my strength to drag this heavy head through this jelly.

I struggle and kick to get free, but the Grue laughs and climbs up my body until its face is before mine. It spits words through sharp teeth. "You had to open that egg. You foolish boy." Its eyes are wide with glee. "Now you're mine."

The Grue slashes open my belly and drags me under. I muffle a cry into the sticky goop, my stomach spasms and muscles clench in pain. My pretty pink intestines spread out before me, and I hug them to my body. I kick free and surface, but the Grue covers my mouth and pulls me against its unexpectedly soft body. Despite its harsh words, the monster hugs me to it, comforting and cradling as it sinks me into the unknown. I give in. With submission comes serenity. I wonder if this is what it feels like to die.

Its soft breasts press to my back, its breath cold and inhuman against my ear. It whispers, "I think he's already coming out of it."

As I blink the jelly from my eyes, I see bright amorphous blobs which come into focus as industrial lighting hanging from a white ceiling. I appear to be in a room of massive proportions, maybe a gymnasium.

I will myself to lift a numb arm and stare at my hand, while pins and needles tingle to my fingertips. Wires and tubes emerge from the flesh on the back of my hand, from my bicep, and, as I look down at my body, many more emerge from beneath a shroud laid over me — a rainbow of wires and tubes connecting me to bags of fluids on chrome stands or to softly humming machines dangling from chrome hooks. I touch my numb face and discover I'm wearing an oxygen mask. With equally numb fingers, I sink fingernails into my cheek, and when I do it hard enough, pain blooms.

I'm alive.

I attempt to rub the goo from my eyes, but I jab my eye socket with my thumb, which shouldn't happen if I had my glasses. I search for a bedside table and realize that not only is my bed narrow and a few feet off the ground, but I'm also boxed in with metal rails. Across the blurry room, I realize I'm only one of dozens, maybe hundreds, of others. They've arranged us in perfect rows, wall to wall, head to foot, with only a few feet between us.

Between the silent, still bodies move slender, ethereal keepers in blue robes who float effortlessly from one cot to the next. They check feeding tubes and oxygen — they ensure we're properly hooked up and thriving in our convalescent dream worlds. A throaty groan echoes across the gymnasium, the dry, phlegmy kind old men make when they rise from the dead and hunger for flesh.

Pain lances into my stomach where the monster clawed me, and I reach down, massaging padding under the sheets. As I explore over my stomach, pain spiderwebs up my chest and deep inside to hidden places I didn't realize felt pain. I grit my teeth, stomach muscles tensed and quivering as I'm forced to pause my explorations. Once the intense agony subsides to a dull throb, I can once more think clearly.

It seems unlikely that someone could save me from . . . but as I think about the attack, I realize how ridiculous it sounds.

"I told you he was awake," says a woman floating to me. She leans close enough that I realize she's human. I can't read her expression because of her medical mask, but her eyes are dark and kind.

"You must be really strong," the woman with kind eyes says. "You weren't supposed to wake for another hour or two."

"Where am I?" My voice is little more than a croak.

"You are in a surgical staging area. You just woke up from surgery, and I have been told that it went well."

My brain is racing to catch up. I try to remember what could have happened to my stomach to make it hurt so badly — it clearly can't have been clawed open by a monster.

"Please don't try to get up — you're tangled in cords," the woman says. "You're safe, and everything is okay. You might have to wait here a while before we can move you into a recovery room. Can I get you anything?"

"My glasses?"

She searches the gurney. "They don't seem to have come in with you."

She reviews a clipboard that seems to materialize in her hands. "Your surgeon left a note saying he's going to speak to you in your recovery room. I'll find your glasses and inform your surgeon that you're awake."

She touches my arm and fades away into the room.

"Thank you."

A flood of realization washes over me, sinking me beneath the surface of an icy lake, leaving me breathless.

I remember my mom's friend ambushing me in the pre-op staging area and trying to scare me into accepting Jesus as my saviour.

I remember Karen's veneer of supportive strength cracking — her face pinching, and her crying when I blew her a kiss as they wheeled me out to be prepped for anaesthesia.

I remember the distracted, flirting anaesthetists trying to give me an epidural, twice, and failing. Then the two of them laughing at some inside joke as I sink under.

I remember the nurses that marked my stomach.

I cup my right side through the sheets, looking for the surgical site, to confirm the ostomy is temporary. For a moment, my anaesthetic-soaked brain wonders if they abandoned the surgery, but then I reluctantly slide my hand to the left and discover bulky, taped-down padding. Beneath all that gauze, something alien pulses in response, firing painful electric shocks that nearly overload my system.

While thinking is difficult right now, I'm certain I remember that the pain shouldn't be on this side of my stomach. I reach farther down, exploring the padding of what may be a diaper, and, reasoning I can't be remembering this correctly, I wrestle the sheets to my waist and pull back the taped gauze.

Beneath the gauze is a transparent colostomy bag. A clear plastic colostomy bag containing a swollen, angry tomato of abused intestine, red and wet and pressed against the plastic like a cheeky window kiss.

I realize I'll never be the same. Everyone from this point on that sees me naked will pretend they're not repulsed by the bag of shit attached to my stomach. I'm suddenly unsure if this is a worthwhile trade-off for only potentially being cancer free.

Snippets of memories seep through the sludge clogging my brain: being told there would be spectators in the surgical room and strangers advising Dr. Teller — medical advisors who didn't know the face of the person they'd condemned to this *thing*. The infuriating, helpless unfairness of the situation overwhelms me, and tears slip down my face; I can only feel them in cool tickles over the thawed portions of my cheeks. I allow my hands to fall to my sides, resting on the surgical cot I've woken too early on.

I feel abandoned — a number on a clipboard among countless rows of sleepers. With luck, they'll wake to better news, to news of surgeons who didn't betray them. I ball up my fist and thump it on the bed.

The nurse returns with my glasses. Seeing the wet, windowed colostomy bag in high definition is so much worse. There are really only two reasons why anyone would put a clear colostomy bag on someone like me, both cruel to the patient: the first is that it's more convenient for caregivers, and the second is because they want me to be smashed in the face by its undeniable reality and accept it.

"What's wrong, dear?" The nurse takes my bedsheet and tries to cover the colostomy, but I clumsily shove her hands away. She recoils as if I'd struck her. Maybe I unintentionally did. Admirably, she maintains composure. "Your surgeon should be here soon," she says, and she offers a hopeful smile before leaving me to speak with the other nurses.

I hope she tells him I'm a monster.

I hear Dr. Teller's Kermit-like voice talking to the nurse across the room before I spot him. He says, "Already? Okay, I'll talk to him for a minute." He moves through the sea of sleepers and looms over me.

"Well, hello there, young man." His practised enthusiasm is glaringly obvious. "All splendid news. We believe we removed all the cancer."

"Good, but —"

"Four of your lymph-nodes were likely infected," he continues, cutting me off. "We removed those and sent them for testing. I am afraid the cancer was a little larger than we would have liked, so after conferring with my colleague in the operating theatre, we decided it would be safest to remove your anus."

I reach under the blankets to check, but I'm thwarted by a diaper. "I don't have an —" I start to ask.

Dr. Teller grips my arm, stopping me from disturbing the surgery site. He says, "Not to worry, we sent that material away for testing as well. Because we were so careful, I am confident in saying that we have got it all."

"Can you reverse my colostomy?" I ask before he can interrupt again.

For the first time, my surgeon appears at a loss for words. His brows knit as he considers something, then says, "Not with today's technology, no. We felt your best chance to recover without the possibility of remission would be to remove as much of the potentially affected tissue as possible."

"You promised me."

"This is excellent news, Paul. But I will let you rest. I will speak with your family, and we can talk more soon in the recovery room. Don't worry, you will be back home before you know it."

As he disappears and I'm left on the cot, I wonder if — during our first meeting on that busy day all those months ago — he had given me enough information to make such an important decision. I wonder if things could have been different if I had insisted on surgery immediately instead of waiting months to shrink a tumour that instead exploded in size. I shouldn't have allowed others into the operating room. Since when can others, outside of my surgeon, make decisions for me? Did I sign that right away? Why didn't I read that document?

I wonder if Mom or Karen will cry when they hear the news.

The thing on my belly throbs and seems to have swollen larger. I grip handfuls of bedsheets and think about how often I had envisioned this worst-case scenario. I stare at the thing on my belly, glistening under harsh hospital lighting, and wonder if I had somehow willed this outcome into reality through the power of my imagination.

⌐ 9 ⌐

C'est Toi

I look up from my book to see how far the glowing plane icon has travelled across the digital map. The screen refreshes, the icon stutters, and the ETA updates.

Approximate landing time, 20 minutes.

My phone flashes awake when it registers a single bar. A beacon of white light in a dark plane cabin, eliciting annoyed groans from sleeping passengers. It buzzes obnoxiously, dancing on the plastic fold-down tray.

I fumble for my phone and say, "Calm down." I press my thumb against the touch pad until it buzzes with acknowledgement. The camera activates, realizes that it is dark, and politely dims. One hundred and sixty-two Facebook updates? I don't even get that on my birthday.

I tap the number crowding my notification bell, and a list of wholesome messages flashes onto the screen.

"Good luck, Paige!" writes some guy I kind of knew in high school and didn't realize was still following me.

"You deserve this, you're so brave!" writes a guy that puts a heart on everything I post and slides into my DMs a few moments after I post a selfie to ask me how I am.

"Be sure to take some time to visit the sights," writes Bill, a trans man who facilitated the first trans group I came out at, and who helped me raise money for this trip.

My mother writes, "I love you. Come home safe. I know you don't believe in it, but I'm praying for you."

"I loved your story, you are so strong," writes a girl that bullied me in public school.

"You are an inspiration," writes an old ex-girlfriend I dated when I was Paul.

A chat bubble flashes onto the screen:

Sarah: Look out the window!

Blocking my view to the window, a woman snores in an eye mask that reads "Wake Me When It's Wine O'Clock 🍷," her coat pulled over herself like a blanket. If you're going to sleep the entire flight, why sit by a window? I imagine she's returning to California on yet another boring business flight and not bubbling with excitement and eager to be under palm trees.

Paige: I can't. The blind is closed.

Sarah: Tell them to open it!

Paige: I don't want to bother them. Take a picture?

Sarah: Aw, okay.

- Picture Loading -

A black square leaps into the chat. There's a hint of white wing, an overexposed red light at the wing's tip, and a sea of white twinkling blotches stretching to the horizon.

Paige: Looks pretty.

Sarah: Can you see it?

Paige: Kinda.

Sarah: I think that's California!

Rows of lights flicker into life on the ceiling. The dim illumination stirs the airplane sleepers and a moment later a disembodied Howard Stern–sounding voice says, "Good evening, ladies and gentlemen, this is your captain speaking. As we begin our descent, please ensure your seat backs and tray tables are in their full and upright position.

"We will land in San Francisco earlier than predicted, at seven ten p.m. local time. The temperature is a cool fifty-three degrees with light rain. Whether you are stopping over or staying in sunny California, we thank you for flying with us this evening, and we hope that you enjoy your stay."

Paige: I guess we should turn off our phones.

Sarah: Okay baby, almost there!

I hold my thumb on the power button. My phone buzzes once, goes dark, and rests. The sweaty guy who butt-squished Sarah in her seat heads for the bathroom. My neighbour opens the window blind, and the view is incredible, even from where I am seated. A bright, sprawling landscape of lights stretches to the horizon. They creep by the window as we bank and circle, then speed past as we descend. Then there is a black void spanned by a string of lights. A bridge? We are almost there.

﹀﹀﹀

Movies have taught me that California is an idyllic paradise of palm trees, warm weather, and days at the beach in the company of scantily dressed superstars. Perhaps that's true for L.A., because my first impression of the area surrounding the San Francisco airport at night is dark streets and smashed out streetlights. Even though my rental car reeks of stale cigarette smoke, it's an improvement on the unusual wet-dog tar smell of the sticky pavement outside.

Something claws at the inside of my stomach, and the head-ache that's been plaguing me for the last two hours of the flight has now progressed to a growing pressure behind my eyes. All I want is a bug-free motel with soft pillows, but Sarah talked me into picking up Taco Bell and wine. Exploring financially desperate areas of America after dark as a trans woman, especially one without a lot of street smarts, has always been on my list of things to avoid, but most trans women I've spoken to said California is probably safe. From what I've experienced, "probably safe" is the highest standard trans women can aspire to in our society, so I agreed.

We wait for an awkward and painfully obvious drug deal to complete between a couple of teenagers and the Taco Bell employee. I've seen enough sly, palm-down hand-offs in movies to know what's going on. They eye me as I enter and order, but I'm looking tired or trans enough that they realize I couldn't possibly be a cop. The two dopey-eyed white kids finish their deal with some kind of finger-snapping handshake.

As we arrive at the motel and wheel our suitcases to the room, I'm annoyed to discover that they've closed the pool for a winter so warm that I had to take off my jacket. The elevator is out of order, so we drag the bags up the stairs and let ourselves in. I take a few steps and plant my face in the closest bed. Sarah and I don't usually do the two-bed thing, but I figured it would be easier to recover from surgery without Sarah elbowing fresh sutures.

Given the effort it took to get here, I feel like I should cheer for joy, or scream "I made it!" from the balcony, but all I want is sleep.

Sarah asks, "Can you believe they've never heard of Fries Supreme?"

I say, mostly into the pillow, "We're closer to Mexico now. They have to compete with the taco trucks."

"They have taco trucks? This place is amazing." Sarah unwraps a Cheesy Potato Burrito, takes a bite, and swoons onto the bed, "Baby, you gotta try this."

"Put it in my mouth."

"Phrasing!" Sarah muffles a guffaw. "I don't think this place has a corkscrew. Do you think they'd bring us one?"

I motion to the rusty air conditioner. "This kind of place doesn't have room service. They might have some at the front desk."

"Would you go?" She smiles sweetly to me. "You still have shoes on."

Though my eyes burn, I drag my aching body to its feet, grab the room key, and step into the cool night air.

Sarah calls after me, "Matches too?"

Sitting on the stairs is a skinny girl wearing neon leg warmers and a matching scrunchie in her hair. Her pink lipstick is smeared onto her cheek, and she jams something small into her jeans pocket. Standing in front of her is a muscular guy hurriedly pulling up the front of his baggy, chain-covered JNCOs.

Both stare at me in surprise, then the guy smiles and winks. I lower my gaze and hurry past, head down the stairs, and take my time at the front desk. When I get back into the room, I say, "You wouldn't believe what I —" but Sarah is wearing the green dress with the diving neckline, which pushes her milky breasts out on display. She hands me a large plastic cup of wine.

I impishly grin and ask, "How did you remove the cork?"

"I just shoved it in. Cheers, baby. Welcome to California."

We clack cheap plastic pre-wrapped motel cups and drink. The wine is bitter and warm, and when I draw it into my mouth, it pastes itself against the insides of my cheeks and dries out, leaving a foul, gummy aftertaste. But after I take another, longer sip to wash away the funk of the last one, the heady rush of alcohol kicks in, and I resign myself to drinking the rest.

Sarah smiles with purple teeth. "Not bad, eh?"

"Not bad," I lie. When I met Sarah she worked for a local wine shop, and she must realize this wine tastes like it's mixed with mop water from the corner store we bought it at. Sarah always tries to make the best of a situation, and I appreciate her for that. I lie beside her and prop pillows behind my head. When I close my eyes, the room spins. Ghosts of headlights slide behind my eyelids, and authoritarian customs officers demand compliance. A wave of exhaustion overwhelms me, and a splash of wine spills onto my hand, waking me before I drop my cup. I squeeze my eyes, then open them. "Wow, I'm tired."

Sarah places her cup on the night table and straddles my hips. "I was hoping you might be in the mood."

"I'm exhausted."

She arches her back and leans over until her plush breasts push against my chin. She nibbles her lip. "Who said you had to do anything?"

"You know I don't enjoy that. It feels nice, but you're still blowing me."

"I was thinking of doing a Venus Flytrap."

I struggle not to spit out my mouthful of wine and force myself to swallow. "Are we still calling it that?" I down the rest of my cup in two big gulps. I'm sure wine isn't supposed to be gulped, but this vintage tastes better that way. "Let's do it."

"Fuck yeah!" Sarah cheers and crawls down, unbuttoning and tugging at my jeans. In her eagerness, the band catches on the edge of my colostomy bag and the gooey wax adhesive rips at my skin. I yelp and double over, grabbing my stomach. Sarah gasps and surrenders her hands. "Are you okay?"

I'm not bleeding, and only a little tape tore away, revealing red, raw flesh. I hold the adhesive against my belly until it sticks again. "I'm okay, but be gentler?"

"I'm sorry. Did you still wanna do a Flytrap?"

"Oh my God, stop calling it that." I hold her pouting face and laugh against her lips. We kiss. Her breasts engulf my smaller ones as she fumbles with my fly. I wriggle free of my jeans.

She pulls down my gaff, freeing my tucked, flattened penis, sweaty and stung from being pinched so long on the trip. It slowly peels away from between my thighs. As life rushes back, the pinched creases sear with pain.

As she kisses me, I try to go somewhere else and alternate pretending that her eager, nimble fingers are playing with my pussy, or that a guy is rubbing himself against me.

"You're really turned on," Sarah says against my lips, "I don't think I'll have to go down on you." She squirms out of her panties, and I spread my legs for the next step.

She pushes my knees back and then straddles herself over my hips. Our butts briefly touch as my ankles rest on her shoulders. She reaches behind her and guides me into her. The trick to getting off with the Venus Flytrap is to avoid looking down. Once I see my dick penetrating someone else, it's over. Instead, I concentrate on Sarah's face, her breasts, anything else at all. I let my imagination go wild and leave the details out of it.

Is this what it feels like getting fucked after surgery?

"Baby?" Sarah asks as she stops "thrusting" for a moment. "Are you in your head? You fell out."

Went soft, she means. I slipped off the parallel bars during mental gymnastics. I got caught up thinking about the mechanics and now the Russian judge is having a field day.

"I'm just tired."

Sarah reaches back and tries to encourage me. I close my eyes and try to only think about how sexy and slippery that sensation is. She asks, "Did you want to stop?"

"No, give me a second." If she were a guy, he'd be rubbing his cock against my pussy. I feel myself swelling and I kiss her again so it's not too obvious I'm closing my eyes. I imagine Sarah's tongue against my slit, licking, poking. Sarah slides herself back on. If I think about it just right, it almost feels as if she's thrusting her cock inside me, instead of the other way around.

Sarah says, "There we go." She shallows her thrusts and says, "Grab your tits."

I obey and cup my underdeveloped breasts and twist my nipples. If I focus on the pain, I distract myself better and prevent myself from thinking about my cock. *My pussy . . . with*

Sarah's strap-on . . . her cock . . . don't go soft and fall out . . . not my cock, her cock.

Sarah moans into a kiss, and my exhausted brain ignites. I focus on our kiss as she thrusts her pent-up lust into my pussy. A guttural groan that must have been mine vibrates into her mouth and she grips me tighter, knowing how I enjoy being forced. Her ass slaps against mine and I almost lose hold of the fragile illusion, but I concentrate on a mental picture of her cumming inside me and — and — I grip her shoulders. My fingernails bite into her flesh and I tense while my body floods with electric panic, then I whimpermoan into her mouth as everything explodes and I let go.

Sarah lets me ride out the orgasm, then slides off. She rolls over, letting me lower my legs and ease my aching hips. I lay there, bathed in waves of relaxing disgust and shame. Although wholesome memes and comics encourage me to be trans and proud like them, to love the things I can't change about myself, it's difficult to do when I'm held back from happiness by money. While I'm sure this surgery will help me feel more confident during sex, what about when I'm applying for a job, or getting bullied on a bus, or being stopped by police? Like most things in this world, it's the rich trans women who get to look and feel empowered; the rest of us just get whatever the government thinks we're worth.

And everyone knows what that is.

"Wow, baby," Sarah says between breaths, "that must have been a great one by the sound of it."

Part 3

Download

◥ 10 ◣

Computer Love

Back in 1989 — A two-bedroom apartment
above a pizza parlour in rural
Southern Ontario

In the shadowy recesses of a haunted house, Lydia Deetz searches for answers in an ancient tome. She stabs her finger into a page. "It says it right here, Beetlejuice, the only way to get rid of skeletons in your closet is . . . to tell the truth!"

"There's gotta be another way," Beetlejuice whines as he clings to a chandelier, scrambling to avoid the skeletal hands grabbing at him.

Lydia lowers the book as spirits chase Beetlejuice behind a couch, and she implores him to tell the truth about something . . . anything, "Like, who's your best friend?"

Despite the ghoulish bones reaching for him, Beetlejuice smiles. "Well, shucks, Lydia — *you're* my best friend." Dad positions himself between me and the television, looming with folded arms. He's dressed to drink in his best pub vest and reeks of Old

Spice. "Fack, Paul," he says in a thick English accent. "You are impossible to talk to."

Dad's accent becomes more pronounced when he drinks, and today I don't think he could say fuck properly if he tried — my friends love it. Me, not so much.

I try to look around him and groan as I seem to have missed an integral plot point as skeletons float into the sky and pop like balloons. "Dad, I can't see. This is the new cartoon for Beetlejui—"

"You're fourteen facking years old and it's a facking cartoon." Dad sighs. "Did you hear what I just asked you?"

On the television, credits roll as the triumphantly sinister *Beetlejuice* theme fanfares. The Saturday morning announcer tells me *Alvin and the Chipmunks* is coming up next. The screen flashes to a commercial, and people are screaming and running from silvery flying saucers in a black-and-white movie. Mario buzzes in on a pixelated prop plane and shoots at aliens. "The Martians are coming! Yes, and Mario is your only hope. Team up with him in the new *Super Mario Land*. Guide him on the Nintendo Game Boy —"

"Paul!"

"Sorry," I say, though I continue to monitor game footage.

Dad gathers his wallet and keys. "Do the facking dishes, will ya? There's shepherd's pie in the freezer."

"I heard you the first time," I lie.

"I'm not sure if I'll be back tonight."

"Whatever."

Dad leaves, keys jingle, and the door locks. A wave of relief washes over me as I hear that metallic clack. On the television, Alvin slides on his knees strumming an air guitar. I shut it off and toss the remote.

Dragging myself to the kitchen, I turn on the water and pull dirty dishes from the sink. I squirt probably too much soap into the water, pick a few of the crustiest pots, and submerge them. As I wonder how long it will take for the concrete-like potato residue to soften, I inspect a wineglass with a lipstick imprint from one of Dad's latest conquests.

I dry my hands on my pants as I head to Dad's office and boot up the Amiga 500. The computer clicks, the speakers hiss with static, and a picture of a hand holding a floppy disk appears on the screen. Though it's now several years old, and even though I updated the workbench to version 1.3, the boot sequence takes forever compared to some of my friends' new rigs. I let it crunch and buzz, and figure it can be left to load properly while I clean the dishes. When I return to the office, the bright blue AmigaOS dashboard illuminates the room.

I pull up the Smartmodem dialer and input the connection details of my local BBS. The rectangular box rings. Someone answers, but their voice is garbled and squeals like microphone feedback through the tinny modem speaker not designed for human voices. If I had to guess, the voice belongs to an annoyed older woman. I disconnect, but I try again because it's the only local BBS that has a portal to the internet.

This time my modem rings and clicks and screeches. The host computer screeches back triumphantly. Together they howl and beep and stutter in harmony until the screen registers:

```
- You have connected to Hamilton Dungeon BBS -
Login?
Nosferatu
Pass?
*****
- Welcome, Nosferatu -
- You have no new messages -
```

And upon the screen one row at a time, a gorgeous full-colour fire-breathing ASCII dragon appears. The menu below the artwork lists some dated BBS door games: *Drug Wars*, *Trade Wars*, *The Pit*, and my favourite, *Legend of the Red Dragon*. Below these are the file trading database and local forums, but the BBS master also recently added a new link: CONNECT TO THE INTERNET.

I click on that, and while the host computer negotiates a connection, I open my notebook and find the address to the IRC sex room my friend told me about.

A seemingly endless list of chat rooms appears when I connect to the address. Some are clearly labelled, like #VideoGames, #Horror, and #Rabbits. I'd probably have to clean the gunk out of my mouse three times just to scroll through them all, so I enter the room name into search and #IRCAfterDark appears.

I click to enter.

When I reach for the door, the handle disappears and an androgynous, featureless humanoid springs into life before me. In a husky, vaguely feminine voice, it says, "Welcome noobie, I am a greeter bot. Please type your nickname, age, sex, and location to continue. By selecting a nickname, you agree to our rules, which include —"

I open my terminal.

```
/nick Raven
- nickname taken -
/nick Rayven
- Welcome, Rayven to IRC After Dark! -
```

The robot bows, the door swings open, and I'm dragged into a crowded room with men in smoking jackets and women in lacy lingerie, though all of them have blurred faces. I walk in and wave, but no one seems to notice me.

I feel as if I've just walked into a party where I'm the only outsider. Eventually, I give up trying to get anyone's attention and sit on one of the many lounging couches to eavesdrop.

EternalHippie talks to KinkyBoots21 about his trip to Bermuda.

PinaColada says to the room, "— and he says to his brother, 'He must be fucking her up the ass!'" The entire room bursts out laughing, while others politely raise their drinks.

"Good one," says LongDongSilver.

A woman named PurrPrincess approaches PinaColada, and they kiss. In a flash, the door robot appears beside the kissing couple and pushes them into a bedroom. I consider getting up and trying to talk to a woman, but the ten women here are surrounded by at least forty guys, all vying for their attention.

"Hey there Ray," says a man beside me. His nametag reads Goldenboy69. Like everyone else, he seems to have anonymity features enabled and looks like every other man in here — and probably what I must look like.

"Hi, Goldenboy69."

Goldenboy69 leans closer and whispers in my ear, "You must be new. Type /msg and my name before replying so we can talk privately."

I whisper back, "Thanks. I am now . . . new. How did you know?"

He taps my name tag. "You didn't include your age, sex, or location. Someone will tell the bot to kick you if they notice. You should fix that."

"Shit, thanks." I open the console and type: /nick Rayven (14/M/Ontario).

GoldenBoy69 slaps his hand over my tag. "Quickly, set your age to eighteen or the moderator will ban you. I don't care about things like that, but people here are uptight."

Hurriedly, I change the age. GoldenBoy69's nametag says that he's thirty-six.

GoldenBoy69 says, "It is my pleasure, Ray. Listen, why don't we go to a private room? I can help you get other things set up." He leads me through a door into a bedroom. Inside is a bed and a softly bubbling jet tub tucked into a corner.

I say, "This place is so cool."

"Comfy, right?" GoldenBoy69 sits on the side of the bed and pats the comforter. When I sit by him, he asks, "Where in Ontario are you from? I'm from Mississauga."

"Near Hamilton," I say, figuring the nearby city is big enough he could never find me if he turns out to be a weirdo.

"So close! We should meet for a coffee or a beer. What do you look like?"

Though I'm unsure why he's asking, I feel that I've come this far and say, "I have long blonde hair, brown eyes. Kind of skinny, I guess?"

GoldenBoy69's avatar freezes for a long moment. His avatar's cheeks flush and he says, "You sound cute. I bet you look amazing in shorts."

I roll my computer chair away from the screen and stare at the words, but the bright neon font flickering upon my monitor confirms it.

. . .

[11:18] <Rayven> I have long blonde hair, brown eyes. Kind of skinny, I guess?

[11:21] <GoldenBoy69> You sound cute. I bet you look amazing in shorts. *^.^*

. . .

[11:35] <GoldenBoy69> I'm sorry, Rayven. Did I say something wrong? :(

He's a fag? How did I not realize that? My heart races, and I roll the office chair even farther back to scout the empty apartment and reassure myself that I'm still alone.

The thought of anyone discovering that I've talked to a gay guy is enough to make me feel sick, but I can't remember ever being pursued like this. I enjoy the rush of the chase too much to write this excitement off as flattery.

[11:41] <GoldenBoy69> If I've said something wrong, I can go. But you seem fun, and I enjoy talking to you.

This really *is* fun, even if the shorts comment felt weird. It's just make-believe, after all. I say, "I'm sorry. I've never done anything like this before."

"Do you have any pictures of yourself? I can send you one of me." A minute later his picture transfers and his form solidifies, becomes clearer, and he could be any guy you might meet on the street. He appears a lot younger than my dad, but way older than me. Stubble of a beard, glasses, hairy legs, curly blonde hair the same colour as the golden retriever by his side.

I search through the few scanned images on my computer and find one of me standing by a pool. I'm wearing shorts and an oversized tank top and am playfully cocking my hip. I send it to him.

"I was right," GoldenBoy69 says. "You're cute, and so feminine."

Feminine? There's another first. "Is that okay?" I'm surprised at my self-consciousness.

"Perfectly fine. Feel free not to answer, but have you ever fooled around with your guy friends?"

While it feels as if I should keep the encounter a secret, my veil of anonymity makes it easier to say, "I touched my friend's dick once. We were in a closet, and he asked me to hold out my hand. When I realized what he put in my hand, we laughed, and he kissed me. It happened only once."

GoldenBoy69 rubs my knee. "Friends are the smartest way to experiment. Having a friend who knows what they are doing is even better. It can be fun and feel amazing."

Within me, two raging storms collide: a tornado of stranger anxiety crashes against a swirling vortex of curious arousal. My heart pounds and I don't know whether to scream, run, or play with myself. A tiny whisper from the eye of the storm entices me with "kiss him, touch him back, see what happens."

GoldenBoy69 says, "Did you want to cyber? We can try a few things, and if you like it, we can meet and try in Real Life sometime. I'm in Hamilton all the time for work."

That muttering voice in the centre of the maelstrom grows louder, takes control of my mouth, and says, "Okay."

He asks me what I'm wearing, and I tell him I'm wearing shorts.

Immediately, he presses me to the bed, and his lips are on mine. I pretend he's a girl and open my mouth, guilelessly slashing my tongue against his as he rubs my belly. His hands slide down, pull up my shirt, and he tugs open my pants. His fingers slide over the front of my underwear, and as he massages, that panic builds, alarm bells screaming, and I pull away.

"Just a second, please." While I can't put my finger on the exact sensation I'm feeling, I imagine it's similar to an animal being petted in the opposite direction of their fur growth. My whole being shudders at the thought of him touching me there again.

GoldenBoy69 surrenders his hands. "I'm sorry. I suppose you aren't ready to be touched yet. Were you okay until then?"

I debate leaving, but I say, "I guess?"

"Would you like to touch me instead?" He undoes the tie on his robe and pulls it open over his lap. He takes my hand and guides me back to the bed. We kiss again, but he's guiding my hand, touching his chest, over his belly, and then onto his cock. I'm surprised when I don't feel the same rush of panic and discordant note of static I felt when he touched me.

He guides my head down to his lap and says, "Open your mouth and touch yourself." Even though I know he can't see me, not in a way that matters, my hand shakes as I tug down the front of my pajamas and pull myself free. He pushes himself into my mouth, and as he does, I know I just crossed a line I'll never be able to retreat from. Even if my friends never find out, I will always know that I've entertained the most forbidden desires that any straight guy in the 90s could dream up. And this emerging part of me wants more.

It wants it all.

The way he whispers praise as I lick him sends my heart racing, and soon I'm panting over the keyboard and thinking of doing the things I'm so far only describing, and eagerly waiting for the next thing he'll say. I'm there, in that motel bedroom with him. I can feel it, smell his cologne, and I can almost taste him until he groans, "Good girl."

I grab the phone cord and yank it from the modem so hard that the plastic casing breaks away from the drywall.

I'm on my feet in a heartbeat and staring at the screen with my dick pointing at those bizarre, strangely confirming words. Tucking myself back in, I run out of the room and pace the kitchen, hyperventilating, staring at the filthy linoleum tile and wondering who the fuck I've become.

I pace until my erection calms, then I storm into my bedroom, grab my pack of Player's, and rush out of the apartment and down the stairs before throwing open the door to stand on the sidewalk. Lighting up is more difficult than I expected because I'm shaking so badly, so I lean against the doorframe to steady myself. Overeager for nicotine, I suck in a full lungful of hot smoke and splutter. My lungs ache, and I puff out a cloud only to suck in another. The ember sizzles the cigarette paper, leaving a length of glowing ash hanging flaccid a third of the way.

An old couple passes and politely tries not to stare. My face feels like it's burning, and I wonder how flushed I look. I wonder if they can tell I was just virtually blowing a guy. I wonder if a gay guy happened to walk by right now, could he tell I'm one of them? I wonder how I'll ever be able to face my friends or my mother again. I feel as if I've somehow branded this societal transgression onto my skin and I'll never be able to scrub it off. I pull long drags off the cigarette until my head swims and I'm dizzy from the nicotine.

As I calm, I try to determine if there is any way GoldenBoy could ever find me. I conclude that he can't, even with my photo. Though I've stopped shaking, my body is paralyzed as my brain overclocks, and I blankly stare at the concrete while I inwardly argue about the possibility of being gay. Certainly, that must be the case, but if so, why would his calling me a girl feel so fulfilling?

I take another drag, slower this time. I scrape the cigarette ember against the sidewalk and blow the smoke out before stuffing the nub back in my pack. I climb the stairs, lock the door, and reattach the partially broken phone cord enough to get a dial tone.

I dial the BBS, connect to the internet, find the door, and type.

/nick Lydia (18/F/Canada)

- Welcome, Lydia to IRC After Dark! —

Return to Innocence

"It's not real life, I get it," Kris says. He sits hunched over in his chair, eyes bloodshot and staring at a grilled cheese. "I've played roleplaying games before." His clothes are at least a size too big, and he looks paler than he did when I first met him at his dealer's place across the street.

I ask, "Why do you hang out with that guy anyhow? He's too stoned half the time to understand what he's talking about." I place a well-loved copy of the Palladium Fantasy rulebook beside his plate.

"He always has weed." Kris flips pages in the book and stops at a picture of a dragon. He takes an uninspired bite of sandwich and slowly blinks, his head nodding. "What am I supposed to be doing again?"

"You don't have to stay there — you're welcome to hang out here as much as you like." I press play on my boombox. The tiny reels of the cassette squeak and turn, speakers hiss, and "The

Sign" by Ace of Base thumps into life. I lean over Kris and flip pages until he's at the beginning of the book. "Start here and make a character."

Kris stares past the page, blinks twice, and chews his sandwich. "I can't think with this song playing."

"It's good though, right?" I stop and eject the tape. I toss it in a drawer of loose cassettes and clatter through the pile to extract one with white reels and neon swooshes that's labelled in marker as "chill tunes."

"Kinda gay, but it's okay." Kris tosses the book on the table. "Why do I want to play this again?"

"Just try it." I jam the tape into a tray with a broken closing hook. I hold the tray shut as I press rewind. The tape stutters and buzzes as the cog whirs magnetic tape onto the growing left reel. The spinning abruptly stops, the rewind button buzzes and clacks back into its neutral position. I press play and the cog grabs the reel, both playing the song and holding the tray shut. "Return to Innocence" by Enya sighs over my speakers. "This is all Enigma and Enya. It will help you get in the mood."

"It's putting me to sleep." Kris's chewing slows as he clocks out. The window to reach him with my game is closing.

I open another drawer filled with binders and loose paper and fish out a pre-made character. "Here's one I made. Why don't you play this for now and make your own later?"

Kris looks at the sheet. "Do I have to play a robot? Got any humans?"

Since I know he won't stay up for another hour to go through the process of character creation, I say, "Half the fun of a role-playing game is being something you're not. Just try it?"

He stares at the sheet, processing. "Be anything. Like a girl, you mean?"

"No," I say too quickly, hoping he didn't notice. "You could, but I mean you can be an elf, a monster, a kind of person you can't be in Real Life. You can get outside of your head and escape."

Kris blinks again so slowly that I think he has fallen asleep. "All right. How do I play?"

"I tell a story and —"

"There's so many fucking numbers on this page," Kris interrupts.

"If I need any numbers, I'll ask for one specifically. All you need to do is react to the story I'm telling as if you were your character. Cool?"

Kris shrugs. "Cool."

I sit behind my tri-fold game master's screen. On Kris's side are knights and dragons, and fantastic green landscapes, but on mine are the true mechanics of my world — printouts of tables filled with combat modifiers, lists of cities and characters, and other house rules taped over the screen's preprinted information.

I say, "While your long-term data recovery subroutines are too damaged to remember what first brought you to this world, you remember flying through a portal using your booster rockets. You also recall falling toward a lush jungle. The last things you remember are snapping branches, the buffet of leaves, and then solid ground rushing up to meet you — then, nothing."

Life is hard for the people of the Menan nation. Recently, strange, pale, round-eared beings came to these shores from across the sea and encroached upon their borders. They hunted without permission on protected lands, and they stole crops. A war was brewing with these newcomers that they feared they could not win — yet its inevitability loomed on the horizon the same way every man, woman, and child knew they must one day face their Uru and answer for every selfish choice they made in life.

"How long is this going to take?" Kris asks as he rests his chin on his hand.

"Not much longer, I'm getting to you."

To avoid these violent outsiders, Hevron and Rho'den expanded their hunt east into sacred lands, hoping to secure a fallow beast to feed their village. As they pushed deeper into the jungle, there was no way they could realize how their actions would change their lives, and the lives of their people, forever.

Rho'den, the older and wiser of the two, led the way, pushing aside branches for his younger charge. It was he who had gone against the —

"This is taking forever," Kris interrupts. "Am I Rhodo? I thought you said I was a robot?"

I choose to take a sip of tea rather than react negatively. "You are a robot, and they haven't found you yet." I make a mental note to hurry the plot.

After a time, the hunters discover the tracks of an adult fallow beast. Excited at their fortune, they follow them far from their village until they reach a sacred hill known by their people as the Breath of God, a holy place where Wise Women gather their omens and signs.

As the hunters draw close, Hevron spots a strange object poking out of the hill.

"Is that me?" Kris asks.

"Yes. I'll tell you when you can say something."

The sight of the mirror-like object gleaming on the hill is impossible to resist. Before his protector can stop him, Hevron lays his bare hand on the metal. An electric charge tingles through Hevron's body, and his hair stands on end. He knows then he is in the presence of his god.

Too late, Rho'den recognizes the sacrilegious transgression and pulls his charge away from the now vibrating object.

Deep within the hill stirs something which had slumbered for generations. Long before colonizers first came to these shores, longer even than the Menan people had migrated south to these lands, something had fallen to this spot, was critically damaged, and has since been running on low power reserves for nearly one thousand years. Meticulous subroutines assessed damage and safety, used crude energies the robot's receptors could leech from the ground to refill its batteries and power its repairs. But when its defensive systems register the touch of that hand, the metal man within the hill is stirred by the possibility it may need to defend itself.

Kris asks, "Can I move?"

"First, you think you can't, but the ground around you shifts and falls away. You climb to your feet as dirt rains from your limbs. Your vision, long used to viewing only worms and tiny digging mammals, perceives two pointy-eared men. Flashing red warning beacons target the spear and bow they hold — but logic dictates that neither poses a threat to you. The two humanoids shout in a language you don't understand."

"Do I have weapons?"

Out of the mound steps a shiny metal man, easily a foot taller than either of the hunters before him. Rho'den, worried his ward has awoken one of their gods, drops his spear and begs for their lives. Hevron follows suit. In response, the metal man glances at his arm and assesses his weaponry. Reflexively, a panel lifts, slides smoothly back, and a cylindrical object emerges.

"Cool. I shoot them."

I cringe. "Are you sure? They're kneeling before you and look afraid."

"Fine, I'll just shoot Rhody, or whatever his name is."

The metal man thrusts his fist toward the old hunter. The cannon on its arm whirs as it powers up, a red glow flaring within the barrel. Before the weapon discharges, and though Rho'den had never witnessed a gun before, he rises from his knees, smiles, and spreads his arms invitingly, happy he could pay the god's price for his ward's mistake.

Mercifully, the metal man's weapon is so destructive that there is little suffering. What remains of the old hunter falls lifeless to the ground.

Hevron screams in pain as if he were the one shot. He cradles the head of Rho'den into his lap. Rho'den was a man who took him in as a child and was the only father he had ever known. Ignoring the blood pouring down his legs, Hevron says something that sounds as if it may be imploring.

Kris's grin fades. "What is he saying?"

As the remaining life form mourns the loss of the other, internal databases awaken, linguistic subroutines calculate syntax, pragmatics, morphology, and phonology, and build a workable lexicon that expands with every word it speaks.

The young man begs, again and again, that the metal god before him bring this brave, worthy man back and take his life instead.

Kris stares at the dice, the ones he just eagerly rolled to see how much damage his gun would do. "I feel bad," Kris says. "I want to bring him back. Can I do that?"

"You killed him. You have a lot of weapons, but nothing to heal anyone."

"Please, my lord," Hevron begs, "I apologize for offending you. I who do not even know your name, beg this wish of you."

Kris says, "My character's name is blank."

"That's because you have to make one up."

Kris writes on the sheet and says, "You may call me Tinman. What do you guys do with your dead?"

Hevron says, "We bury them, Lord Tinman, so they may return to the land."

"Then that is what we'll do." With the greatest of care, Tinman cradles the body of the fallen warrior and places him in the hillside. Together, the young warrior and the metal man bury Rho'den in the sacred hill. By the time they finish, the sun has sunk below the horizon.

When I look at Kris, I recognize a familiar look in his bloodshot eyes. How he relaxes his grip on reality and allows Tinman to emerge. He's forgotten, at least for now, about being homeless and living on a can of mushroom soup a day. If I'm right, he would now prefer to be here, exploring this world, instead of escaping with drugs. If the hook is deep enough, he'd rather be in my fantasy world than anywhere in this one.

He asks me what he should do next.

I say, "Anything you want."

◖ 12 ◗

Oh My Goth!

**1999 – Three years later,
still in the same room**

"We should head out soon," Kris says as he hovers in the doorway.

I pull a brush through my hair, activating the ammonia stink of cheap boxed hair dye. Poker straight and darkest black with a hint of blue. I finger comb a part in the middle and pull waves over my shoulders and then begin applying thick eyeliner. "Yeah, give me a minute."

Outside of my bedsheet-covered window the sun is setting and KMFDM's Fuck MTV Mix of "Go to Hell" shakes my boombox. I pop the cap off my lipstick and lean into the mirror, puckering as I paint my lips tar black. A wave of euphoria tickles through me as I turn my head, admiring the way my eyes pop and how the lipstick makes my pillowy lips look feminine, but in a borderline masculine way.

I slide knee-high industrial boots over pleather pants and work on fastening the buckles. At least twenty of them on each leg means this is probably the most time-consuming part of club prep.

"Cool." Kris folds corded arms over his chest, which flexes through his sports jersey. He's been training a lot since he's moved out on his own again. His naturally broad shoulders and square jaw reflect his heavy Germanic heritage, yet his appearance is softened by his hip-length golden hair. "You always make your eyes look so cool."

I say, "I thought you didn't like eyeliner."

"I might try some."

"Sure, man — here." I hold out the pencil.

Kris considers it. "Would you put it on for me?"

I sit on the couch and pat the cushion. "I'll try not to stab you in the eye."

Kris sits and looks through his eyelashes. I pull down his bottom lid to expose his water line and draw.

In those early days when we first met, Kris seemed like a pitiable, broken boy obscured within clouds of pot smoke. I later discovered that his veneer of vulnerability concealed wells of perseverance. He's been cagey about the details of his parental abuse. Many times, I've inadvertently stumbled across his tells when someone mentions his family — his averted eyes, the concealed shame, and his persistent urgency to change the subject. While I may never know what truly happened, it was bad enough to push a fourteen-year-old kid into the streets, with parents uneager to bring him home.

Lately, he seems focused on getting his life on track by going to school and learning to be a mortician. As goth as I am, I don't think I could do that job, but I'm proud of him.

"There," I say. Kris's eyes tear up, and I'm thankful the eyeliner is waterproof. When he reaches to wipe his face, I catch his hand. "Don't rub your eyes."

"It stings."

"That's the devil's price for looking cool."

Kris examines himself in the mirror and asks, "You think it looks good?"

"Yeah, man." I hand him a tissue. "Dab, don't wipe."

He takes it and slaps me on the back. "Thanks, man. Let's go."

⌇⌇⌇

With a deafening hiss, dry ice pours fog into the club from the DJ booth. Purplish grey rivers snake through twisting dark shapes on the dance floor. A wave of it flows over the table where I sit, and I close my eyes, basking in the chill against my flesh and that familiar fresh, chemical stink. When I open them again, the shadowy ghosts of goth kids sway within the fog, reaching and twisting invisible apples from invisible trees before elegantly tossing them away. The DJ activates a bank of laser lights that slice knife edges through the clouds. Bauhaus bleeds into "Mother Russia" by Sisters of Mercy, and a sea of fists pump in the air as everyone bounces on Docs and knee-high fuck-me boots.

Reverend Fester pushes through the crowd to our table. He's wearing a priest collar, befitting his station. His black mohawk has a lean to it, like his hair is reaching for one of his smudged eye sockets. He says, "Hey, man, thanks for coming out. Been a while." He holds out a beefy hand, and I clap mine to his. He leans in and we hug before he excuses himself to socialize.

Several of the regulars stop by for hugs and to shake my hand. In fact, there's only one unfamiliar face in the entire club — some skinny, pale guy with long black hair. There's something unmistakably familiar about him, though. I write it off to looking a little like me, and I wonder if he's from Toronto and slumming it in our club.

Kris appears through the smoke, holding two frosted pints. He clunks them on the table and yells, "This one's on me. You grab the next?"

I give a thumbs-up and sip a mouthful of chilled, nearly tasteless domestic beer that washes away the sour tang of carbon dioxide. I motion with my chin. "Hey, who's the new guy?"

"Who?"

I aim Kris's chin toward the skinny guy and motion. "The one that kinda looks like me."

Kris excitedly leans in. "That isn't a dude. It's that girl you used to disappear outside with. What's her name?"

A confusing sensation that isn't unlike panic flashes through me. I stare after this person moving through the crowd, hugging people — that familiar grin, that same long, stringy hair. But it couldn't possibly be Anatole. "No way," I say, mostly to myself.

"Yeah, dude, I was talking to Fester about her. Apparently, she's trying to turn herself into a guy. She's injecting herself with testosterone and everything. Her face is covered with acne from the injections."

A second wave of the feeling rises, but this time laced with anxiety. It's as if a race began, but I didn't hear the pistol. Anatole was already rounding the first bend, and I was still standing at the starting line, too afraid to spill my beer.

Kris asks, "Didn't she have a thing for you?"

"Something like that."

Kris chuckles into his beer. "I figured. Be careful, dude, she's always been a bit of an odd duck." He circles his fingertip around an ear.

I'm unable to stop watching them . . . should I say *him* now? Should I ask? Did they . . . dammit, he, not notice me? He would have said something. I try to ask as casually as possible, "Do you know if they go by he now?"

Kris shrugs. "No idea, dude. Probably?"

"I'm going to ask." I chug the rest of my beer. The carbonation stings my nose and makes my eyes water.

"Why?" Kris searches my face, then shakes his head. "Whatever. Get us that beer on your way back?"

I cross the club and tap Anatole on the shoulder. An unmistakable face looks back. A face more gaunt than before, and undeniably more masculine. Bushy brows and a struggling attempt at facial hair

— though mostly covered up with pale face powder over acne. A dawning look of recognition flashes upon his face, and then a smile splits his cheeks. He throws himself into my arms, hugging tightly.

Anatole yells, "Paul, I —" but the nearby speakers drown his words. He gestures animatedly with his hands. I cup my ear when he repeats himself. Though my ear vibrates painfully as he yells, I can't distinguish his words from Concrete Blonde's "Bloodletting" anthem blasting on the nearby speaker, accompanied by nearly every person in the club singing along.

I give up and point at the door. He grabs his jacket, and we head outside.

We walk away from the club as we once did, as if it hasn't been years since we saw each other. I'm momentarily humbled in contemplation by the transformative nature of time. Dry, curled leaves roll and scrape, dragged by chilly autumn night breezes across sidewalks under the dim glow of streetlamps. I pull my Hot Topic Matrix Neo coat tighter. Hugging the thin fabric against my body only seems to make the night even colder.

"You want my coat?" Anatole asks. His voice is an octave lower than I remember, with a helium lilt that betrays the voice he used to have. Even by moonlight, it's clear that Anatole's previously porcelain face is more plagued by zits under his makeup than I previously thought.

"I'm okay," I lie. "Damn, how long has it been?"

Anatole thinks, his hands pushed deep into coat pockets. "A couple of years?"

"You disappeared."

"Yeah," Anatole says. "Bad relationship."

"I'm sorry."

"He wanted a girlfriend." We walk under a streetlight, maybe the one we met under. Anatole's stride is confident, yet without the dramatic flair he used to show. Under that confidence there's a brooding melancholy, and it's clear that life has beaten the joie de vivre out of him.

"I was surprised to see you in a dress before you disappeared." I pull a slender purple pack of clove cigarettes from my pocket, draw one out, and light it.

"The alcohol helped for a while."

I draw in a lungful of spicy fumes. I let the smoke fall in a wave from my mouth and inhale it into my nose. Together we hurry across the road between cars and continue walking down an alley with a few discarded bike frames piled next to a Dumpster. I say, "I think I understand. Sometimes we need to escape." I hold out the pack to Anatole.

"I don't smoke, remem— oh wait, are those cloves?" He slides one from the pack. We stop at the mouth of the alley, and I cup my hand around his cigarette to light it for him. A Tragically Hip song whines from a jock bar somewhere nearby.

I ask, "Should I call you *he* now?"

"Please."

"Is your name still Anatole?"

Anatole grins. "I changed that before we met. You never knew my old name. Do you want to know what it was?"

Something tells me that would be too personal. "No, you're Anatole to me."

We walk through a small parkette and pass a government building then turn down a commercial street filled with shops, heading toward the sounds of nightclubs and bars. Anatole says, "I missed our talks. I missed you."

"I missed you too," I say. "We used to be able to talk about anything."

"We still can." Anatole considers the cigarette, holding it with his fingertips, and draws on it like a joint. He stares at his boots. "I want to cut off my tits."

I stop and cringe. "Jesus, Anatole."

Anatole stops with me and shrugs. "Sorry if that grosses you out. Do you want me to stop talking about it?"

"No," I say, but I consider my options to pivot. "Your voice sounds really great."

"It's still too high."

"I heard estrogen doesn't make transgender women's voices higher. Testosterone must be a one-way street with vocal cords."

A smile tugs at the corner of Anatole's mouth. "I knew it."

"Knew what?"

"You just happened upon that kind of information?"

I stammer, trying to think of a plausible excuse as heat rushes to my cheeks. "I must have heard it somewhere or . . ." I let myself trail off before I hang myself.

Anatole stops in front of me and looks into my eyes. "Are you trans?"

I feel like I'm being lured into some kind of mind control — if a trans person confronts you about being trans, and you suspect you're trans, are you compelled to tell them? It feels that way. I stammer and defensively begin a lie, but then I stop myself and say, "I've thought about living as a woman." However, my *thought about it* actually means I've wished it more than a few times.

I change the subject before he digs any deeper. "Can they make you a penis?"

"I wish." Anatole walks again, and I sigh in relief.

I search my memory for things I've learned about trans men's surgeries that I've picked up on the periphery while pulling up gory pictures of surgical penile inversion techniques on WebCrawler until I nearly passed out. I say, "Don't they make one from your leg that you can inflate it with your testicle?"

"Not exactly. I'm not satisfied with what is currently available. The penises they can make right now aren't real enough for me." He sighs. "You probably don't understand."

"Try me?"

"Okay, I want my tits gone. I feel like they shouldn't have grown there, but they did, and I hate them, and I can't hide them, even with this fucking binder. With the binder, it's only a little better. And who needs to breathe, right?"

We pass a bar decorated with inflatable palm trees and Hawaiian leis. Yet another Tragically Hip song laments over the street-facing speakers, and the contents of the overcapacity bar filled with girls in micro dresses and guys in sports jerseys spill onto a patio. Some of the braver patrons appear to be wearing shorts and bikinis and fake tans, and those people huddle close to the afterburner-grade patio torches that are so hot I can feel the heat on my cheek from the sidewalk.

I say, "I think I understand what you mean."

"Hey Paul, since you asked a personal question — can I ask you one?"

I unconsciously fidget with my pewter bat buckle. "Of course."

"Do you like your penis?"

Did he seriously ask me that? I decide that he's been forthright enough to deserve my thinking through his question aloud. "I guess I don't like it in the way most guys do. It's kind of there and performs its job. Most of the time, I don't think about it." I tastefully omit my conflicted feelings about masturbation.

"I miss my penis," Anatole says.

Miss his penis?

"Hey, ladies," yells some jock bro with surfer hair and Hawaiian shorts. He holds himself up against the bricked alleyway with one hand while he pisses on his feet. "Come party with us. You freaks are hot."

My heart leaps with joy, then plummets through the floor. The void it leaves fills with panic.

"Hey, buddy — fuck off," Anatole shouts.

I grab Anatole's arm, hurrying him along. "Do you have any idea what those guys will do to me when they find out I'm not a girl?" A quick glance confirms the jock is swaying in place, watching us leave.

Anatole seems to have already forgotten the jock as he walks on. "It's hard to explain. I think I used to have a penis in a past life." Cars whoosh past. "I'm not describing it right. It's like a vague memory of having one. I know it sounds crazy, but I dream about it all the time, and sometimes the feeling is so real it's like I still have it."

I can now see why Kris and others must think he's crazy. However, they'd think I was too, if I admitted the similar things I hide from them. Those sleepless nights staring up at glow-in-the-dark sticker constellations and wishing on adhesive comets that I would wake up as a girl and no one would remember Paul the boy.

Anatole asks, "You know what I miss most about having a penis?"

I shake my head.

"Pissing on trees."

I blurt out a laugh before I can contain it. "Pissing on trees? Like a dog?"

"Yeah!" Anatole's eyes light up. "Just like a dog. First damn thing I'd do. I'd piss on every fucking tree I could find."

I shake my head and casually check over my shoulder for jocks. "It's handy being able to pee anywhere, I guess. You know, I've dreamed about having a vagina, sometimes even having sex. I wake up relieved and invigorated, but disappointed as reality sets in."

"Are you sure you're not trans?"

I've barely admitted considering that possibility to myself, let alone another person. If Anatole hadn't disappeared all those years ago, I feel like I may have eventually opened up to him. Maybe he could have helped me work through these feelings. And if we go years before seeing each other again, I might lose my chance to discuss it.

I say, "I don't think I'm ready to throw away my life, you know? What if I don't look like a girl? What if I become a freak?"

"There are great facial feminization surgeons these days."

"We can barely afford food. If I knew I'd transition well, I think I'd try, but I'm too old now."

"You're not old."

But I am. The most passable girls I've seen on the internet transition in their early teens. Once testosterone warps your bones, it's over. Not even surgery can change that kind of thing back. "I'm already twenty-four years old. It's not worth going through all that humiliation for nothing."

"I understand why you feel that way," Anatole says. "But you're wrong."

"About being too old?"

"No, you said transitioning is throwing your life away. I'm not doing that — I'm starting to live."

His words slap me across the face and leave me breathless. I say, "I didn't mean that. I meant for myself, because —"

"You definitely mean it, and that's okay." Anatole holds out his hand. I take it, and we smile to each other. He asks, "Hey, wouldn't it be cool if we could swap parts?"

We turn another corner to round the block. One turn more and we should see the Frat House again.

I say, "It would. In fact, it would be pretty damn awesome."

"Yeah, it would be."

I squeeze Anatole's hand. "Would that be like a genderfuck take a penny, leave a penny?"

He bumps his bony hip against mine. "Take a penis, leave a penis?"

I can't help but snort, laughing far louder than I mean to, and it echoes down the empty street.

"Oh shit," a guy behind me says. "I think that's a dude."

Anatole and I turn to find three jocks trailing a half block behind us. One of them has surfer swooshed blonde hair and sleeves rolled up over veiny biceps. He might be the guy who pissed on his shoes. When we turn, the surfer jock yells, "Hey, freak — are you a dude?"

A second, doughy guy says, "I think the one is." He's much quieter, as if afraid to speak up.

The third guy, wearing a football jersey, leaps on the surfer's back and cackles. "Oh shit, dude, you're fucking gay!"

Anatole takes a step toward the jocks and says, "Why don't you go fuck each other?"

I briefly wonder which one of us they think is a guy. In the time it takes Anatole to bravely step forward, I've mentally calculated how far the club is from this spot, whether I can outrun an athlete in sneakers with my industrial boots on, and wondered if Anatole has been in a fight with someone like this before. I conclude that Anatole likely doesn't have a lifetime of experience presenting as a skinny, effeminate geek being beaten up by guys to realize what a colossal mistake he's making.

I tug Anatole's arm, and he stumbles as I drag him back. His face is red and creased with rage but softens into concern when he sees mine. We run, the chilled night air biting at my cheeks, our dark coats flapping behind.

"We just want to talk," one of them shouts.

Then they're chasing us, and we burst through the doors of the Frat House. Thankfully, the place has filled even more and resonates with the comforting drone of Bauhaus. While it's doubtful they'd follow us into the club, I run to the edge of the dance floor and bury myself within a writhing mass of leather, lace, and clove.

But they enter.

The three of them gather in the doorway and scan the crowd, but they're looking for a couple of pale, dark-haired skinny people in long coats, and they'll need to be more specific to find us. I try to point them out to Anatole, but I've already lost him in the crowd.

Besides lifting weights and learning kung fu, Kris bounces at a trashy country bar on the weekends — and I can't think of anywhere safer than by his side. I find Kris chatting with a tall girl with snow white hair and thigh-high boots. I grab his shoulder and shout, "THERE'SJOCKSINTHECLUBANDITHINK-THEYWANTTOFIGHTME!"

Kris holds up a finger to the goth girl. "Just a sec, hun." He raises his eyebrows at me in a can't-you-see-I'm-busy kind of way.

I try to calm myself. "There are jocks in the bar, and I think they want —"

A loud bass-filled thump interrupts the track, then the music cuts altogether. A familiar drunk voice booms over the speakers. "Everyone, tell him to play Tragically Hip." When the only thing he gets in reply is a couple of shouts and a fuck you, he chants, "Play the Hip, play the Hip."

A chorus of boos fills the club, and our DJ snatches for the mic, but the surfer jock holds it above the DJ's head like an abusive older brother. When the DJ finally grabs the mic and pulls, the jock releases it. As our DJ falls, the jock punches him in the face. A blood spray is briefly illuminated in the club's laser lights.

"Fuck!" Kris shouts and leaps out of his chair and bumps the table. His pint tumbles to the floor and shatters. Accompanied by triumphant cheers, Kris and another guy drag the surfer jock out of the booth. I spot the football jock trying to chat-up the white-haired girl, but she's yelling something into his face that I can't quite hear.

Then the doughy, quiet jock is suddenly standing in front of me. "You're the guy from outside, right?" I immediately back into a table in my attempt to avoid the inevitable punch, but he holds out his hand. "Wait. My friend isn't usually like this. I wanted to say I'm sorry, and I think you're really —"

Before he says anything more, Kris pushes through the crowd and grabs his shirt, ripping it as he tugs the doughy guy away. Then Kris shoves him toward the door hard enough he slips on the spilled beer and falls on his back.

Kris points at the door and shouts, "Time to go."

As the doughy jock with kind eyes struggles to sit up, he's surrounded by pale, willowy creatures who float around him, laughing at his tearaway pants. Something makes me want to stop Kris and tell him this guy isn't trying to cause trouble like the others. But I don't. I've spent too much time investing in the goth lifestyle's social currency. I know their ways — I dance to their music and meet their expectations. As long as I stay under the radar and don't contradict them, I remain one of them.

The doughy jock is pulled off the floor, and Kris escorts him to the door as others guide his jock friends. Surfer dude yells about freaks and pussies and faggots as he's pushed out the door.

Half of the club follows the jocks out, and Fester grabs my shoulder, his chest heaves, and one of his eyes looks as if it's about to pop out of his skull. Fester points to the DJ, who is lying in a group of fawning girls that tenderly dab at his bloody nose.

"Where's the fucker who did that?" Fester asks.

I point to the door, and Fester storms off. Despite his size, I've never seen him upset before, and neither have others, judging by the way the rest of the club follows him outside.

On the sidewalk, Kris shouts, "Take your friends and walk away." His words form cloudy puffs that drift into the chilly night.

The surfer jock with the bloody knuckles bumps chests with Kris and asks, "What are you gunna do, faggot, brush my hair?" But Kris doesn't escalate, he only repeats himself.

Fester storms past Kris and shoves the big jock hard enough that he stumbles and nearly falls. "Go."

"Fuck you."

Fester uses his momentum to step forward and bring a thick fist down onto the bridge of the jock's nose. A meaty slap echoes down the street, along with a sound like a snapping twig.

The jock is pistoned to the ground so quickly that he bounces off the concrete and somehow finds himself back on his feet. Around me, the crowd draws a collective breath. Fester is already walking back to the club before the jock takes three steps in completely different directions. The jock's eyes roll, and he crumples onto the sidewalk.

"Somebody call an ambulance," the white-haired girl says.

I didn't realize I was staring until Kris grabs my shoulders. He says, "You're shaking. Are you okay?"

I look past Kris at the two remaining jocks, still surrounded by a crowd of sickly looking twenty-somethings. The doughy guy's expression probably resembles the one on my face when Anatole yelled at them. I say, "I'm fine. It was the guy on the ground. The other two did nothing."

Kris nods then points to the semi-conscious jock. "Take your friend and get out of here."

They pick up their friend and limp away down the street.

Kris slides his arm around my shoulder and leads me toward the doors. "Did you see that fucker bounce?"

"You saw that too?" I ask. "I wasn't sure if I imagined it."

As the doughy jock leaves, he smiles at me. It's a heartbreaking, gentle, stiff-lipped smile. I smile back, and in that moment, we share something. His smile communicates that he's thankful I spoke up for him, but there is more. The way his soft, imploring gaze lingers on mine, his tightened lips suggest the frustration of a missed opportunity — and while I could be reading into this moment too much, I think he wishes he had more time to explain how he feels. The moment leaves me confused, but curiously interested, and wondering if I will ever see more smiles like that — but then Kris pulls me through the doorway.

"You saw Anatole. Is she really turning into a dude?"

We walk through a rolling cloud of purple dry ice. "Turning into? He's already there."

⌐ 13 ⌐

Today Was a
Fairy Tale

Emerging from a cloud of rose-scented mist, Kali's face is lit electric pink as we pass a buzzing neon heart on the tunnel's rocky wall. We float together in a giant rubber duck that pulls us along a submerged track toward an expanding arch of light. As we pass through the cave's mouth, sunlight gleams off the duck's droplet-sprinkled plastic wings and the sequined lining of my bridal gown reflects shimmering rainbows across the water's surface.

Kali caresses my ears. "What did you think?"

"Best honeymoon ever," I say.

"We're only getting started." A sly smirk hints at the corner of Kali's mouth as he pulls me close. I rest my cheek against his suit-covered chest, allowing myself to melt into the relaxing vibration of his affectionate purring. Being here, having him holding me, sharing this moment together in an actual tunnel of love with my husband, has made all the fuss of the past two weeks of wedding mayhem worthwhile.

This does truly feel perfect, even though I know that none of this is real — not in the way most people value realness. I know this amusement park we're in, this plastic duck boat, and even our avatars are just lines of code stored on a softly humming server somewhere. Despite that, I feel an authentic bond with Kali, which is no less valid than the intimacy and trust that accompanies sharing your bed and life with someone in the Real World.

In loving relationships, we seek reassurances that our partner cares for us. Grand romantic gestures may be beautiful and sweep you off your feet, but they are easily staged. We communicate true love through a multitude of selfless moments. Love appears as an unprompted cup of tea just the way you like it on a tough day, or when you fawn over a beautiful sweater and a week later, it appears on the dining room table even when it's not your birthday. Genuine gestures of love can even appear in an act as simple as being cuddled as the little spoon while you drift off to sleep.

Despite what you might think, these gestures can mean more online.

Kali's wedding suit is an excellent example. If he and I married in Real Life, he might buy or rent a suit. A tailor then measures and makes alterations, but all Kali has done is point and pay and pick it up when it's ready. Here, Kali inevitably tried on multiple suits from multiple online vendors, still spent real money to buy it, but then he also sank hours in an editor, carefully tweaking the suit's proportions to accommodate his unique furry body. It took me three days to find and fit a bridal dress that showed my tail, and then edit a veil so that it didn't cut off my ears.

Kali proposed with an emerald ring. While he likely didn't spend too much to buy it, he took the time to learn I prefer emeralds to diamonds. Communication and attention to detail matter just as much here. He also scouted this abandoned amusement park for us to be alone. Thoughtful kindnesses like these are more than I have ever experienced in a Real Life relationship.

In some ways, online relationships better illustrate commitment and desire. In Real Life, you and I might walk together — your hand might bump mine and we might like the feeling of that accidental touch enough to hold hands. It could be sweet, but there's a casualness to this act that cannot occur online.

In virtual worlds, we might similarly walk together, but you would intentionally position your character closer to mine, target me, and initiate a command like /hold hands with Lydia.

While stepping out of a romantic moment to type may sound detached, if my online partner values the time required to specifically write an affectionate gesture because they want to build a connection, doesn't that add something? Describing a character's intention is not only precise and deliberate, but every descriptive pose my partner writes is only for me, for us, to create our memorable moment. Whether we're holding hands, or fighting, or fucking, we craft line after line of descriptive prose — a conscious, poetic rededication to the value of our relationship. So, yes, I know that our relationship, our marriage, and this moment are not "real" in the way society might define it, but for a lonely and sick trans woman, they are everything.

Besides, don't scientists say reality, as we understand it, might be lines of code, anyway?

The smiling duck carries us toward the turnstiles, and the grandiose vaudevillian majesty of the amusement park blooms around us with disembodied shouts of "STEP RIGHT UP" and "GET YER POPCORN HERE!" which shatters our private moment.

I just hope the park's owner hasn't installed security cameras in that tunnel.

We float along in the warm afternoon sun, the duck's bill gleaming wet and pumpkin orange as the boat clunks into place at the turnstile. The automated gate squeaks open, awaiting the non-existent next couple.

There's nobody in the maze of chromed queue fencing, nor is there anyone lined up for the roller coaster, which rockets riderless along its tracks — though ghostly screams pierce the air each time it plummets to earth. All the games are unstaffed, and the popcorn cart's lights strobe, unattended, in the middle of the pavilion. I'm relatively sure there are no vendors, no carnies, no security, and no other living players in this entire amusement park.

I wrap my arms around Kali and pull myself into him, smelling him, not wanting the moment to end. "I had a tough day," I mutter, feeling needy.

Kali takes my hand and helps me stand as I gather up my dress to avoid stepping on the hem.

"I'm sorry, baby," he says, "did you want to talk about it?" While his tone is warm, and sincere, how much should I reveal without disgusting him?

Learning about each other's Real Lives might have deepened our trust, but by releasing that information, we've forever dispelled some of the magic that inspired our shared fantasy. I've learned that Jason, the man behind the cheetah, is a self-proclaimed straight man. Even though I tell him I have always, secretly, wished I was a woman, he certainly must wonder how a Real Life relationship with me would play out.

What would he tell his friends? His family? Is such a relationship even possible? "Hey Mom, hey Dad, this is my girlfriend, Paul. I realize she looks like a guy and sounds like a guy, but she's actually a girl. Don't believe me? You should see how hot she is online! Rawr."

Augh.

While I've told him I have cancer, cried to him about losing my hair, and he's aware I'm often sick, weak, and tired, I've been hiding the most graphic, unappetizing aspects from him. What if that information is enough to destroy the fragile illusion of feminine beauty I've woven? What if it installs a picture in his mind of holding the hand of a bald, sad, sick boy rather than the curvy, sensuous, and loving female rabbit he's leading toward the snack cart?

"Chemo stuff," I say. "I'll be okay." I raise myself onto my toes to kiss him.

"You know you can talk to me," he says in a resigned tone.

Instead of putting him through that, together we enjoy the post-apocalyptic aesthetic of the amusement park. Kali gets me cotton candy, we go on as many rides as I can stomach, and as evening approaches, we bore of the desolation, and he walks me to the parking lot. Beyond the ticket booths, a black Triumph motorcycle awaits. Two helmets with leather retro goggles rest on its sun-warmed seat.

Kali asks, "You said no more rides, but how about one more? Two if I'm lucky?"

I snicker to myself as I pull on the helmet and adjust my ears to dangle out the back. "How long have you waited to say that?"

"You love it." Kali pulls on a leather jacket, which melts away his wedding tux. Blue jeans and leather. With the practised swagger of James Dean, he mounts the motorcycle and kickstarts it into life. The bike roars as he cranks the throttle a few times for effect.

"I do." I tuck my dress between my legs and climb on behind him.

For a moment he lets the bike idle — long enough for me to wonder if its code is glitched. Kali glances over his shoulder. "You understand I love you, no matter what, right? You'll always be my bunny."

"I know," I say too quickly. A lump swells in my throat, and if I say anything more, I'll cry and ruin the moment. Sometimes, I wonder how he can puzzle out my inner struggles. "I love you too, my kitty."

He grips my clasped hands around his waist, then he engages the bike, and we roar out of the park and onto the highway. Simulated wind whips my wedding dress against my bare legs. I marvel at how perfectly someone must have sampled the bike's ratcheting engine. I close my eyes, and, for a moment, I am there — completely.

I can taste the salty brine of the nearby seaside, feel the wind in my hair, even sense the subtle creak of the soft leather seat. I cling to Kali and lose myself to the sound of the throaty, growling motorcycle as it vibrates throughout my body.

The sound stutters as we pass a zone boundary.

It tears me out of the moment like a record skip.

The seaside road with its endless beaches, boardwalks, inviting deckchairs, and tourist-less sun umbrellas disappears, and we drive on a featureless grey plane. A highway appears under our motorcycle, cracked and old. A field of apple trees spring into existence to our right like a regiment of soldiers, telephone poles fold out of the ground all the way to the horizon, and suddenly we're driving through a desolate stretch of highway that could be anywhere in small-town America. Ahead are failed building developments, abandoned houses, pointless intersections, and a single gas station. Kali stops at a gas pump, hooks the kickstand with the heel of his boot, and settles the bike.

I can't help but admire the dedication it must have taken to recreate such a mundane and forgettable part of the world. Endless hours of coding and referencing photographs and street maps for what? To enjoy the luxury of driving past such a forgettable location?

Kali climbs off the bike and grins, looking suspiciously proud of himself. I feel myself getting annoyed that he'd interrupt such a potentially perfect day to take me here. It would have made more sense to bring me back to a beach, like the day we met. Does he think I'm happy to be taken to a gas station?

"Pretty cool, don't you think, Suzy-Q?" Kali finally asks. He takes my hand and helps me off the bike.

Suzy-Q? He's really committed to this fifties thing.

"It's a really clean gas station, Daddy-O." I say it as enthusiastically as possible. Then a wave of chemo fog creeps through me, first rising as nausea, filling my mouth with bile. Then fingertips of exhaustion smooth over my brain and tug at my eyelids. These are the typical warning signs before I hit that invisible wall where sleep is non-negotiable.

It's coming, sure as anything.

"Turn around," Kali says.

When I turn around, the sun disappears and we stand on the cool pavement before a dimly lit restaurant called the Bobby Socks Diner. Finished in gleaming red paint and polished chrome, it has those familiar wrap-around windows where one might expect to spot James Dean smoking inside. Beyond the diner, a single dim streetlight barely illuminates the oil-stained parking lot. Three moths batter against each other to be closest to the bulb.

I fight the chemo. I say, "You remembered." I draw nearer to the diner, and through the windows is the most iconic fifties interior I could have imagined. There are Naugahyde booth seats, and hanging globe lights illuminate a checkerboard dance floor. On the walls are autographed pictures of Ella Fitzgerald, Billie Holiday, Doris Day, Clark Gable, Etta James, and others I don't recognize. In a strategic place of honour are portraits of James Dean, Marilyn Monroe, and behind the counter is the inevitable Elvis, surrounded in gold and flashing marquee lights.

Kali stands by the door, a smug grin on his face and a poodle dress hooked on his fingers. The looming chemo coma is beat into submission by the wild pounding of my eager heart. I race and take the dress from him, and at the press of a button it springs onto my body, cinches in my waist, and fluffs up my tits. Flared collar, bright blue skirt, neck scarf, and complete with bobby socks in saddle shoes.

"How do I look?" I spin in front of him, skirt flaring.

Kali leans, cigarette hanging from his mouth. His loose leather jacket reveals a skin-tight white t-shirt beneath. "You're the bee's knees." He opens the door, a bell on a metal coil jingles. "After you, doll."

Inside, I marvel at a rotating pie display while Kali flips through song lists on the jukebox, clacking selection panes over one at a time.

The jukebox accepts a coin and rings a tiny chime of acknowledgement. Inside the illuminated casing, the dime rolls along internal metal tracks and registers a satisfying *ka-chink*. With a mechanical whir, the selection arm hums over, lifts and twists a record, then drops it perfectly onto the spindle. The turntable spins up, speakers crackle to life, the needle *thuts* into place, and "Earth Angel" echoes through the diner.

They say you can't appreciate the blues until you've experienced loss. Perhaps in the same way, in that moment I understood these lyrics for the first time. As Kali leads me to the dance floor, I realize that "Earth Angel" isn't about a heavenly romance, as I had once assumed.

I drape my arms around Kali's neck and press my cheek to his. We dance as the Penguins sing, and chills tease up my spine. Unlike the romantic ballad I once believed it to be, I now hear a story of misguided, unattainable love based on someone's appearance — a song about unhealthy and unrealistic obsession.

I ask, "How did you find this place?"

We circle the floor, Kali leading me under the appreciative gaze of the framed greats. "It took me a while to find the perfect one." The smirk playing on Kali's lips makes me question whether he's talking about me, or the diner. He pulls me closer and whispers along to the lyrics. Kali's warm, deep voice vibrates the headphone speaker against my ear, promising eternal love, and asking for mine.

I close my eyes and imagine him holding me, his cheek against mine, singing only to me. He knows the woman behind my avatar is far from beautiful, so I find it difficult to trust these beautiful professions.

Choking back a sob, tears blur the screen and I mute my microphone. I know I should be happy. This is, perhaps, the most tender moment we've ever shared. However, I know a virtual world isn't a place where love can last forever. Despite my doubts, and all the years of building walls between reality and my virtual life, just for a minute I allow my heart to wish I could truly hold Jason.

I wipe my eyes with the sleeve of my hoodie and force myself to take a few deep breaths and compose myself. I unmute.

"This is perfect," I whisper.

"I love you," Kali says.

Gritting my teeth, I force myself not to mute the mic, and in a wavering voice I say, "I love you so much. I'm sorry, I —"

"We don't have to talk," Kali interrupts. He noses my cheek, and our eyes meet, and he presses his lips to mine. We slowly twirl as we kiss, and the lights of the diner dim. We hold each other and sway — virtually dancing, virtually kissing in the most perfect virtual diner I have ever virtually seen.

My throat hurts from swallowing hopes best left unsaid. I rest my elbows on the desk, clasp hands over my mouth, and try to remain as quiet as possible while I focus on the sound of Kali's breath in my ear.

Perhaps it's the heaviness of emotions, or because it's nearly three in the morning, but my chemo fog creeps back. It once again arrives as a wave of nausea, but this time sends me reaching for the trash can. The nausea sinks away, but what replaces it is a demanding pressure behind my eyes, a fogging in my skull, and the room spins. I won't be able to fight off unconsciousness much longer.

The jukebox whirs and clicks as it queues up "The Great Pretender."

"Kali, I have to go."

"It's late for you, I understand. Thank you for spending so much time with me tonight."

"I had the best time."

When I step away, Kali holds my hands. "Can I see you tomorrow?"

Tomorrow. Time is an abstract concept when you rarely leave the house. Somewhere between countless appointments, comatose afternoons, and sleepless nights, I can no longer locate specific days within definable time.

What do I have to do tomorrow? Go in to the hospital and have my chemo bottle changed. I promised Karen we would decide on wedding venues.

I say, "I might be on in the evening."

"Send me a quick message before you sleep tonight?"

"Okay, Kitty."

My avatar waves and poofs out of existence in a shower of glowing particles that swirl on the dance floor, then everything goes dark and I'm back at the *Second Life* load screen.

I shut down the game and pull up Skype. Kali is already on and waiting for me to message. I roll my office chair away and use the desk to pull myself to my feet. Swaddled in my oversized hoodie, I didn't realize how much the winter chill had crept into the apartment over the past few hours. I scrape my feet to the bathroom.

My heart still bubbles over, remembering how perfect it felt to be in Kali's arms. I resist the mirror, knowing how profoundly my reflection will ruin this delicate, fluttering joy. I shuffle back to the computer, fighting the now overwhelming cotton candy in my brain, fogging out everything, shutting me down, deleting any thought that doesn't involve sleep.

Kali's icon is yellow, waiting. I click on his adorable cartoon cheetah face and type.

You say: Night night, kitty. Tonight was wonderful. I love you so much! *mwah!*

Kali's icon flashes green and three dots cycle.

Kali says: Love you too, my bunny! Have a good rest. We can explore more of the amusement park tomorrow. <3

The moment Kali's message appears, a loud *ping* echoes from the bedroom down the hall.

My heart seizes.

I realize what that sound must be but don't allow myself to believe it.

In a panic, I shut down the computer and stand quietly in total darkness. I wait and listen, swaying with exhaustion. I pray Kali doesn't message again, doesn't make the tablet I forgot in the bedroom ping another notification. He doesn't.

What's the worst-case scenario?

The worst thing that could happen would involve Karen somehow still being awake this late and using the tablet. She sometimes does, but she has to work tomorrow.

Best-case scenario?

She slept through or ignored it. Surely if she saw that message she would call out or make a sound.

I wait.

I shiver from the cold, from nerves, while the room spins and chemo presses behind my eyes. Nothing. I creep through the kitchen toward the open door of our dark bedroom.

Karen's face is illuminated in blue light as she sits in bed, holding the tablet. She stares expressionless at the screen, scrolling up and up with her finger. I step into the room, convincing myself she hasn't seen the little bubble with Kali's words of love pop up from the conveniently self-installed Skype auto-notifier.

Karen says to the tablet, "You forgot to sign out."

I wrack my brain, trying to think of something to say. That she and I haven't been exclusive for some time, that we agreed online flings were okay, that last week she bought a webcam to chat from the bathtub "with her sister," that recently I caught her chatting to a full-blown dom who gave her commands to follow in our apartment. Hell, Kali and Karen even know each other's real names.

I could try to turn the tables and weaponize one of her past transgressions to distract her long enough to reframe the argument, but I can't think of a fair way to say any of it because I understand I've crossed an unspoken line.

I knew I'd crossed it even before I noticed the strategically concealed creases of pain on her face.

I knew it the moment that hideously harmonic *ping* echoed through the darkness, within this room, from the tablet in her slightly shaking hands.

"I'm sorry, I —"

Karen asks, "You love him?" She resists looking at me.

"I said that, but not the same way I love you." This is the best half-truth I can construct as chemo fog crushes me. My eyes strain to see past the digital glow shining up against her chin like she's telling an ominous campfire story.

"You call him *Kitty*?" She spits the name like a curse and swipes at the screen.

Karen is the first girlfriend in whom I've ever confided my previously secret online encounters. Of course, I hid how cathartic and euphoric "being female" truly was for me. I always couched these online relationships in sex, and she understands sex. She's able to disconnect sex from emotion, and therefore she's deemed online play allowable. I used to be able to keep my emotions out of it, but I somehow lost that ability after I met Kali.

Karen says, "'I love you *so* much.'" She sighs. "'Mwah'? Ugh."

"Those are just words," I lie. I realize how meaningless that sounds the moment the sentence clears my lips.

Karen mercifully puts down the tablet and faces me. Her eyes glassy and bloodshot, her mouth open and jaw quivering as she searches for something to say. She's usually so cool and stoic, and while she might put on a good show of emotion when she needs to, I've never seen her cry. But this is real. I truly hurt her. She says, "This isn't what we agreed to."

"We didn't say anything about —"

"I shouldn't have needed to," Karen interrupts. "You need help. You need to talk to someone, Paul."

For the first time in my life, I cringe at the sound of my name. I'm not sure if my revulsion is rooted in the way she spit it at me, so filled with contempt, or because I've spent so much time being Lydia. Maybe it's a mix of both, soaking in a vat of chemotherapy.

No matter the reason, I realize that I no longer want to be Paul. Lydia could have dealt with this easier. She would have been faithful to her convictions, and her relationships, and not act like the petty coward that rises within me.

"What about your boyfriend, Mikey?" I ask. "You two talk all day, almost every day."

"It is just sex with him," Karen says in monotone. "Besides, he's not my boyfriend. I don't love him." And she's far too good of a liar for me to decipher how much of that is true. I crawl onto the bed, but she faces the wall. She asks, "Do you even still want to get married?"

I'm surprised how fast my brain embraces this opportunity of escape. Despite this instinct, I do genuinely love Karen. Since I've been on disability leave with only a fraction of my wage, Karen has stepped up and worked many hours to support us, and then sometimes spends entire weekends performing at festivals. She's justifiably exhausted all the time, and on top of that does all the shopping, the cleaning, and our meal prep.

I don't think I could have survived this long without her help. I sometimes suspect she has developed caregiver burnout and me and my illness have become loathsome to her. However, if this is the case, she's never admitted it to me. The only thing she ever truly wanted from me was marriage, and I wanted to give her something back.

I entertain the thought of saying, "No, I don't want to marry you."

If I did, we would have a messy fight that would last for days. We would divvy up our belongings, and I would need to move out. I'd move in with my mother because I can't support myself — I can barely walk. But if I told her that, it would open the possibility of being with Kali in Real Life.

The realization of this opportunity triggers a note of confusing static within me, the same one I always feel when I think of our meeting each other. A relationship with Jason couldn't possibly compare to our online romance. I've seen the real him in pictures, and I find him incredibly handsome, but the thought of being with him as Paul doesn't fit with the fairy-tale romance I envision.

Would breaking up with Karen mean I could transition? Start hormones? Perhaps it's an opportunity. The thought briefly elates me until I consider the consequences of doing so. My body might change a little at my age, but my face can only change so much, my bone structure not at all, nor my voice.

I'd be that comical, try-hard wanna-be woman people snicker at when they talk about shemales and trannies. I'd be the "fucking faggot" of my small town. And when I'm well enough to go back to my job, what then? Are they progressive enough to accept a trans woman? I'm almost forty — too old to start a new career. Would my bosses still consider me part of their family if I said I wasn't a man, admitted I loved a man, and made them call me by a woman's name?

No, of course they wouldn't. I'd probably lose everything. What if I end up homeless? Even if I sacrificed all those things, would Kali even find me attractive? Would he ever truly love me . . . as me?

Karen pulls the covers over her and buries her face in her pillow.

I touch Karen's shoulder. "I do want to marry you."

◖ 14 ◗

Born This Way

2011 – One year and a crumbling marriage later, in The Beaches, Toronto

The house is unmistakable. A decorative iron fence restrains an overgrown yard filled with explosive blooms of assorted pollinator flowers. Swaying over the door is an oversized Pride flag. In a sea of postage stamp lawns and "good morning" neighbours, at least I can be sure I've got the right place.

Next to the house, down a darkened laneway hides a nondescript side entrance, the one Craig told me to enter. On the phone, he made me think this house was his office, and his home was an estate in Brampton. My psychologist made this guy out to be a rare trans advocate who, out of the goodness of his heart, travels to Toronto once or twice a month to sprinkle titty skittles on all the good little trans girls so they grow up buxom and fabulous.

Yesterday he called to tell me to come a little early as there is a bike race this weekend. For someone who was raised on the genius of Hamilton's alternating one-way street system, Toronto is, at the best of times, a traffic nightmare. It took me an hour to negotiate the city's congestion, blockaded intersections, construction, and needlessly aggressive taxi drivers as I attempted to navigate through detours, only to discover all the street parking had been gobbled up by spectators. I ended up walking over six blocks in this late summer heat with beads of sweat creeping down my spine and no doubt soaking into my jacket.

Now my hair is stuck against my forehead and sweat stings my eyes. My stomach twists into knots as I approach the dimly lit lane. I was already worried that Craig wouldn't prescribe me any pills, but now I wonder if he'll cancel the appointment that took me months to secure. It could be why I'm feeling so cynical about being shuffled down a side door out of sight instead of welcomed through the queer secret garden.

I find the door unmarked, but unlocked, so I knock and open and pray to the chokered patron saint of trans women that I'm not walking into some dude's man cave.

"Vanessa, is that you?" a campy voice calls from down a flight of carpeted stairs.

For a moment I wonder if I've stumbled into someone else's appointment slot, but then I realize I had signed off on an earlier email with the name Vanessa. I had been trying the name on, but hadn't yet heard it aloud, and now I realize it doesn't fit at all.

"Yes, sorry!" I slip off my shoes on the provided mat and descend the pillow-soft steps into a cozy basement consultation room.

"It is almost half past. I told you not to be late."

I stop on the stairs. "I'm sorry? I drove an hour from Hamilton. It's confusing here and —"

"That is why I said to come early," Craig snaps, cutting me off.

I creep down the last few stairs. From around the corner, Craig rustles pages and mutters. I'm now convinced I've screwed any chance at talking him into prescribing today. When I step into Craig's consultation room, his forehead creases flash away, and, like a flipped switch, he pivots back to an upbeat, campy trill. "Oh well," he sings, "we'll have to hurry since I have someone coming after you."

Craig sits on an overstuffed couch, writing on a slip of paper inside a folder. Slender, athletic, and dressed in designer business-casual clothes, and he's wearing shiny brown shoes, a stark contrast to the ones I left on his mat. I'm ninety percent sure my sock has a hole, so I curl my toes to hide it.

Craig leans forward and offers his hand. He gives me one of those trademarked "bro confidence" handshakes — a firm, tight grip with a single, purposeful shake. It's the kind of greeting that suggests he's courteous and professional, but too busy to waste time shaking a hand more than once. It also makes me want to remind him I'm a woman, but I try not to read into it too much since I chose not to wear the dress my psychologist suggested.

The room we're in has the curated aesthetic of a comfy living room rather than an office, but there's nothing personal enough to make it feel like a home. There's a portrait by some nature artist showing a misty lake with overhanging trees, and a shelf with a bonsai tree and wooden cut-out letters that spell *Born This Way*.

Better than *Hang in there, baby*, I guess.

"We should start," Craig says. "I understand you were referred to me hoping to be prescribed hormone replacement therapy?"

"Yes."

As Craig refers to his folder, I realize I don't know what to do with my hands, so I clasp them together. What kind of question is that, anyway? For Craig to even consider me as a patient, I had to see a psychologist for at least three months until they would agree to make a referral, then I spent another four months waiting for an appointment slot to open, and then I battled through Toronto traffic and Craig's pissy mood. Maybe he just gets off hearing trans women ask for it?

No, I'm sure that's not the case. It's more likely a legal loophole. I'm hot, and irritable, and probably nervous. I try to smile.

Craig says, "I want you to be comfortable. This isn't an interview. Think of it more like a conversation."

Sure, a pleasant conversation where you decide my future. I nod.

"To help you relax, I'm going to take some anxiety off the table. At the end of this appointment, I will write you a prescription for spironolactone, if you want it. But I'll need to see you for three months after today before I prescribe you estrogen."

My heart sinks. I drove an hour for this?

"You won't prescribe me estrogen?" I ask. I can tell by his tone that he thinks he's doing me a favour.

Craig smiles as if he's had this conversation before. "I can't. I am required to see you three times over three months to prescribe it to you and —"

"I saw my psychologist for over a year, isn't that enough? He referred me to you months ago."

Politely, Craig waits for me to finish. "I trust your psychologist, and I have heard good things about his work, but I haven't seen you, personally, for long enough."

That would have been nice to know a year ago. However, I've lived without estrogen for thirty-six years. What's three more months? I say, "Okay."

Craig nods and puts on what I'm sure he believes is an empathetic frown. The faux compassion he's projecting sickens me. "I'm so sorry about this. Did you still want me to prescribe spiro? Because there are things we need to chat about first if so."

"Well, yes, of course I do."

"Okay. I'll tell you a bit about spiro and estrogen alternatives so you understand the various risks. First —"

Like the voiceover at the end of an American drug ad, Craig lists the potential side effects of both spiro and estrogen supplements. He tells me how the cheapest estrogen, the stuff low-income trans women use, is actually refined from horse urine, but if I have good medical coverage, I could use more efficient synthetic variations in patches, or injections, or tablets that dissolve under my tongue. He warns me that I won't see many changes from taking only spiro, or any testosterone blocker, but I might observe some breast growth and my skin may soften. He then briefly mentions that there's a higher chance of breast cancer, but I'll lower my risk of heart attack, which I think is a nice trade-off. He concludes by saying that experts don't fully understand these risks or if they influence my life expectancy.

From what I've read, when he says *experts* he means absolutely no one. Trans women's hormones were originally designed for post-menopausal cis women, or for people with heart and liver problems. So, I only half pay attention because I'm relatively confident that what he's saying is bullshit and speculation, and he's talking a lot for someone who claims he's behind schedule.

I reason that it's possible these warnings are a test of my conviction, and I consider cutting him off to tell him the truth — that I'd drink literal poison if it meant I could live as a woman for just five years.

You can't scare me, I've survived cancer.

Craig finishes with, "It's slow, but it is a start. You want to block your testosterone, correct?"

"Absolutely," I say. "At least that might stop me losing more hair."

He glances at where my hairline has been sneaking up my temples, Craig's own having fled to near the middle of his scalp. "Not everyone reacts the same. Spiro won't bring back lost hair, but it should prevent further loss. Are you okay to chat more? If so, we'll call this session the first of the three I need to legally prescribe you estrogen."

If I say no, do you yell psych! and rip the scrip from my hands?

"Sure, why not?" I say, just happy he's finished his "side effects may include" spiel.

"Great! How do you identify, Vanessa?"

"As a woman?"

"Right, I should have been more specific." Craig mimics bopping himself against the side of his temple. "That was my next question. But how do you identify sexually?"

"You mean, am I straight?"

"Yes. Gay, straight, bi, asexual?"

Is it only in job interviews where they aren't allowed to ask that? I hope this isn't a qualifying question and say, "I used to think I was straight, but I might be bi . . . or straight, but for men? It's complicated. Does it matter?"

Craig hurriedly waves his hands. "No. It doesn't make a difference for prescribing you. I just want some insight into your home life."

"It sucks. I think my wife wants a divorce."

There's that fake compassion face again.

"These things are unfortunately common for transgender women. By the way, not wearing women's clothing today is perfectly fine, though most transgender women do. You might wish to experiment with your feminine presentation soon if you are considering surgery. Anyhow, we don't have to talk about your real-life experience prerequisite yet. All that's important for me today is that you identify as female."

Great, am I going to have to go through this Harry Benjamin shit again?

"I identify as a girl — a woman, yes."

Speaking that aloud while wearing men's clothes, and in a man's voice, and without a digital persona to hide behind feels unusual, and I'm suddenly aware of how strange I must appear when I say it.

Unfazed, Craig writes something down. "Would you tell me how you came to this decision? Or describe how you recognize you are female?"

I chew my lip to avoid blurting out my reactionary response, the one I've prepared for the trans-uninitiated. But what's the *correct* answer? Does he expect me to say I like pink and dresses and want to wear my hair long, or that I like to paint my nails?

Those don't make anyone a woman. While I'm sure saying so would satisfy him, I decide to be as honest as possible.

"Men's presentation and bodies seem foreign, and I've always struggled to relate with other men. Leaning toward feminine presentation and mannerisms just feels *natural*. Beyond that, I've never cared about women's clothes or makeup. It's always been about my body — about *being* female, not dressing as one. I don't like what puberty did to my body, and I want to correct it."

Craig busily writes notes. He holds up a finger. "You don't have to be male or female, you know. Some people live in between."

In between? What an awful way to say that. I say, "I know that. Do you mind if I tell you exactly how I know?"

Craig smiles. "I would not mind at all, please go on."

"I imagine I'm standing in front of a magic doorway. Have you heard of this exercise?"

Craig looks up from his watch. "No, I don't think so."

"There is a magic door. If I close it and walk away, I could be a man without doubt in my mind. However, if I walked through the door, I would be a woman. Not a trans woman, but as if I was born that way, a cis woman."

"Interesting." Craig writes, pausing only briefly to emulate a smile.

"If I wanted to, I could walk back and forth between the threshold, becoming a man or a woman at will —"

Pointing with his pen, Craig says, "Which is completely valid. Is switching back and forth between genders something you wish was possible?"

"No, that's the point. The possibility of being unarguably female made me cry with relief the first time I performed this thought experiment. If that magical door existed, I would walk through, close the door, and throw away the key. It was then I realized the reason I have never seriously considered transition wasn't because I was unsure if I wanted to present as a woman, but instead because I was afraid of society not accepting me."

Craig gently rests his pen on the folder and reclines in his plush couch. His gentle smile is convincingly compassionate for the first time. "So, what changed?"

"I'm still terrified about being the freak who is pointed at, beaten up, or killed, but this is the only body I have. One thing surviving cancer taught me is that I need to embrace important things in life while I still can. Hormones and surgery are the closest I may ever get to that goal in this lifetime. So, I suppose transition isn't a goal for me — it's a compromise."

Furiously writing now, Craig says, "That was eloquent, Vanessa. You've never dressed in women's clothes?"

"Not the way you probably mean. All I want is to look in a mirror and see a woman. If you're asking if I wore my mother's clothes as a kid, I did. I also wore my father's. Sometimes I dressed up like a rabbit, or I ran around with no clothes at all. I didn't even think about myself as a boy until I hit puberty."

Craig finishes a sentence with a stab of his pen. "We should talk about what you went through during puberty more next month. Was puberty when you realized you felt like a woman?"

"Not clearly like a woman, no. I just felt . . . wrong. Until puberty, my sister and I looked and sounded similar, but then I couldn't sing as high as she could anymore. I felt as if I was turning into a monster, and I assumed everyone felt that way. If I had to pick the first moment when I *knew*, it was when I was eighteen or nineteen. I recall wishing I would wake up as a girl and nobody would remember I used to be a boy. I still wish that."

"It sounds like you've struggled with this for some time."

Until he said that, I had never considered how long I had trapped this secret inside me, and the tragedy of all those lost years sideswipes me and the room goes blurry. I reflexively cover my face. "I'm sorry, I just —"

"It's fine." Craig hurries a box of tissues into my hand. My glasses fall into my lap as I shove Kleenex under the lenses. "We're almost out of time. I want to give you your prescription, and I need your signature on another form."

The promise of a prescription and escaping these questions sobers me. "I'm okay, go ahead."

"First, here is your prescription." He hands me a slip of paper and applauds me. His face alight in overenthusiastic celebration. "Congratulations!"

"Thank you," I say. I take the paper and stare at the messy way he's written spironolactone.

Craig laughs and crosses his arms overdramatically. "Most people cheer or want to hug me. They seem more . . . excited."

"I'm sorry, I'm overwhelmed. There's a lot to process."

Craig turns the file on the table to face me. "This is a form to put you on a waiting list for GRS — a procedure we used to call SRS, or bottom surgery. While we haven't discussed it, this sounds as if it may be something you might consider one day. The wait-list grows longer every year, and it's over a year right now, so I thought you might wish to get in line."

"I don't know if I'm ready to do that yet."

"This is for an initial consultation, not a surgery date. If a year goes by and you realize this is not something you want, there is no pressure to continue further."

"I guess it's possible." I sign the form despite my body involuntarily shuddering at the uncertainty and risk associated with another major surgery.

"Exactly. Do you have any further questions for me?"

Absolutely not. Get me the fuck out of here.

Little Talks

2011 — Two months later, in Karen's car in Hamilton, Ontario

Karen checks her blind spot and merges into traffic. She says, "We need rice, salt, butter, and milk. Was there anything else?"

Kali says: How are you, my bunny? Did you pick them up?

I lower my phone. "Did you say you needed hairspray?"

"I swear I'm forgetting something." Karen notices my phone. "How's Jason?"

She doesn't really want to know, of course. Lately, I try to avoid conversation, when possible, because there is always an unspoken "I have to live with you, so I'm attempting civil discourse, but I don't actually care about you, or your perversions, and I resent you more every passing day" kind of vibe when we do. Refusing to answer also causes Karen to brood, which is preferable to another fight, so that's what I do.

Karen sighs — no doubt an attempt to remind me of the emotional burden I place upon her.

I type back.

You emote: Lydia throws her arms around Kali's neck. "Good morning, Kitty! I'm out getting them now."

I shut off the screen before he answers and bury the phone in my pocket. It's too weird talking to both at the same time. To soften the impending question, I decide to reply to Karen. "He's okay, thanks for asking."

Karen falls silent, her brow furrowing. I brace for a fight.

Before she can speak, I ask, "Can we stop at the pharmacy?"

"Are you okay?" Karen checks her blind spot and signals. She briefly locks eyes with me for what feels like the first time in days.

Her sudden compassion is unnerving. I absently twist the dark tungsten of my unreasonably heavy wedding ring. It reminds me of the many visits she made to my post-surgical recovery room over my month-long stay. She would always smile when she'd enter my quiet, internet-less room, carrying cheesy movies and news of her day. Her selfless kindness made me fall in love with her all over again.

I had planned on hiding the reason for my pharmacy visit. However, hearing her genuine concern, and once more tasting a hint of our previous connection, I am inspired to tell the truth. I say, "I need to pick up my new pills."

This additional information washes away her fragile compassion. Her expression hardens. "They actually gave you estrogen?"

"Yes."

"Will you grow tits?"

"Hopefully."

Kilometres of tense silence follow.

I give in and pull out my phone, hoping to see Kali's loving encouragement, but he hasn't answered. He plays even more computer games than I do, so it's possible he's doing that. I hate being reminded of how little I know about his day-to-day activities. He's so private. Could he be filling this time with other girls?

Other girls. I smile despite myself. When I glance at Karen, she flicks her eyes back to the road. Was she watching me? Is she mad that I'm smiling? Her nostrils are flared.

Karen says, "I'm going to New York on Friday."

She teaches belly dancing, and sometimes vends at ren faires. It could be for one of those, but it's a little late in the year.

I ask, "Are you visiting your boyfriend?"

"Yeah."

The callous betrayal lances through my chest and stings more than the cold finality of her statement which informs . . . no, *gifts* me that information. She's pulling away. This is the last push, the disconnect. A second small heart leap of elation follows as I realize that a life with Kali might still be possible, a life I thought I had lost when I married Karen.

I say, "We agreed that outside relationships are only online."

"You broke the rules first," Karen immediately snaps back, as if she had been waiting for my line.

"I thought we were past this. What happened to being open and talking more?"

She purses her lips, thinking, pretending she's concentrating on driving. "You started this. And I've been thinking — I don't think I can be married to a woman. Date, or make out with, maybe, but not marry."

I take off my glasses and rub a palm into my eye socket. Is she alluding to divorce?

Karen says, "Besides, I already visited him once."

I jam my glasses back on. "When?"

"A couple of weeks ago."

I search my memory. "You said you were visiting your parents."

Karen shrugs.

"You've had sex with him?" The phone buzzes in my lap. Probably Kali.

Karen signals and takes an off-ramp, ignoring my inquisitive stare until we've slowed at a stoplight. "That's none of your business." She turns into the grocery store plaza. "But yes."

Is she testing me? I want to roll the window down. Is she trying to lure me into asking for a divorce? I need to be bigger than this. I must be supportive if this marriage is going to work.

I want to be eloquent, but my lizard brain asks, "Like real, naked sex?"

"You fuck Jason all the time."

"Sure, online."

"You talk to him on your headset thingy, it's more than that. Don't lie. You should go visit Jason." Lately everything Karen says is part of an agenda, so this must be one plot point closer to her endgame. She's pushing me away.

I take a moment to calm myself, to not play into her hands, and to stop myself from sounding too excited about the suggestion. "You want me to go to Texas and have sex with Jason?"

Karen's smile flicks on. "You definitely should."

I hadn't expected to see Kali in Real Life, at least not for a long time. Certainly not before I was ready, and not while I still look like *him*. I envisioned this moment happening years from now, when I am far enough along to feel comfortable in my skin — and then Kali could hold me, as me, and we would do all the wonderful, naughty things we've only ever done online.

But these days, I feel like I'm playing a game for which only Karen knows the rules.

She's definitely winning.

I say, "Maybe."

"Don't you want to?" Karen's expression could pass as concern.

"I want to see him, but not like this."

Karen nods sagely. "You video chat with him sometimes, don't you? Doesn't he love you for who you are?"

"He says so. We rarely use video, usually just to say goodnight."

I'm sure her stumbling upon my biggest fear was a coincidence, and she likely just wants me gone. Kali says he's straight — so what happens when I get there and he can't even kiss me? If that happens in Texas, what should I do? Go home? Hang out with him like we are just friends while inside I curl up and die? I thought I had more time to think about how this would unfold.

Karen asks, "So, what does he call you? Does he call you Paul or does he always use your game name? Was it Lydia?"

My in-game name sounds so strange when she says it. "He uses Lydia, and I call him Kali." I suddenly realize it sounds odd when I use those names in Real Life.

"Is that what you're going to use when you transition? Or are you going to put an *a* at the end of your name?"

"Paula feels wrong, and I don't want people being reminded of my old name. I want something pretty and feminine. I like *v*-names. What do you think about Vanessa or Victoria?"

Karen clicks her tongue. "Those don't sound like you." She pulls into the grocery store parking lot. Cardboard bins overflowing with pumpkins are displayed outside of the automatic doors. "Besides, what if people shorten them? Vic and Van can be guys' names."

She has an excellent point.

As we hunt for parking near the doors, she says, "You should visit Jason for Halloween."

"Halloween is our first wedding anniversary."

Karen shrugs. "Don't worry about that. I'm not. Besides, I've asked Mikey to come over this year."

Another electric lance of warning pierces my chest as I realize that there's no fight to be had here. This is already over.

I say, "I'll check whether work will give me the time off on short notice."

Karen pulls into a spot and switches off the ignition. She turns to me, and though our bodies are close, we are miles apart. She asks, "Have you told anyone at work yet?"

Working in a small country town is bad enough with all the gossip and the scrutiny. Over the years, my bosses have been like family, but I've heard that people lose their families over transition all the time.

I say, "I'm still getting back into the swing of things. I've only told you, my sister, and my mom so far. You still haven't told anyone, right?"

Karen gathers her bag and checks her phone before she answers. "No, I haven't. You can't expect me to stay quiet forever, though. How long until you do?"

"I need to save some money first, just in case." I follow Karen past the pumpkins and through the doors. "I can't afford to be fired right now. But they've been so supportive with everything else in my life, I could get lucky, and they might understand."

Karen walks beside me, clicking at her phone with her thumbnails. "I don't think they're legally allowed to fire you for coming out. You should try."

Easy for you to say.

I check my phone. There's a notification from Kali. Even after all this time, I still get butterflies when I see his name. I stuff the phone back into my pocket, determined to diffuse this situation first. I want to reach out and hold her hand, but I don't. "How are you doing with all of this?"

Karen asks, "With what? With you?" She doesn't look up.

"With me, with . . . us."

Karen finishes typing, her gaze flicks up to me, and she shrugs. "You're not okay?"

"Look, Paul, this is still really new to me. I'm trying."

"It's just that you won't even look at me most of the time, or hug me or —"

"I said I am trying," Karen interrupts, loudly enough to draw stares from surrounding shoppers.

I slow my pace and slink behind her. She's the one who holds the power of my secrets. It's not out of the question to imagine her calling me out in the middle of the grocery store. I imagine all the shoppers turning and pointing at me, mouths agape and howling. Karen wrenches a basket free from the poorly fitting nested stack and starts bagging produce.

I unlock my phone.

Kali emotes: Kali purrs and grabs your hips, running his fingers in your fluffy tail fur. "That's great, baby. I miss you, though. I know you've been busy."

I grab a loaf of bread, put it in the cart, and write back.

Lydia emotes: Lydia grins, her slightly bucked teeth showing. She nuzzles your face. "If you miss me, I've got some exciting news. How would you like to have me come visit you for Halloween? We can dress up." <3

***

I lean my gleaming chrome Lambretta into the turn. A dozen mirrors branch out from the scooter's shield, an homage to *Quadrophenia*. I twist the throttle and the chainsaw-like engine screams. Down the road, the leafy majesty of a giant tree renders into existence. It's the largest weeping willow I've ever seen. The dangling fingers of its leafy branches provide the perfect picnic shade. I ease the throttle, guide the front tire onto the walkway, and coast to park beside Kali's motorcycle.

When I shut off the bike, the sound of its ratcheting roar is replaced by seabirds and wind hissing through willow leaves. The repeated crack of a hammer and rasp of a saw echoes from the backyard.

I find Kali building an expansive deck that stretches into the shallows of the beach. Wearing only cut-off shorts, his orange fur gleams in the afternoon sun and his striped tail lazily swishes over the deck. Kali gathers some nails, holds a few in his fangs, and slams the hammer into a board again and again, the sharp clack echoing across the bay, and another section of deck materializes, ready to be stained and finished.

I sneak behind him and cup my hands over his eyes. He jumps and barks a strangled "Erk!" and a section of deck glitches and reappears fifty feet offshore. Waves noisily splash against the sides of the tiny wooden island.

"Guess who?" I say against the back of his ear. "You're cute when you're scared."

In a single fluid movement, Kali pulls free. His claws dig into my shoulders and the world spins. I reach out, clutching for support, but my back slams against the deck, knocking the wind from my lungs. Kali pounces on top of me, straddles my hips, and pins my biceps to the deck so hard my arms go numb. I look up helplessly into the feral grin of a triumphant hunting cat.

"You know," Kali whispers, letting a hint of growl play in that deep voice vibrating my headphones, "it isn't safe to sneak up on cheetahs. Bunnies find themselves in the most compromising positions that way."

He's so damn hot. I struggle again, testing his strength, but not too hard. "Who said I didn't want to find myself in a compromising position?"

Kali steals a kiss. I lean into it, mouth opening against his, and as our tongues wrestle, he breathes a frustrated growl into my mouth, then leans back, sitting on my hips. "You are so cute like that. I have half a mind to keep you there. I thought you couldn't make it on today?"

"I found a little time, but not much privacy." I try to conceal the slight pant in my voice.

"I guess that means there's no chance I can show you how great our new bed is?"

"I shouldn't. Just think, soon I'll be there, and you can show me in Real Life."

Kali climbs off and helps me to my feet. "I can't wait, baby." He leads me to some deck chairs. "Do you have time to talk?"

He's obviously having second thoughts about meeting me. "Sure," I say as calmly as possible. We face the waves, watching them roll across the bay and wash over the misplaced section of deck. Someone down the coast is playing calypso, the steel drums barely heard over a motorboat.

Kali reaches across the gap and gathers my hand. "Are you still nervous about seeing me?" Unsupported by the rest of the building, the piece of deck breaks apart in the waves and washes away.

"A little." By that I mean a shitload — not only because of what Kali might think of seeing the real me, but also because going means I'm conceding my marriage.

Since our little talk in the car, Karen has been increasingly aggressive with me, and more openly affectionate toward her boyfriend. Visiting Kali will only light the fuse that will surely detonate the life she and I have constructed.

Perhaps it's for the best. I need to try for a better, more honest life. One with someone who wants to be with the real me. Until now, I've lived my life according to other people's expectations, and I've done my best to be what they've wanted, but that time is over.

Kali squeezes my hand reassuringly. "You don't need to be worried. We don't have to do anything you don't want to do."

I squeeze back. "I want to do everything, but I'm scared you'll find me disgusting."

"I could never be disgusted by you. You're beautiful."

Bullshit. I can't imagine how he could hold the real me and think it beautiful. Kali tries to meet my gaze, to show his sincerity.

I say, "I don't understand how you could say that, even with the lights out."

"Your cheekbones are so sexy, your lips, your legs. Those things are already feminine and will never change. There is a beautiful woman in you. When you grow your hair, it will completely change the way you view yourself."

I sigh. "I feel so lucky I found you. I'll bring my wig. That might help."

"For sure, and you'll probably be more comfortable when you have your costume on. Are you still bringing that? With that gorgeous rabbit mask you showed me?"

"I'm bringing something else too." I wheel away from my desk and pick up the box with the silicone tube inside.

Kali laughs. "You got me a present? Are you going to surprise me?"

"It's probably better that you see it. Hold on, I'll send you a picture." I take a photo with my phone, then plug it into the computer and upload it to email.

After a few minutes of Kali sitting motionless, he laughs. "Cock sleeve? Is that for me to use on you?"

The question catches me off guard like a punch to the gut. "No," I nearly shout into the mic but then soften my tone, "no, it's for you, baby."

"I don't understand how it works, I'm sorry."

"It's a jelly tube that you . . . lube up and fuck. I thought that since you can't fuck me the way we do here, maybe I could hold it when we fool around? If I didn't have that surgery, we could have done butt stuff, but I can't now."

There is a soft *thut* sound as Kali mutes his mic.

Kali's avatar freezes, and he's silent for an excruciatingly long time. I realize that I've screwed up. Obviously, he wasn't ready to talk about actual sex yet, even though it was an unspoken assumption that such a thing would certainly happen. I switch from first-person view and swing the camera around so I can watch Kali and me holding hands.

Occasionally my avatar will cuddle up to him and we'll look lovingly into each other's eyes. This sunny, perfect day is just like every other. How can Real Life ever compare to this? Kali says we don't have to do anything, but I want those things. I want what we have online. But that's not possible for me, and it maybe never will be.

I write.

Lydia says: "If you don't like it, we don't have to use it."

Kali unfreezes and smiles. "Sorry, baby, my roommate came in and I had to get rid of her. I'm so happy you thought of me. We could try it, but I'd be perfectly happy to just have your lips around me."

"We can do that too," I say.

Yeah, a straight guy is looking forward to someone that looks like a guy blowing him — an inexperienced one too. What the hell am I doing? This is going to be a disaster.

Kali tugs my hand and nearly pulls me out of my chair. "Come here." Reluctantly, I let him guide me on top of him. I straddle his hips, and he wraps his arms around me. "You get up in your head too much. You have nothing to be nervous about. I would honestly love to be with you just like this. If the only thing I get out of this trip is the opportunity to hold you in my arms — my real bunny in my real arms, that would be the best thZRRRRkkkkTVVIKK—"

Kali's avatar glitches, stutters, and then freezes, holding me in a death grip.

His voice warps into a horror show of garbled digital chaos. His mouth is frozen open and one eye is half-closed like he is suffering some kind of cyber stroke. Strange, coloured blocks pixelate across the sky.

I say, "What the . . ."

– WORLD DISCONNECTED –

"Fuck!" My screen turns black with just those two white words floating in the void. I exit the notification and double-click on the program shortcut to bring the world and Kali back.

Ding

I ignore the Skype app on my phone. It's probably Kali telling me I've disconnected. The loading wheel spins much longer than it should.

– GRAPHIC CARD NOT FOUND –

What the hell do you mean, not found? A small yellow warning triangle appears in my taskbar. I click the symbol, and it informs me I do not have an active video card. I realize it has finally fried.

You've seen a lot, video card, and only you and our federal spying agencies can truly understand everything we've been through. I guess I need to buy another.

I check the time: 6:40 p.m.

Kris was coming to visit for eight. I've been putting off coming out to him for long enough and planned to have him over for *the talk* tonight. Coming out to family is one thing, but this is the big one. Kris has stuck with me through poverty and cancer — is it realistic to hope he'd stick with me through this? However, if I've got him in the car, he'll have to at least hear me out.

I pick up my phone and Kali's notification flashes. I dismiss it and dial Kris.

Kris asks, "Hey, what's up?"

"My video card fried, and I wondered if you could drive me to the store? I need to talk to you about something as well."

◖ 16 ◗

Midnight City

Thirty minutes later

Headlights slice through the darkness of the dusty country road —
they flash like lighthouse beacons as they pass between trees. That
must be him. I realize too late that I should have rehearsed. I could
still chicken out, but if I don't tell him now, then when? Kris signals
his turn and rhythmic orange light strobes as he slows. A best friend
of twenty years who's lived with me for half of that time doesn't
deserve to find out through Karen's impatience.

I squint and shade my eyes from the high beams. His car
creeps up the drive, gravel crunching and popping under the tires.
He needs the truth from me, even if it means this will be how our
friendship ends.

Kris turns off the car, and I walk to the passenger door. The
cooling engine ticks quietly in the night. Within the darkened car,
Kris smiles, nodding his head in time with muffled heavy metal
music. I walk slowly, mentally practising what I'll say. Listen, we
have to talk. No, too dramatic. Hey, so remember when everyone

used to say I was gay, and I said I wasn't? Yeah, funny story, they weren't entirely correct, but . . .

No, under all his rugged dude exterior, Kris is a sweet guy and more observant than he lets on. I'm sure he's noticed how distant I've become, even if he's too polite to say anything. But if he thinks I'm no longer the friend he believes me to be, who knows what he might say.

I open the car door and Pantera's "Cowboys from Hell" blasts into the night.

"Hey!" Kris shouts over the music. He leans into the passenger seat and tosses a few DVDs, his boy's Bratz dolls, and assorted plastic animals into the back seat. His blond hair is swept back and buzzed on the sides. He's muscular and hides his geekiness from all but his closest friends. He turns down the music, clearly satisfied with his arrival performance.

"Thanks for picking me up." I slide in and shut the door.

"No problem." He starts the car, rests his hand on the back of my seat, turns, and backs down the driveway. We roll away from the house, from Karen's judgment, from Kali and my computer, and soon it's just Kris, and me, and Phil Anselmo, driving into the night.

"We headed to Tiger?" Kris asks.

"I think it's the only tech store still open."

"Sure, give me directions when we get to the Hammer."

Any other person would ask how I've been with my cancer recovery, what's going on with my life, or probe for conversation points. It's been painfully obvious to everyone there has been trouble with Karen since she has teased our imploding marriage on Facebook. While I can't address her statement because of the block Karen put on my account, she claims she hasn't told anyone why we're separating. But Kris never pries. He has a unique, Zen-like way of being. If given the opportunity, he would be perfectly content to live in a moment like this — two friends in a car on the way to the store listening to metal. He never bothers to ask about —

"How's the chemo treating you?"

So much for Zen.

"They took my licence away. Thanks again for coming."

"I guess you're still seeing double?"

"Yeah."

How do I start this conversation?

I came out to Mom with a letter, my sister over a burger, and my dad by email. I sat Karen down and told her — and she played it off like it was nothing. Of course, that changed. Now only Kris and those at work remain.

Just two more anxiety-inducing, awkward conversations, each with the potential to destroy my life. In theory, two chats sounds simple, but I stand to lose my best friend and my job. Losing one or both sets me on a potential path of self-destruction: either rudderless without supportive friends, or unemployed as an awkward, coming-out trans woman. Who knows, maybe this time next year I'll be living on the street and complete the stereotypical, tragic trans experience.

However, a potential future of two positive conversations keeps me motivated, and the promise of freedom is intoxicating. No more lies, no more sneaking around, and no more Paul. I could finally shut down my email and make a social media page under my new name.

Maybe someday Kali will move in with me and we'll look back on these uncertain times and laugh. Kris will come over, and all three of us will play Dungeons & Dragons and Diablo on our couch.

But first, I need to open my mouth and ignite the possibility.

Along the unlit expanse of rural highway, shadowy trees crowd the pavement and rush past the car. I attempt to regulate my breathing and build up my nerve. Once I start, I'm committed. Off like a band-aid. All in and roll the dice. It's never been an intelligent strategy, but it's mine, and one I can live with. Calculated chaos, the only way to live.

I say, "I'm sorry for being distant lately."

He risks a glance away from the highway. Concern creases his forehead. "Sorry? You've had a serious surgery. I thought you needed some space."

"I guess I needed space to figure things out, but it's not what you think."

"You've been through a lot. I think anyone surviving cancer needs some time to figure things out."

I consider joking about just how much I've figured out, but decide against it. Instead, I say, "That is the thing. I almost died, and it helped me to see there are things in my life that need to change. I realized I haven't been authentic to myself."

Kris stares straight ahead as yellow dashes rocket toward the car like Pac-Man Extreme. "You getting a divorce?"

"No," I begin, but then correct myself. "Well, that's coming down the pipe as well."

Without missing a beat, Kris asks, "You gay?"

Christ, a guessing game isn't how I wanted this to go. I need to take control of this conversation. "Gay?" I chuckle nervously.

Kris gives me a side glance, one eyebrow cocked and looking suspiciously like The Rock. "Yeah. Are you gay?"

"No, but you're on the right track."

Kris turns down the music so that Phil is whispering in the background. "What's . . . uhm . . . what's going on then?"

"I'm trans."

I get The Rock again.

"Transgender." We drive in silence for almost five minutes, my heart hammering my chest, but I dare not add to that statement.

I half expect him to pull over and let me out. Instead, he says, "Huh," and turns the music back up.

He stares forward. A tiny crease in his brow is the only hint he's thinking about anything at all. I wonder if he's thinking the same thing that goes through everyone's head when you tell them you're trans.

People like to think they can tell a trans person from a "normal" person, a trans woman from a "real" woman. So, everyone needs this moment to consider all the potentially queer things they've ever witnessed over the years. Then they take all those grouped up memories and compare them with every woman they've ever known, every gay man they ever thought they knew. Finally, they examine the mannerisms of both and see which one fits the categories in their head.

They soon realize that my mannerisms don't fit anything, and they're confused and annoyed that they have to create a fresh box in their head labelled "trans" to put me in. Because now this person — me — doesn't fit into the old trans box they used to have, the one filled with "yaaaaas kween" and drag performers, man-in-a-dress comedic acts, and off-colour jokes that end with punch lines about their date secretly having a dick.

"Okay," Kris says.

Wait, what? "Did someone already tell you? Do you understand what I mean by trans?"

Kris shrugs a shoulder. "You're saying you're a transgender."

"Not *a transgender*, but I am transgender, yes."

"Isn't that what I said?"

"No."

"You're saying you're a girl, right?"

My mouth is dry. "Yes."

"Okay then."

"Seriously?"

Kris glances in the rear-view mirror. "It doesn't matter to me. Gay, transgender, a girl, a video-game addict, the best Dungeon Master I've ever known. Whatever. You're still my best friend."

The lump returns to my throat, and I choke as I try to swallow it. My eyes well with tears. "Thank you." I push my glasses up my nose enough to wipe my eyes.

Kris pretends not to notice. "Do Rick and Tyler know?"

"You're the first to know outside of Karen and my family."

"You gunna tell them?"

"Probably next week."

"That'd be tough. How did Karen react?"

"Like I said, I think we're getting a divorce."

"That makes sense. Hopefully, you don't lose your job."

It's been my experience that the first time you come out to a person, you can expect two reactions: You receive the first when you come out, and the second about a week later. That first reaction leans toward the idyllic and is full of support and hope. I'm sure this is a knee-jerk way people deal with distress. Since they're in shock, they try to say what they believe good people say. What they *think* people *should* say, not what they truly *feel*.

Reality sinks in about a week later, after they have had time to digest.

This person they've known all their lives, the one they *knew* was a guy, is now telling them he is a girl. The personal proximity of trans-ness as a friend, co-worker, or lover shakes their world view. Trans people are no longer something on the periphery of their social circles to be observed or debated, they are now something that must be normalized if life is to continue as usual. They realize the trans person not only needs to be treated as a *normal* person, but they will now also be responsible for defending the idea of "trans as normal" to friends and colleagues who disagree. Then the question is, is the trans person worth that level of personal embarrassment?

I say, "You're seriously okay?"

"I was your best man at your wedding, and I'll be your best man at whatever wedding you have as a girl. Playing games with you helped me get off drugs, and you probably saved my life. You will always be my best friend."

"I was terrified to tell you."

"You don't have to worry about me." As the streetlight changes to green, he speeds through the gears, the g-force crushing me into my seat as he adds, "Does that mean you like guys now?"

"I'm kind of seeing someone online."

"I guess everyone was right about you, in a way. You don't think about me like that, right?"

"No," I say too quickly. I study his face, trying to determine if he's being sincere, but I don't think Kris ever isn't. "Just try to think of me as a girl, that's all you need to do."

"It's hard for me to think of you as a girl when . . . you look like a guy, but all I can do is try."

"You're being really cool about this."

Kris sails through a red light. "Wait, where are we going again?"

Right, the video card. "We need to make our way downtown. Keep following this road and head down the mountain."

Kris signals toward the mountain brow. We drive in pregnant silence until we arrive at the store. We get out, and Kris hurries forward and holds the door to the store open for me.

"Why thank you, sir," I say as I pass.

As we walk toward the cabinet-locked graphic cards, Kris leans over and says, "As long as you're you, we'll always be friends. Just don't tell me the details about the surgery if you get it — I don't think I can handle that."

17

Scars to Your Beautiful

I squint at the small brass plaque under a black and blue pen-drawn depiction of a woman and cat. "Get this, it's called 'Black and Blue Pussy.'"

Sarah taps on her phone. "No way."

"Marci even has a sense of humour."

There is a knock on the door, and a well-groomed blonde woman walks in holding a clipboard. "You must be Paige?"

"Yes."

"My name is Stephanie." She hands me a folded surgical gown and towel. "Please put this on. You can keep your socks, but everything else off. Doctor Bowers will be in shortly."

"Just think," Sarah says, "this time tomorrow you'll be in surgery."

I stare at the ground. The sayings "we're only human" and "everyone makes mistakes" take on new meaning when you trust a relative stranger with a knife and your body.

Major surgery requires an act of faith. While I don't worship any deity, I still think it's a form of faith to pray that my surgeon doesn't get drunk the night before my operation or discover their spouse has cheated on them. No matter how much research you do on your procedure and the person performing it, at some point you need to surrender and hope for the best. Sometimes, surgeons make mistakes. When they do, the patient wakes up changed, wakes up wrong, or doesn't wake up at all.

Sarah lowers her phone. "Baby, are you okay?"

"I'm sorry, I was thinking about something."

Sarah wraps her arms around my neck and pulls my cheek into her breasts. She breathes into my hair, warming my scalp. "Are you scared?" I nod once, hugging back.

"I'm scared about waking up different, like before." I motion toward my stomach. "I don't want any surprises, you know?"

I allow myself to go limp as Sarah cradles me. She says, "I understand."

Marci Bowers walks through the door, tailed by Stephanie. Outside of a single Skype video chat, I've only seen Marci in news articles and on television. Marci is a true California girl, tanned with feathered blonde hair, and, as she spots me, her authentically warm smile lights up the room. She practically glows with life.

Most of my experience with other trans women has been online, sharing moments of struggle and frustration with a world that seems eager to shove us under a rug or down a well. But seeing this successful, powerful, and professional woman before me inspires me to look beyond all of that, at least for the moment.

"Paige, how are you, babe?" Marci hugs me to her before I know what's happening.

Is this reality? Are doctors allowed to hug their patients? I hug her back. "It's nice to be here."

"Had a pleasant trip from Buffalo?"

"We flew out of Buffalo, but I'm from Ontario."

Marci puts on her glasses and takes the clipboard from Stephanie. "Right, you're my Canada girl. We're going to treat you right."

"I hope so."

"We will." Marci wheels over a stool. "I have your surgical notes, but tell me again why you're here and not with Doctor Brassard's team in Montreal?" She quietly flips pages on the chart.

"After my diagnosis was confirmed by psychiatrists at CAMH, I received a letter from Doctor Brassard to arrange a surgery date, and then they emailed me a package to fill out. I disclosed my cancer surgery and returned it. A couple of days later, a nurse contacted me to say they weren't sure they could operate, because I had cancer, and they needed my surgical notes to be sure. Weeks later I received a call from a surgeon who works with Doctor Brassard, and she informed me it was impossible to have normal GRS, but they would be happy to give me a surface procedure."

Marci furrows her brows. "A surface —?"

I interrupt her, "Like, they would aesthetically shape a vulva with no —"

"Without a vaginal canal."

"Right."

"So, zero-depth. Did they say why?"

"The surgeon said it's because of scar tissue from my previous surgery. I insisted that zero-depth wasn't good enough, so the next day Doctor Brassard phoned me himself. He was curt with me, sounded impatient, and said for me the procedure is literally impossible."

Marci looks up from her notes. "He actually used the word impossible?"

"But you don't think so, right?"

Marci shakes her head. "Not impossible. Did he say it's impossible because of the scar tissue? Because that is a concern of mine as well."

"Yes, but he also said that there's no place to attach the vaginal canal."

Marci eyes me skeptically. "I'm not sure what he could be talking about. You don't need to attach it to anything. You can add a stitch at the end for healing, but that's not common practice. I've worked with Doctor Brassard before, and he is a skilled surgeon. I'm sure he only wanted your surgery to have the highest chance of success."

"Or because he doesn't want to ruin his monopoly in Canada by taking chances."

Marci continues writing. While she says nothing, I think I catch a corner of her mouth tug into the briefest of grins.

I ask, "But you can do it, right?" A queasiness bubbles in my stomach, accompanying dizzying déjà vu.

Marci sobers when she notes my expression. "Yes, I believe I can. According to the surgical notes, it's true that you likely have extensive scarring close to where I need to dig."

That's a pleasant visual.

Clipping her pen to the board, Marci stares up into the corner of the room. Her eyes lose focus. I recognize that look and wonder if she's in surgery right now, mentally slicing up my insides. Still miles away from this consultation room, Marci says, "The scar tissue would make healing difficult, so that may limit the depth we can achieve."

"How shallow are we talking?" I wonder if I've waited five years and negotiated international surgery coverage with my government only to find out that, when it comes down to it, I still won't have a functional vagina.

Marci turns away from the corner, her eyes focused. She motions to my lap. "Mind if I have a peek to see what we're working with? We can ask Stephanie to leave if you like?"

"She doesn't have to. I'm sure she has seen lots."

Stephanie laughs to herself and nods.

Marci chuckles. "Okay, Paige. Knees apart and lean back."

I obey and she lifts my gown onto my thighs and cool air washes over my naked lap. Marci leans in for a closer look.

Nothing was quite as devastating as the moment I came to terms with the fact that hormones would never magically change me. Even after a lifetime of neglecting my body, hormones changed my breasts, my hips, softened my skin, but they can't change bone structure. Hormones fine-tuned the discordant notes of my body, but doing so only highlighted the ones I couldn't fix — my face, my shoulders, my penis.

While the Canadian government is kindly helping me take care of my little penis problem, there are no financial supports for the working class or poverty-stricken trans women like myself whose face or body has been irreversibly changed by testosterone. It is a cruel gift to offer a kindness to remedy a single dysphoric aspect yet deny all others, especially when many trans women are enviably comfortable with their penis.

I live in a country more interested in my genitals than my desire to integrate with society or avoid poverty and violence. Canada is more obsessed with what I have in my pants than my face or my mental health. Despite that, some people still have the nerve to call *us* perverts.

Marci's hands are cool and deft as she lifts my scrotum and covers me again. The entire process takes only a few seconds, and the chill of her fingertips against my flesh remains long after. She says, "I'm glad to see you still have your scrotum and foreskin — that extra material will make a big difference. I think we can give you five inches of depth."

"That's pretty decent, right?" Alarms klaxon in my skull; I've heard promises like this before.

Sizing with her fingers, Marci says, "Most girls have between four and six. It will also depend on your scar tissue."

I imagine every penis I've seen in Real Life, which aren't many. Little ones, like what mine became on hormones, would be no issue at all. Of course, depth would never matter for my relationship with Sarah. But for someone like Jason, five would never be enough. I absently wonder if guys ever bottom out in cis women's vaginas.

What if that's something trans girls are known for? What if something happens, and I break up with Sarah and date a guy who fucks me and bottoms out with only half his cock in me? Does he keep hammering at the back wall of my surgically constructed vagina? Does he say, "What the fuck, are you trans?"

But that scenario is ridiculous. He would already know. It's too dangerous to let anyone fuck me before they know. Trans girls die that way all the time. Besides, everyone can tell I'm trans. How could they not?

"Five inches is great!" I smile as authentically as I can.

Marci smiles back. "I will visit with you before your surgery tomorrow morning. You know where the hospital is and have arranged a ride?"

"Yes, we're taking an Uber."

"Lyft," Sarah corrects.

"Right, whatever."

"Lyft is better."

Marci nods along. "Are you taking in some sights today?"

"Definitely," I say. "But nothing to eat, as you instructed."

Marci hesitates. "Since you have a colostomy, I see no reason you can't. You mentioned you flush?"

"I irrigate my ostomy every two or three days."

"Irrigation is like an enema, correct?"

"Yes, that way I don't have to feel dirty." Carrying the cleaning kit around when travelling is a pain, but when swimsuit weather arrives, I'm thankful for it. I ask, "So, I can eat before surgery?"

Marci smiles and nods. "Go ahead. Please rest up and have a light breakfast tomorrow morning."

"Deal!" Overwhelmed by the prospect of being able to eat before my surgery, I hug Marci.

"No problem, babe," Marci whispers in my ear.

⋙

Twelve hours later, squinting to read the key in the darkness, I say, "I think it says nineteen." I realize I'm looking at a courtesy card for eyebrow waxing, and not our hotel key. The world spins around me for a moment, I lose balance, and I stumble dangerously toward the motel door but brace myself at the last minute by pressing the box of wine against the frame.

"Are you drunk?" Sarah presses against my back and laughs into my hair.

"I am not. Besides, you had way more than me." I wrestle with my purse, digging for the key card. "This would be easier if you weren't leaning against me."

I get the door open, and Sarah runs for the bathroom.

I set the wine box on the dresser, rip the nozzle hole open, and wiggle out the spout. I fill two plastic wine glasses we bought at the dollar store. "It's criminal how much cheaper booze is here."

Sarah moans in relief as her bladder empties. "And booze is everywhere." She sways as she emerges and takes her glass. "Cheers?"

"To a new nooni."

Sarah laughs and clacks her glass on mine. "To noonis!"

I drink the bitter wine, letting it cleanse the gummy aftertaste of our dinner away.

Sarah falls onto the bed and reaches for the remote. "Wanna put on American Netflix? I think they have *Alias Grace*. I know how much you love Atwood."

"There's no one better." I slide onto the bed. While she figures out the remote control, I unlock my phone and scroll through the day's pictures.

I swipe through and stop on a picture Sarah took of me just before we had dessert. Low through the windows of the restaurant, the sun blazed orange on the horizon and shone golden upon my face. Sarah caught me as I gazed out of the window. In the photo I wore a contemplative smile and shadows accented my dimples. For a moment, I'm stunned that anyone could take a picture of me that I couldn't mentally dissect into a categorized list of my most hated features.

"I have an idea," I say as I pull myself out of Sarah's grasp. "I'm not going to 'jerk it' one last time, but I was wondering if you could do something for me?"

Sarah cautiously says, "Sure, I guess."

"Can you take a picture of me without my clothes on?"

I hand her my phone and pull my sweater over my head and dump it on the bed. I step out of my jeans and reach behind to unclasp my bra. I pull my gaff away and my penis stays stuck, pinched, and flattened for a few moments before slowly peeling away and dangling free. I step out of my pants. "Okay, do it."

"You don't want to lie down?"

"We'll take a few."

Sarah snaps pictures, the flash blazing and burning flares into my retinas. When she is done, I take the phone from her. I sit and open the first picture.

The horrible lighting of the dimly lit motel does me no favours in this photo. Mercifully, I shaved myself completely out of compassion for the surgeon and anyone else in the room when I'm unconscious. Still, the image in this picture is one I expect.

I haven't exercised recently, so there's a paunch of belly over skinny hips, with wide shoulders that make my immature breasts and tiny, underdeveloped nipples look ridiculous. I'm glancing toward the floor, accenting a second chin. Between my chubby thighs is a comically small penis, maybe the same size as the one I had when I was fourteen — not that the one I had before hormones was much larger. A "girl dick," as Sarah calls it.

There is nothing in this picture I like. Everything perfectly reflects the things I obsessively hate about myself. There is nothing showing the person I wish myself to be, but it's unapologetically the person I am. This is the person people in public stare at in confusion, or apologize to when they stumble over which pronouns to use, or smirk at when they damn well know I am a trans woman and "sir" me, anyway.

"Baby?" Sarah asks. "Are you sure you should look at pictures like that before you go to sleep?"

I nod. "I'm ready for tomorrow now." I turn off my phone and pick up the wine.

Part 4

Logout

⌐ 18 ⌐

Parking Lot

2011 — Five years earlier,
approaching the U.S.—Canada border
on my way to meet Kali

"In three ... hundred ... metres ... turn right," my tablet echoes in the darkness. It's two o'clock in the morning as I pass the point of no return where the Peace Bridge connects Fort Erie with Buffalo. My eyes burn from lack of sleep, too nervous about this border crossing and my eventual rendezvous in Texas.

Ahead, flood lamps illuminate a line of empty customs booths. With no line-ups, I'll have time for a diner breakfast, some relaxation, then my check-in. I'm familiar with the procedure that always goes, "Citizenship? Where are you going? How long? Have a pleasant stay," then I'm gone. The only thing different is I'm visiting my boyfriend this time, and while border guards are supposed to be impartial about such things, I can't dispel the uneasy butterflies fluttering in my gut. My psychologist's pep talk helped. "Be honest," he said.

The border guard leans out of his kiosk and impatiently waves me forward as I hesitate at the stop sign. I creep up, put the car in park, and crank the window down. The middle-aged man leaning out of the booth looks tired.

"Good morning!" I say, trying to start the customs interview on the right foot.

"In two . . . hundred . . . metres . . . merge left."

He leans on his elbow. "Sir, please turn off your radio."

"I'm sorry." I fumble with the tablet and repeatedly press the volume button until it finally mutes.

"Would you mind turning off your GPS?"

"It's a tablet programmed with directions. If I turn off the power, I won't be able to find my way to the airport."

He sighs and puts down his coffee. He reviews something on his desk and asks, "Where are you from?"

I try to calm myself with a deep breath, then say, "Cayuga, Ontario." I hand over my driver's licence, and he flips it over, examining it.

The man's brow creases, but he doesn't face me. "Where's Cayuga?"

"Near Caledonia?" I offer. The border guard grimaces, so I add, "Close to Hamilton?"

Recognition dawns on the guard's face. He leans out of the kiosk, examining my car. "Isn't Hamilton close to the Rainbow Bridge?"

"Well, yes, Hamilton is, but Cayuga —"

"Where are you headed?"

"To Buffalo airport."

"Where are you travelling to?"

I try to convince myself that this is going well. I say, "Houston, Texas." I dig in my bag and hand a stack of directions and flight itinerary printouts to him.

"This says your flight isn't until six thirty. Why are you here now?"

Does he think I'm going to sell drugs before I go? "I thought this bridge would be quieter and I wouldn't have to wait in a lineup."

"All the bridges are quiet this time in the morning." He stares at my itinerary. "How long were you planning on staying?"

"A week."

He clicks on a flashlight and beams it into my back seat. I avert my eyes as he waves it back and forth, scanning, "Two suitcases, for a week's stay?"

"I'm checking one and taking the other with me on the plane."

"That is a lot for only one week, don't you think?"

"I filled one with costumes," I say, hoping that is enough of an explanation this close to Halloween.

He looks at a screen in the booth. "What is the purpose of your visit?"

I remind myself to be honest despite my quickening heartbeat. But what should I say? He'd be confused if I said I'm a trans girl visiting her boyfriend.

The guard looks impatient. What if he wants to open my suitcase? I'll have to explain my costumes, and *oh, shit, the cock sleeve.* Panic overrides my reason, and I realize that the longer I delay, the more I'm screwing up this interview. He knows that things are not "normal," and I have to tell him something. I reason that a half truth is probably the safest bet, and that I'll tell him I'm visiting my boyfriend, but I'll let him assume I'm gay. He'll at least understand that.

I say, "I'm going to meet my boyfriend and we're going to a Halloween party." Judging by the slight eyebrow quirk, I'm guessing it was a sufficient surprise. I'm secretly proud of myself that I didn't have to lie too much.

The border guard pauses, squints at me, and then stares into his booth for a long time. So long, in fact, I'm wondering if he forgot to let me go. Finally, he glances over. "Are you married?"

Oh, fuck. "Yes."

"To a woman?"

"Yes." Shit! He can see my marriage status? How much does he know about me? I resign myself to one hundred percent honesty and pray he doesn't dig too deeply. Besides, what could he do if I told him I'm trans, that my marriage is in shambles, and that I've never met my boyfriend who lives across a border and a thousand miles away? Maybe I should just go ahead and tell him I've also got a Little Red Riding Hood costume and a jelly cock sleeve in my bag so I can jerk off my boyfriend because I don't have the right equipment. What could he do with that information?

"To a woman," the border guard repeats to himself. He frowns. I've never seen a border guard frown before.

The guard asks, "Does she realize where you are right now?"

"Yes."

"And that you're meeting a man."

"Yes."

"Who you're dating?"

"Yes."

"And she's okay with that?"

Okay, I can't be entirely honest about that. He doesn't need to know every detail about my marriage.

I say, "Yes, sir, actually she's the one that encouraged me to go." My palms sweat, and I rest them on my pants, hoping the moisture soaks in. As blood flushes my face, I will myself to calm down, but the blush I'm likely sporting is no doubt hurting my credibility.

The border guard stares, twisting his mouth as he thinks. "I find that hard to believe."

Yeah, me too, buddy.

"The situation is strange, but true," I say.

"If I phoned her right now, with the phone in my booth here, she would say the same thing?"

"Yes. But she's probably sleeping." I'm suddenly aware of how cold it is with the window down. The guard makes a face, so I continue. "But if the phone call woke her up, she definitely would say that."

He rests his hand on something in his booth that I can't see, and I silently will him not to do it, but dare not ask. I doubt Karen would try to sabotage me, as she certainly wants privacy with Mikey, but at this point, I don't know what to expect from her.

The guard stares into his booth for far too long for it to be anything good, then he pulls his hand away. "How much money are you bringing with you?"

A wave of relief washes over me as he changes the subject. "Three hundred dollars."

The guard dramatically leans away. "That is an awful lot of cash."

"Is it?" I ask, immediately regretting saying so.

"Why do you need so much money?"

I'm momentarily stunned as I try to determine how much money other people take on vacations. I say, "I am going for a week. I'll need food, souvenirs, drinks —"

"Okay, sir." He gathers up my papers.

I exhale the breath I didn't realize I had held.

The border guard hands me my itinerary, leans out of the window, and points across the parking lot. "Park by that grey building. Go inside and wait for your inspection."

My heart freezes. What kind of inspection? I thought they only inspected your car for stuff when you returned. I mechanically take the itinerary from him and glance at the cold, military-esque building tucked off to the side of the border lot.

I try to remain composed, but inside I'm screaming. I stuff the itinerary back into the open wallet in my lap, then realize he never returned my licence.

"Sir," I say, trying to hide the quiver in my voice, "you forgot to give me my licence back."

"They will have it in the interrogation room for you."

Interrogation room? "Thank you," I say. I drive past chain-link gates, and under flood lamps so bright I feel like I'm driving along an airport runway.

Even colder than I remember, the breeze coming off the Niagara River blows through my window. I resist rolling it up and let it chill my cheek, mess my hair, refreshing me, waking me up, cooling me down — and, with any luck, calming my burning cheeks.

My car is the only one in the inspection area.

I park and turn off the engine. I can hear cars whoosh by on a nearby highway. From somewhere near the building comes an approaching jingle of keys.

I make sure my tablet is tucked under the dash so it doesn't get bumped and turned off. As I step out, two large men wearing blue rubber gloves approach.

"Sir, step away from the vehicle," one of them shouts. Both wear army boots and uniform tops that I can't quite read, with sleeves rolled over bulging biceps. One has arms covered in tattoos.

They give off a cop-like aura of brazen authority. I realize that, even though I'm not in cuffs, and no one has touched me, I am nevertheless detained. Temporary or not, I can't leave until they've finished doing whatever they want with me.

The guards circle the car. "Leave your keys in the vehicle and open your trunk." They sound twice as bored as the man in the booth.

With shaking hands, I miss inserting the keys in the ignition the first time, and I pull the lever to pop the trunk. "Please don't turn off the tablet in the console. If it's turned off, I'll get lost."

One guard is already leaning into the back seat and unzipping the suitcase with the costumes and the cock sleeve. I try to convince myself that they've seen weirder things.

"Sir, please wait in the building. Someone will be with you shortly."

I back away from the car, watching them pull my clothes onto the back seat, flashlights beam out of the windows.

Wouldn't it be funny, I think, if they fold all my clothes again once they're done?

As I walk to the building, I wonder how long it will take before they find the sleeve. Will they bring it inside as evidence of my perversion? Will they force me to explain it? "Sir, if you're an upstanding citizen, what do you have to say about *this*?" And they'll waggle it in my face. Confronted with such irrefutable proof, I'll be forced to say, "You got me," and hold out my wrists for them to clasp in fuzzy cuffs and take me to perv jail.

The inside of the waiting room is blindingly bright. There are dozens of empty chairs, a single man sitting at a desk, and nothing else. His shirt reads, U.S. Customs and Border Protection.

"I'm here to have my car searched." I strategically word my comment so they don't get any ideas to expand the *car* search to a *me* search.

He motions with two fingers across the room at an empty bank of chairs bolted to a metal pole. "They'll be with you when they're done."

I sit and watch through the window at flashlight beams swinging in the darkness. The lights click off one at a time, and then, through one of the glass walls of the building, I spot the guards laughing with the jerk from the booth.

Waving over his shoulder, the guy from the booth leaves the building. End of his shift, I'm sure. What an asshole. Fuck over a fag and head for home, huh?

The guards push open a glass door and enter the waiting area. They avoid looking at me and gather around the desk. As they talk, one of them thumbs over his shoulder toward my car, and they all chuckle. As they finish, they lounge by the counter, and the guy with the arm tattoos waves me over.

I stand on jelly legs and comply.

As I approach, he asks, "Why do you have two costumes?"

"I'm going to a ren faire and a Halloween costume party."

A Black guard looks as if he's trying to control his face when he asks, "What are the costumes of?"

Honesty. "A pirate, for the faire."

"Definitely some kind of pirate," the tattooed guard says, smirking to the other guard.

I continue, "The other is Little Red . . . Rabbit Hood."

The tattooed guard splutters into his fingers and howls, grabbing his knees, and the room explodes in laughter. I wait for them to stop, my heart racing. Please, God, just kill me right now. Despite having a full bladder, and terrified I'm going to piss my pants, a nervous smile creeps onto my face as I try to share in the joke.

Waving a hand, the Black guard glances at the driver's licence in his hand and says, "Enough of that. Listen, Paul, is it?"

"Yes."

"What exactly is a Little Red Rabbit Hood?"

If I'm being accurate, I would say that it's a red dress, a pink corset, tall boots, long opera gloves, a gorgeous velvet red hooded cloak I bought off Etsy, and a sequined rabbit masquerade mask. Instead, I say, "Imagine Little Red Riding hood, except as a rabbit."

The tattooed guy's face is as red as an apple. It's clear he's trying not to laugh anymore, and I can't bring myself to look any of them in the eye.

The Black guard continues, "And you're going to a party with your boyfriend? What's he wearing?"

Fuck it. "The big bad wolf."

Spinning on the spot, the tattooed guy turns from me and puts his head on the counter. His back shakes in silent, barely repressed laughter.

The Black guard doesn't laugh. "Listen, Paul, go sit tight for a moment more."

I do as he says while he returns to the others. My skin feels numb, and my brain spirals. How could they stand there and mock my costumes and not even mention the cock sleeve? Could they have missed it? It was in that bag.

The Black guy approaches, holding my keys and my licence. He hands them to me. "Have fun."

While I know I should escape before they change their minds, I need to make sure there's no confusion. "I'm free to go?"

"Yeah." He winks and walks away.

I step into the chilly air, thinking about the guard's gorgeous eyes, him winking at me. The air smells twice as fresh as it did before. Now only a plane ride separates me from seeing Kali, for real, and in the flesh.

I open the car and find the suitcases pulled open and clothes unceremoniously stuffed back in. I find the cock sleeve lying in the middle of the suitcase on a pile of tossed clothing, as if on display.

I probably need to wash that.

I stuff everything back in, zip up, and climb in the driver's seat. My tablet is dark.

No. I press the button and the screen flashes white. The UI initializes. I pull up the map, and the loading circle spins in the centre of the screen.

Over the map reads, – `Searching for Signal` –.

I turn off the tablet and toss it onto the passenger seat. I can almost smell the booth guard's bigotry on the off button.

"Asshole!" I shout, and I bang my palm against the steering wheel again and again until my hand hurts. "I only asked for one thing." I glance over my shoulder, making sure they're not watching, and then bang my hand against the steering wheel once more.

I jam the key into the ignition and start the car, back out, and slowly leave the lot, well below the speed limit.

As I drive away, I search for signs to the airport.

✄

Speakers crackle in the airplane cabin. "Hello, folks, this is your captain again. We are now on our final approach to William P. Hobby Airport in beautiful Houston, Texas. The time is now eleven fifteen, and we are looking at clear skies and a balmy ninety-one degrees. We ask that you stow your tables and return your seats to the upright position."

Our plane sinks below the clouds, and the diminutive landscape comes into focus. Individual details separate from postage stamp land parcels and the sea of grey urban sprawl. Then there are warehouses and real palm trees.

Soon we're buzzing past buildings and intersections, and then we're landing. I'm swept up in the whirlwind of baggage claim and customs, but everything breezes by as my stomach nervously flips. I gather my bag and realize that in moments I'll be standing before a man who claims to love me.

I flip open my phone to connect to airport Wi-Fi.

Bing

The screen lights with a notification from Kali.

```
Kali: Hey beautiful. I'm sitting by the baggage
claim. Any idea when you're landing? The ticker
says your plane landed fifteen minutes ago, but I
don't see you. <3
```

Folding the clamshell, I stick the phone in my pocket and scan the crowd.

I spot Kali sitting alone on a bench in the middle of a busy walkway. People wheel suitcases past him, and he's half-looking at his phone and typing with his thumbs.

I knew he was a tall and husky guy from his pictures, but it's different seeing someone in Real Life. He stands, searching the crowd, and I take a private moment to watch him before we meet. He warned me he was tall, but in Real Life he looks to have at least a foot on me, maybe more. The top buttons of his shirt are open to reveal a little chest hair, and he seems to have shaved his beard like I asked him to. His hair looks freshly cut — I wonder if he's as nervous about this as I am.

He sits and looks at his phone. Spotting an opportunity for surprise, I sit beside him and cross my legs. He texts with someone back and forth, but I can't quite read his screen. I wonder how long it will take for him to recognize me.

He looks up, straight past me, and then at his phone again.

Dammit. "Hi Kali," I say. I try to hide my excitement so I can properly gauge his reaction.

He looks past again, then recognizes me. He quickly shuts off his phone and puts it away. A smile tugs at the corners of his mouth. "I didn't notice you there."

"I wanted to surprise you." I spread my arms.

Kali nervously scans the crowd and leans into me. He squeezes and pats my back twice, then pulls away.

Certainly, this can't be the guy that I've been fucking nearly every day, or the man I married. "I didn't notice you there" is the first thing you want to say to me? My chest tightens, I feel dizzy, and I wonder if I made a mistake coming here.

I say, "It's amazing to see you for real." I try to mask my hesitation, though I'm acutely aware of how deep my voice is in this moment.

Kali smiles nervously, his eyes dart around. "It is. We should get moving. We need to get home and change if you still want to dress up and go out tonight."

I grab the handles of my luggage. "Of course."

I step closer to Kali, wanting him to take the lead as he has done so many times before. To snap out of whatever is holding him back and to pick me up, swing me around, grab my face and kiss me, cry happy tears at being together . . . finally.

As I lean in, Kali's eyes light with panic, and he recoils. "We shouldn't."

Right. Texas.

¶ 19 ¶

Girl on Fire

2012 - One year later

Click.

6:30

"Sure, Cindy," a male radio host teases in a charming baritone, "chickens always cross the road for you."

I close my eyes, allowing myself a moment to bask in the fading sensation of being born female like in my dream — never knowing dysphoria or the fucked-up ways society criticizes and calls you crazy for saying your trans body is female.

"Roger, are you trying to say I seduce chickens?"

I stare at the ceiling. My pussy still burns with lust — warm and tingling — and I reach under the blankets to check. But as my fingers slide over my boxer briefs, I don't touch the equipment I hoped for, but instead a flagging half erection.

The dream was so vivid.

It's one of the few times I've dreamed of myself that way. I lie in bed wondering if it's ever possible to feel that way after hormones and surgery. If it does, it has to be worth trying. The path ahead feels so clear and attainable.

I grab my cock through my underwear and squeeze, hard. I squeeze until my nails bite into the flesh of my penis through the fabric, squeeze hard enough that I have to grit my teeth through the pain, and I imagine forcing the blood out of my shaft. I close my eyes, and a tear slides into my ear.

I can't start the day this way. I still need to get through work.

A foul stench crawls from under the covers — like baby shit blended with a rat that has decayed in the wall for a week. Despite having had my surgery for over a year now, I'm still getting used to new surprises. Being sick enough to stink through the colostomy bag is technically not possible. A hint of stink, perhaps, if you have a filter, but this is much stronger. Though afraid to check, I tug down the bedclothes to discover a dark semi-liquid pool spreading across my mattress.

This is one of my worst nightmares.

My colostomy bag, filled with gas and feces, sometimes puffs out like a balloon if the filter gets clogged. I must have shifted in the night and ruptured the adhesive seal. And now a lumpy stream of shit has mixed with the black beans and corn that has been squeezed out of the fissure. When I lean forward to assess, shit spills down my hip and into the larger pile spreading on my mattress. I must have rolled onto it in the night.

I've mostly trained myself not to sleep on a full pouch, but there have been accidents recently with the increased stress at work. Ever since I came out to my bosses, things have been tense. My workload has tripled, and there seem to be quibbles with everything I do. Certainly, a few more errors than usual have been made under the stress and the scrutiny, but many issues slapped on my desk were never problems before. I can't risk being late or calling in sick, as that would give them a legitimate reason to fire me, which I'm sure they would appreciate.

At least estrogen has worked. A month ago, painful, hard lumps grew under my nipples, which was admittedly terrifying after all of Craig's cancer warnings. Those painful buds swelled, spread breast tissue, and collected enough fat to shape immature breasts. While seeing them form has been incredibly exciting and reaffirming, binding them every morning out of fear that they'll freak out my bosses has been torturous.

6:42

I do the math and realize I need to be out the door by seven thirty to drive quickly, arrive before eight, and open the office. The laser hair removal is working too, so I can probably get away without shaving.

Cradling the front of the warm, wet colostomy bag, I lift and arch my back to cautiously sit. Warm dribbles drip over my fingers and a wave of nausea threatens to gag me as a thicker wave of reek assails my nose.

"... and be careful on your drive to work this morning," the radio host warns. "Cold fronts are coming. Watch for black ice on the roads ..."

"Fuck this," I say, and grab the corner of the bedclothes with my free hand, untuck the fitted sheet, and wipe my stomach clean. I shuffle to the side of the bed and precariously balance the colostomy bag as I waddle to the kitchen.

I turn on the water and push in the sink plug. As the sink fills, I dig one-handed through the drawer for sandwich bags. Balancing the colostomy bag on the side of my hand, I unseal a sandwich bag and toss it on the counter. I pinch the edge of the adhesive that holds the colostomy bag to my stomach and peel it away. The flange tugs and tears at pale, sunless flesh and exposes the puckered, shit-covered rosebud of my stoma.

The edges of the stoma are red and irritated, and some parts are bleeding, which is, apparently, normal. I stuff the full colostomy bag and flange into the sandwich bag, zip it shut, and dump it in the trash. I wipe my belly with paper towel, which I then ball up and toss it in the trash as well. Gone.

". . . you can look forward to that after the next song," says the silky-voiced radio announcer. A moment of silence and then "All Star" by Smash Mouth buzzes my cheap clock radio speaker.

Seriously?

The cool air on my stoma in the breezy one-bedroom apartment makes that exposed nub of my intestine crinkle and retreat against my stomach like the mouth of a lamprey eel withdrawing into its cave. I gather up all the shit-stained bedclothes and bunch them around the pool of waste. Thank God that sales agent upsold me the mattress protector. I wrap the plastic-bottomed sheet around all the blankets, carry them to the kitchen, and submerge them in scalding water.

I dig in cupboards for detergent, then squirt half a bottle of dish soap into the sink and mix all the bedclothes in. The water muddies, and I'm thankful the horrid stench is now masked by artificial lavender. The apartment now smells like someone crapped on a pile of flowers. I wipe my hands on the sides of my underwear and check the clock.

7:07

Too close.

I hurry into the shower, pour a handful of shower gel and soap myself up. I crank up the heat until my flesh stings, even hotter than I normally prefer, but the pain reminds me how sanitizing fire is, and I burn the filth away. The dream about Kali is faded now, but I still remember him fucking me against a wall. My cock stirs and I close my eyes. Not now.

I burst out of the shower, dry myself and drop the towel on the floor. I squeak open the cupboard and grab two colostomy boxes. I tug out a freshness sealed prepackaged bag and split it open. Holding the rubbery flange in my teeth, I grab the pouch from the other box. I take my spritz and spray the acrid mist around my stoma to sanitize the area. A lancing pain bites into my flesh from the exposed bleeding fissure, and I double over. I grab the sink for support.

"Fuck!" I shout, and my cat bolts out of the room.

The pain lasts only a moment. I put down the bottle and peel the backing off the adhesive flange. I straighten my back to avoid creasing the seal and carefully position it around my stoma. I drip some anti-odour juice into the colostomy pouch, align it with the flange, and clip it on.

Clean and secure.

Straightening to examine myself in the full-length mirror on the back of the bathroom door, I realize I'm a mess. Stealthily growing out my hair, I've now reached the point where it's awkward no matter how it's styled. I run my fingers through to slick it back. It's messy enough now that I am sure it won't be long before my bosses complain.

I must be crazy to want another surgery. Caring for my colostomy takes up a lot of free time already — I would have to be insane to take on more routines. Hormones are one thing, but if I ever figure out how to talk someone into performing bottom surgery on me, that means I need to dilate several times a week for the rest of my life.

And for what? I'm thirty-seven years old with broad shoulders, a receding hairline, and a heavy brow bone. My penis is shrinking, I think. And if I turn to the side, my small, coned breasts are ridiculously tiny with very male-looking nipples. What if they never grow larger? Then there is a literal bag of shit dangling from my belly, fat and long and clipped on the end to make emptying easier. Colostomy bags only exist in Hollywood as cruel jokes about old people. Who would ever lust for a trans woman with damaged goods?

It's clear that I'll never pass, and even if I do, who would love me like this? Pinpricks sting my tear ducts, the reflection of my body mercifully blurring.

7:26

Fuck. Keep it together.

Tugging open the drawer, I pull out my size-too-small sports bra and wriggle it on, tugging it down over my chest, flattening my breasts. Over that goes the size-too-small t-shirt to hold everything in place and hide the bra, and the dress shirt goes over that. I started wearing ties — they make my boss happy, and I like to think it might offset some of this perceived sloppiness and distract from my now lack-of-beard shadow.

Jeans, wallet, keys, out the door, and into the car.

7:38

I can still make it if I don't eat.

I work in the small rural town where I used to live before I moved to the city for safety. But by moving, I gave up a lot. I traded quiet roads and safe night walks for dusty streets and a lungful of exhaust. Hamilton isn't so bad as far as cities go. After all, it's the waterfall capital of the world. People don't associate us with waterfalls, though, since we were once the second largest steel producer next to some big plant in Gary, Indiana.

Growing up near Hamilton, I remember staring across the city at hazy, sulfurous pollution clouds and the sea of smokestacks blasting Mordor flames into the night. It earned its nicknames of Stinktown and Steeltown for obvious reasons; and the Hammer, because of the tough-ass steelworkers who dedicated their lives to the furnace and built this city. But then Stelco was bought by U.S. Steel, and the people who built this city can't afford to live here anymore. The skies are clearer, and we still call it the Hammer, but the city's slogan has since changed to "Art is the New Steel."

Gentrification, man.

I drive the back way through the countryside, as there are rarely any cops along this route. I speed, and soon I'm driving on country roads and past farmland. This familiar drive isn't as comforting as it should be since I now associate it with another long day of scrutiny and browbeating. The best days involve smouldering side-eyes, brooding, and stomping, and the worst involve yelling matches, slamming doors, veiled threats, and death glares. It has gotten so bad that I started an online journal to record the micro-aggressions, just in case.

I've found that it's always best if I arrive ahead of everyone. Being early gives me time to relax and turn off the alarm, put on tea and coffee, tidy up, and take down messages so that when my bosses arrive an hour later, I'm prepared. But as I signal my way onto the final street, I notice something different. There is already a car in the parking lot.

7:56

At first, I assume a neighbour has parked their car in our lot again, and I'll have to ask them to move before everyone arrives. Then I realize it's my boss's car.

I park and walk to the door. A tightness unrelated to my binder seizes my chest. This feels like a trap. Are they trying to catch me arriving late? Maybe they left the car here last night after I went home.

When I try the door, I find it unlocked. I enter.

The kettle rumbles as it boils over. Both members of the husband-and-wife boss team turn. Helen prepares mugs in the kitchenette, and Rick fusses with paperwork in the boardroom.

I stand in the doorway and say, "Did I miss an early meeting?" Neither answers, but they look questioningly at each other across the office.

Recognizing this red flag, I put down my keys and wallet and hurry to help Helen with coffee. "I'm sorry. Let me get that."

"No!" Helen barks, and holds out a hand as if to fend me off. "I'll get it." She pauses, takes a breath, and with a careful tone, she continues. "Did you want some tea?"

"Sure, thank you."

Helen avoids eye contact. "I'll bring it to you in the boardroom."

I briefly wonder if they've been collecting evidence of my "mistakes" and have them in the folder Rick has on the table. Then I notice there are three folders, and I suddenly realize that it's happening. I told them I'm trans less than a month ago, and they're doing it. My rational brain says that can't happen in Canada, but Rick is great with loopholes.

I glance at the door and the escape it promises. I could retreat to my car and drive away, back to my apartment to clean my shitty sheets, which suddenly strikes me as preferable to this. But I can't do that. They'll say I quit.

Before I took my first spiro pill, I received some excellent advice on a trans women private Facebook group. I don't remember who wrote it, but it went something like this: If you have a job when you start your transition, don't quit. It might get uncomfortable, they might mistreat you, and you might imagine that you don't deserve to stay, but don't quit. Make them fire you. Save money, and when they fire you, you'll at least get severance. You might even win a human rights case.

I've thought about that post a lot. Even though I feel like a cow being led to its slaughter, I enter the boardroom.

Rick smiles at me. He has prepared folders for himself and Helen, and a third, I assume, for me, is across the table from them. He motions and says in a subdued tone, "Please have a seat."

I sit and reach for the folder in front of me.

Rick holds out a hand in warning. "Let's wait for Helen. Don't worry, I have asked everyone else to take the morning off."

I withdraw my hand. This was a great trap. I didn't see it coming at all.

As we wait, I consider the logistics and conclude that Rick and Helen couldn't have done this alone. My co-worker who claimed to be my friend when I came out to her knew about this. And what's worse, my childhood friend Tyler, who works with Rick, must have known as well. While I'm waiting for Helen to arrive, I think back and wonder how long Tyler must have known. I wonder if someone told him before I was able to come out to him — he didn't seem surprised.

I imagine Rick and Tyler sitting together with Rick asking my friend's advice on how best to deal with their "situation." I wonder if firing me was Rick's, Helen's, or Tyler's idea. This office will one day be Tyler's, and he has a family to think about. Wouldn't want a tranny working here and screwing up their bottom line. Am I right, fellas?

Helen serves the tea and coffee on coasters and sits down. Rick sighs, points to the folder in front of me. "I'll be blunt. We have to lay you off, Paul."

"I figured," I say before I can check myself. "But lay me off? I've been here longer than Jenifer."

"You have many excellent traits, Paul. You have been with us longer, and you are good on the phone. Clients love you. You're also very . . . punctual."

Helen nods as if conceding the point. But I know what they mean. They mean I don't put in enough extra unpaid hours and leave when my shift is over.

Rick says, "Ultimately, Jenifer's skill set is more suited to keep on."

I want to say "her skill of not being trans," but I resist.

"And we can only afford to keep one of you. Let us read through the letter together. We all have copies, and I have included reference letters. You will find they reflect favourably on you."

I open my folder, and Rick reads it aloud. It's carefully worded, and no doubt checked over by the lawyer I helped him and Helen schedule recently. Another red flag I shouldn't have missed.

It's also worded apologetically and cites the recent 2008 financial crisis and its "period of protracted financial downturn" as the reason they must let me go. I wonder if they or the lawyer thought that one up.

Rick flips to a page with the company's letterhead. "I want you to read over the reference letter and tell me if you want to change any wording. We really wish you all the best."

The reference celebrates my administrative skills, and again selectively notes my punctuality — clearly a sore point. The letter mentions that "Paul worked with us for four years."

I put down the paper. Rick appears sympathetic, but he's always been quite good at making himself seem teary and empathetic when it suits him. Helen looks furious. Her hands are balled into fists, and her face is crimson. However, furious has been her default mood ever since Jenifer likely undermined me by outing me early. I guess that shows which one of them must have ultimately pushed to have me fired. I mean, "laid off."

"This is nicely worded," I say, "except it only says I've worked four years here. I've been with you for five."

"Only four." Helen says. "You took an entire year off! And we paid for you to go to conferences and I —"

"That is perfectly fine," Rick interrupts, holding out his hand to stop Helen. "We can change that if you like." Helen forces herself to stare at the paper.

Another sore point, apparently.

I say, "I didn't take time off. I had cancer. I was still employed, just on leave while I recovered."

"We understand that," Rick says.

"I was in and out of hospitals during that time. I nearly died! I could barely walk near the end." My voice cracks, and I realize I'm dangerously close to tears. That might have worked in my favour if they saw me as the woman I am, but it's not great when I'm trying to negotiate as "Paul."

"We know that was tough for you," Rick says, "and it's important for you to know that's not why we have to let you go."

I understand perfectly well why they're letting me go. Rick once criticized the way my predecessor fastened papers together with a diagonal corner staple instead of one flush with the top of the page. He told me that "she stapled papers like someone who didn't want a job." I can only imagine what he thinks of the chaos of my current situation.

For the record, my dismissal package was stapled by someone who wants my job.

I look at the sheet again, realizing that after today, none of their bullshit will matter, and I won't have to put up with this hostile work environment anymore. Helen's face has softened somewhat, and she's looking sheepish. She might think I'm a problem, or disgusting, but she was once a kind person whom I admired. I realize I may never get another chance to tell her how much I appreciated the person she used to be to me.

I say, "I worked in the office for six full months with a chemo bottle strapped to my belt because I didn't want to leave you stranded. I cared for you and didn't want to let you down. Doesn't that mean anything?"

Helen just looks at the papers in front of her, but Rick nods, his eyes glassy. "Of course it does. We're sorry we have to do this."

"S—so," my voice cracks and tears blur my vision. Fuck, hold it together.

Rick slides a box of tissues to me.

I take them and hide my reddening face, trying not to sob. It's been increasingly difficult maintaining the male facade of impervious emotions. While I'm sure my hormone regimen assists in crumbling the emotional barriers of male protection I've created over the years, it has made handling situations like this very difficult.

I try again. "Do I receive severance?"

Rick says, "We discussed that with our lawyer. I think you'll find what we're offering is more than generous. We only owe you a fraction of this, but, for all the things you've mentioned, we felt we could do better. All you need to do is sign this paper saying you accept, and we'll give you the full amount." Rick slides over a last piece of paper. Attached to it is a cheque made out to Paul for a full year's salary.

"It's more than you deserve," Helen says.

Rick flashes Helen a look of warning and adds, "Of course you'll also receive your last paycheque, which will include money in lieu of two weeks' notice."

I scan the paper with blurry eyes. It's all too much. I skim the page filled with legalese, no doubt crafted to protect them from human rights lawsuits, but at that moment I'm too overwhelmed by it all and want it over. It's too much money to turn down and would mean an end to ever having to speak with them again.

Rick hands me a pen, and I hover the nib over the signature line.

I say, "I don't know what I'll do. Who's going to hire me if you let me go?"

While I know begging isn't appropriate, and the professional thing would be to sign this paper, shake hands, and walk out the door — becoming a visibly trans job-seeker panics me. The changes in my body are becoming difficult to hide, and perhaps Rick and Helen have realized I'll soon be presenting as female full-time. Working here through my transition would be awkward and difficult, but job hunting will be much worse.

Should I show up on my first day of work and say, "Psych! You hired a girl!" Or show up to an interview as an awkward trans woman, still stumbling through learning how to coordinate women's outfits? Who would hire me like that for administration?

Rick says, "The world is changing. People are more progressive than they used to be, and you have such an outstanding personality. You will do fine."

Helen appears to have changed her tune and nods along encouragingly.

Progressive like these two? Now I know that signing this is a trap.

I'm sobbing now, unable to stop. I say, "No they aren't, you don't understand."

Rick steels his jaw. "We're giving you a full year's pay. Take a trip. Figure things out. This buys you a lot of time."

That kind of money could also pay off all my debts. I could afford a whole new wardrobe. And I've always wanted to fly to England and visit my family. That much money is a ticket to a new life. And maybe I'm being overly emotional, and Rick is right — I might be able to get another job when I get back to Canada.

I sign the paper, and Rick sweeps it away and into his folder.

"Don't worry about the rest," Rick assures me. "I'll get Jenifer to send copies of this to you. Everything else is in your folder." He takes a cheque out of his folder, opens mine, and slides it in.

When I pick up my package, it's heavier than I imagined.

Rick stands and offers me his hand.

I stand, and he shakes my hand firmly. Tight squeeze and two shakes, my chest quakes with restrained sobs.

"Good luck, Paul," Rick says.

"Thank you, Rick. Thank you for giving me this job. And for bringing me food and money when I was sick at home."

Rick swallows and his eyes water. I internally smile.

Rick, still shaking my hand, steps in and hugs me. I consider pushing him away but give in and hug him back. When he lets me go, I grab more tissues.

Helen escapes the room with the mugs.

"Take the rest of the day off, of course," Rick says. "If you have any information you need from the computer, email Helen or Jenifer and they can send it."

But I had sent myself everything I needed weeks ago when they started harassing me. That advice was thankfully also in the post warning me to hold on to my job as long as I could.

"Thank you, Rick." I head for the door before I lose control and make a further fool of myself.

Helen is already clinking mugs in the sink, busying herself with washing and not looking at me. I say, "Thank you for everything, Helen. Bye."

Helen looks up, her face creased in what may be pain. Tears drip down her cheeks. "Bye," she croaks. I quickly leave, confused and overwhelmed, but thankful to have cool air on my face to dry my tears.

I hurry to my car and head for home. I only get a few blocks away before the reality of what happened crushes me. I've now got a ticking clock counting down the amount of time I have left before rent, colostomy supplies, and transition meds tear through that money. Soon I'll become just another unemployed, financially desperate trans woman. Unlike them, I don't even have the safety net of sex work available to me. Who would pay for a trans woman with no asshole and a colostomy?

When it becomes too difficult to drive through my tears, I pull onto the gravel shoulder next to a farmer's field and park. I roll to a stop and stare down the dirt road, watching the cloud of my car's dust flow around me. Cars rocket past as I idle. My four-way flashers click over. I rest my head on the steering wheel and cry. I run the scene through my head over and over, thinking of things I could have done differently.

I grip the steering wheel until my knuckles turn white. "Fucking assholes."

But something changes. There's a pause, and my sobs turn to laughter. It starts as a chuckle, but soon I'm grinding my forehead against the steering wheel and laughing so hard that it reverberates off the windows and rings in my ears.

At first, I don't know why I'm laughing. Maybe it's relief. But then I recognize it for what it truly is. This is my moment. Nothing is stopping me from transitioning now.

A crazy idea flashes into my brain. What if Rick and Helen meant to gift this opportunity to me? Besides being a selfish and bigoted way of protecting the aesthetic integrity of their business, what if they do still love me and gifted this transition opportunity by handing me a cheque this large? I dismiss the idea, but it allows me to hate them much less if I consider that as a possibility.

I stare down the dirt road ahead of me and decide I will drive home, bag up every piece of "boy" clothes I own, and never touch them again. I wipe my face with the cuff of a coat I will own for only twenty more minutes, and I drive.

◣ 20 ◢

Butterfly

I subtly draw the hem of my dress above my knee, exposing milky white thigh and a length of striped stocking. I spread my legs enough that my thigh is conveniently close to the truck's centre console where Kali rests his hand.

We thunder down the highway in Kali's pickup. I hold my leg there as miles pass, but Kali fails to take the bait. He signals his exit. We loop around and under the highway, emerging before the sprawling majesty of Houston's Galleria. Encased in immaculate white concrete, like a towering walled fortress to consumerism, the mall's walls are decorated with glowing signs bigger than houses. Each of them features a different dewy-faced girl pretending to be a woman, though certainly more convincingly than I. Feeling foolish, I pull my dress down and smooth the fabric against my leg.

Kali says, "You're quiet. Everything okay?"

"Great." I place my hand on his. My slender, long-fingered hand, encased in a white, elbow-length opera glove. Kali's hands are thick and strong and charmingly hairy. I trace the veins on the back of his hand with a fingertip, marvelling at how feminine my hand looks next to his.

I flip down the sunshade, happy to find a mirror. My face is already hidden under thick layers of white pancake makeup. I lean in to check for missed patches. I shaved before we left — but even now the ghost of stubble remains.

It's possible the beard shadow isn't even there. Like a foul smell that lingers in your nostrils, it may only be a memory of something I would rather forget. My sister once casually mentioned that she sometimes wears bright red lipstick to hide her flaws — I'm sure flaws, for her, mean acne or eye bags, but it surprises me how well red lipstick also distracts from masculine cues. However, no amount of lipstick can hide my all-too-boyish haircut, or my other insecurities. That's what the mask is for.

We drive under a crowded glass-enclosed walkway, and we're swallowed into the darkness of a parking garage. Perfect for assembling the rest of my costume without strangers thinking I'm putting on a drag show.

I point to the darkest corner of the garage. "Let's park there."

Kali changes direction. "I thought you'd want to be closer to the entrance because of your heels."

That was thoughtful. "I still have to get my costume on."

Kali parks. "I'm fine if you would rather go home." He reaches for my hand, and I let him take it. I can't tell if this consideration is for him or me.

I have two goals for this trip, and both terrify me to my core. One is to dress in this costume and go somewhere in public for the first time dressed as a woman. The other is to fuck my boyfriend. Of these two knee-weakening goals, the one I dread less is public humiliation. Checking this off my list on the first night in Texas seems like the perfect way to break the ice.

I squeeze Kali's hand and collect my wicker basket. "I've waited so long to hold your hand in public. I won't forgive myself if I chicken out."

"Remember, we can always leave." Kali smiles, and I wait for him to lean in for a kiss, but he climbs out and closes the door. The interior lights dim.

I step out and fasten my cloak. Cradling my basket in the crook of my elbow, I position my wig, then tie on my rabbit opera mask, making sure the ribboned bow is tight behind my head.

With my glasses in the basket, I can barely see myself in the passenger mirror and stab my head more than once while trying to pin the mask into my wig. Above the words "objects in the mirror are closer than they appear," a girl stares back. A very blurry girl hiding behind poor eyesight, makeup, and a mask, but unmistakably a girl. My slender jaw, my fortunate lack of an Adam's apple, and even my plump lips which slowly curl into a delighted grin are undeniably feminine. From somewhere deep inside, an orgasmic rush of fulfilment boils from my heart and explodes, flooding the hollow part of me I never imagined could be whole. As tingles spread to every extremity, I'm giddy and light-headed from the unexpected euphoria.

Kali rounds the back of the truck wearing his costume — a torn dress shirt dotted with fake blood, furry taloned gloves, and a disturbingly realistic feral werewolf mask. He activates a hidden button in his glove and his eyes blaze red, his jaw stretches open, warping the rubber mouth, and an ear-piercing howl echoes through the parking garage. He rushes forward, talons raised, and I back against the truck, head clunking on the window.

Kali growls and grabs my waist. Inside the mask he muffles, "Gotcha." For the first time since I've arrived, his caring eyes stare into mine from within the darkened eyeholes.

I say, "You're terrifying." Though I'm joking, my heart still races.

"All the better for catching bunnies."

When he lets go, I grab my hips and strike a pose.

Kali says, "Gorgeous."

"It's your job to say that. But do you think I look normal?"

Kali pulls off his mask. We smudged his eyes with black makeup so they won't show through the eyeholes. I try not to make a were-raccoon joke and ruin the mood.

Kali says, "You are normal. But you're also hot."

More euphoria bubbles.

I say, "Only my voice would give me away."

Kali holds my hips, and fingertips brush my ass. "All I see is my bunny."

"Other people won't."

"You can work on that."

They might, but only if I don't open my mouth. I ask, "If anyone talks to us, will you answer?"

Kali glances toward the brightly lit mall entrance. A group of three girls giggle as they walk past the truck. Once they've passed, Kali grabs my shoulders and pushes me against the truck's door. The next thing I know, his lips are pressed to mine. My heartbeat pounds in my throat, and I squeak a surprised sound into his mouth.

I realize that I've frozen with my arms straight and stiff by my sides. I nearly drop the basket. Feeling it slip down my arm snaps me out of my trance, and I force myself to grab his shoulders and kiss back. He's pressing my head against the truck window — too hard to move, and I desperately want to slow him down. I try lifting my chin to get a better angle to kiss, but then his tongue is pushing into my mouth. I try tilting my head and one of my mask ears catches in his hair and the mask pinches my cheek. It's better than before, so I ignore the pain.

His tongue is thick and circles inside my mouth like a skipping rope. He's still pushing me too hard, and I'm terrified I'm not doing a good job. This is our first kiss — it sets the pace for our entire relationship. I can't have a bad first kiss.

Just as I manage to interrupt his mixing bowl technique and just play, he suddenly pulls away and smiles. He looks like a messy racoon drag queen with my lipstick all over his face. He says, "I'll talk for us, don't worry."

He seems satisfied at least.

I dig in the basket for my makeup bag. Fireworks explode in my head, and I'm eager for a redo, but I know I won't get it right now. I point at my mouth and say, "You might want to . . ."

Kali leans past me to glance in the mirror and he disappears to the driver's side. Through the truck windows, I can see him furiously rubbing at his face. I pull a wipe from the basket and fix my makeup, thankful for the opportunity to catch my breath. When I finish, Kali is standing behind me with his mask back on. He offers me a taloned paw.

I slide my hand into his, and he leads me out of the garage and toward the stream of Halloween shoppers funnelling into the mall entrance. Some of them glance over, grin, and point. I wish I could wear my glasses with this mask. Everyone is too fuzzy to know for sure, but I'm terrified they're telling each other that I'm really a guy — an impostor in their midst.

I brace myself for some hick to wheel me around by the shoulder and punch me in the face. Instead, as we near the door, I overhear a snippet of a conversation with someone mentioning "rabbit Little Red Riding Hood" and my confidence surges back.

Once inside, I realize that my clever plan to debut my Real Life Experience at the Galleria may have been a miscalculation.

My plan was to disappear into a crowded mall filled with time-conscious shoppers too busy rushing about to concentrate on us. And since it's Halloween night, the place would no doubt be full of costumed people. In my mind, it was a flawless plan. I told Kali to take us to the biggest mall in Houston to up my chances of success even further.

What I didn't realize is that the Houston Galleria is primarily filled with teenagers, tourists, the elderly, and the lonely. While I was right about it being incredibly busy, how could I have known we would be the only two people in costume?

I grip Kali's hand tighter. Busy now only means more people staring at us.

Kali rubs the back of my hand with his thumb and asks, "Where do you want to go?"

Blurry faces, warmly lit stores with names I can't read — but being here isn't about shopping. I lean in and say, "You lead. Take me anywhere, as long as it's with you."

He squeezes my hand, and we walk. As we pass a railing, with my poor vision, it appears as if endless levels sprawl both above and below us. Multiple levels of makeup stores, clothing boutiques, and high-end natural-ingredient scent purveyors. It's dizzying to consider that only a few of these shops cater to the person society wants me to be, many more for the person I want to be, but none for who I am. However, I'm increasingly confident that if I were to walk into any of those stores, someone would walk up and ask in a thick Texan accent, "Can I help you, ma'am?" A group of teens snicker and point as they pass.

This was a mistake. And what does being here achieve?

I'm not even dressed like a woman. I'm a woman who looks like a man, wearing a costume designed for a woman pretending to be a little girl from a fairy tale, while also wearing an opera mask designed for an upscale woman pretending to be a rabbit at a fancy ball.

Ceci n'est pas une pipe indeed.

"Can we take a picture with you?" asks a petite Asian woman.

While I have been panic-spiralling, a small group of people has gathered around us. Three women and two men, all smiling hopefully. The man shows us his camera.

Kali's latex muzzle swings toward me. I can only assume he's waiting for my consent since I can't see him through that terrifying werewolf mask. I nod and wave the group over. Kali holds out a clawed arm. The group rushes forward, leaving what I can only presume is one of their husbands to take the picture. They cuddle in close to Kali, and a woman snuggles into my side. I hug her back. Kali activates the mask, and through tiny hidden speakers, a mournful howl echoes into the mall. The woman beside me clutches my waist and screeches in mock terror. The camera flashes. More people gather.

We walk only a few steps before we're once again surrounded, and another photo op happens. Then again.

Over and over, it happens, and we barely make it past two stores before we've stopped a half dozen times for photos. We are smiling and walking away from the last group of photo-takers, and I'm feeling a little like a celebrity when a woman thrusts her baby at me and asks, "Would you hold my baby while I take a picture with your boyfriend, miss?"

Miss.

I nod and take the infant from her.

Inside my head, I am triumphantly screaming. I cradle the baby to my chest, and the woman positions Kali to growl menacingly as she cowers beneath him.

The baby reaches out, touches my face, and some white comes off on its fingers. Sweet and swaddled in a knitted blanket so pink it's almost white, and so soft that I can feel the plush fabric through my gloves. A tiny baby hand grabs my breast, or rather the padding where my breast should be.

Even if I wanted to speak, I don't think I would be able with the lump in my throat. I disengage the baby trying to nurse through my clothing. Despite my dress being a literal costume, and my wearing a mask, this mother sees me as a woman. The baby grabs my jaw again, and the mother cuddles up to my side and waves to her friend. The mother's cheek rests against mine. I can only imagine how authentically enthusiastic my smile must be when her friend takes a picture.

I return the baby and she repeatedly thanks me. My face is sore from smiling as I dig out wet wipes from my basket and help her clean the patches of white on the baby's hand and her cheek.

When I turn around, two cops are grilling Kali.

An officer points, and Kali removes his mask.

I take a hesitant step forward, and the officer motions at me. "Ask your girlfriend to remove her mask."

She called me his girlfriend.

My heart leaps, but then my brain tackles my heart and presses a knee into its back. I walk away from the baby and the happy tourists who are now reviewing pictures on their devices. Kali's eyes are filled with panic.

The officer says, "Ma'am, please remove the mask."

"I can't," I whisper, so quietly I can barely hear myself.

Looking puzzled, the officer approaches. A badge on her arm reads SIMON — MALL SECURITY and not police. The shade of blue of their uniforms, the swagger, the equipment belts all appear exactly like every terrifying American *COPS* episode I grew up watching. The mall cop says, slower, "You . . . have . . . to . . . remove . . . your —"

"I can't," I repeat, enunciating as loudly as I dare.

The mall cop's expression darkens and a peak forms between her eyes as she squints at me. Groups of shoppers pass, pointing at us with their chins. The harmless curiosity we were drawing transforms to scrutiny. While Houston is apparently better for gay rights than most places in Texas, it's still Texas — and still America. The last thing I need is to record "shocking security camera footage" in front of this crowd.

Kali says, "I'm sorry, officers, her mask is pinned into her hair."

My hero.

Their walkies chirp and someone babbles in heavy Texan drawl something I can't make out. The male cop pinches the receiver velcroed to his shoulder and says, "We're with them. Dealing with it. Over."

The male cop says, "She still has to remove it."

Still she.

Kali smiles and steps between the cop and me. "Listen, we're heading to a party after this. If she takes it off, we'll have to go home and fix it. I've removed my mask, no problem, but she can't."

I love him so much right now, all six-feet-plus of him. He stands protectively in front of me, the wolf's head tucked under his arm like a fighter pilot's helmet. He seems to have everything under control. Only I would recognize the slight waver of nervousness in his voice.

The male cop stares at my fake hair and my mask. The female cop joins him, and together they both stare directly into my eyes. I am frozen to the ground, waiting for their verdict. I half expect one of them to snatch the mask off my face or remove my wig like I'm a Scooby Doo villain.

I could have gotten away with it too, if it weren't for those darn meddling rent-a-cops.

I am entirely terrified, but also impossibly exhilarated.

The walkies chirp again. This time I make out the word "Update?" The female mall cop turns her back and leans on a nearby railing, murmuring into her shoulder. I make out something about hairpins and masks. "Ten-four."

She walks back with purpose. "I'm sorry, but you either have to remove your mask or be escorted out."

Kali and I exchange glances. I nod at him.

Kali says, "We'll leave. But you don't have to escort us."

"Then I'm asking you to leave immediately." The female cop rests her hand on her flashlight.

Kali laces his fingers with mine and pulls me to his side. Beside his strength and size, it's so easy to feel beautiful and feminine. And after his rescue, I desperately want to help him feel like a man as soon as humanly possible.

Mall security follows from a distance as we speed walk toward the exit, no doubt followed by lofty security cameras. Soon we step into non-recycled, asphalt-scented night air. The breeze cools the sweat under my mask. The two rental cops monitor us from the doorway until we enter the garage.

Kali helps me into his truck. He climbs in and the interior lights dim, leaving us in darkness. He says, "Baby, I'm sorry. I didn't know they would do that."

I replay the entire event in my mind and chuckle.

"Why are you laughing?"

"They called me ma'am, just like cowboys." I pretend to tip an invisible hat. "Pawrdun me, ma'am. Iff'n you don't mind, it would sure be swell iff'n ya take off that there mask."

"Because you are a ma'am here."

"No — you saved me. I can't imagine what would have happened if my mask came off."

Kali takes my hand and squeezes it. "But it didn't."

I can't help myself. I crawl across to Kali's seat and straddle his lap. My ears scrape the roof, wrenching my head back as hairpins dig into my scalp. I cry out, the mask and half the wig now skewed, but I'm determined.

I press my lips into Kali's before he witnesses the mess I must have made of my face. I vibrate a contented sigh into his mouth as we exchange a few awkward, clumsy kisses, trying and failing to figure out each other's rhythm. We bump teeth painfully, cringe, then try again.

My tongue finds his, and I reach down his belly and over the rough denim of his jeans and squeeze the thick mass behind his heavy fly. He throbs in my hand, waking, filling as I kiss him. I'm no longer afraid of what will happen tonight if I can stir him this easily.

He groans and pushes me away. "Not here."

I reluctantly sink into my seat, but the way his pants tent scores me a victory. As he backs out and drives toward the exit, I can't help but wonder if he's just shy in Real Life, or if he's truly so terrified to be caught with me in public, however remote.

Kali asks, "Did you want to go anywhere else?"

I pull down the visor mirror to fix my wig; I inspect my mask for damage but find none. "I only wanted to be somewhere without needing to hide. My plan worked, sort of."

"It'll make a funny story for your books one day."

I laugh nervously at that prospect. "I'd be too mortified to write this down. Besides, who would read it?"

Kali slaps the steering wheel. "I know. You like gelato?"

·ᵥᴧᴧ·

Kali drives us to a strip mall close to his place. Though it's now past nine, the gelato store is open. Inside is shiny and red, with cute bistro-style tables and high-backed metal chairs ornamented with coiled ironwork. At the back of the shop is a chalkboard decorated with ice cream scoops and Italian flags, and a brightly lit ice cream counter in front. A pair of women sit across from one another.

Kali gets out and opens my door. I mock a curtsey. "Thank you, sir."

"Sir. I could get used to that."

At least one of us enjoys being called sir.

Inside, the women appear startled by our costumed entrance. One of them comically holds two spoons in the sign of a cross, dripping gelato onto her paper dish. After we pass, one of them says, "So cute."

Kali asks, "What would you like? My treat."

"Surprise me."

When he goes to order, I pick a seat and discover the two women are not, in fact, seated completely across from each other but closer together to one side. They're intently smiling at me. They're both dressed in office outfits — lawyers, maybe.

I smile back. One with a grey pencil skirt and a lot of buttons undone on her blouse says, "You two are adorable."

"Thank you," I say, louder and deeper than I intended. I knew I should have practised my voice more, however neither seems to care. Here the lights are bright, and it's impossible to hide my bone structure. Do they think we're gay?

Kali places a cup filled with a scoop of something green onto the table. He rests his mask on the table beside. His raccoon-like black-smudged eyes are kind and warm. "Did they say something?"

"They said we look good together."

Kali toasts a spoonful of his gelato toward the women. They smile, and as I turn back, in my periphery, I catch one of the women feeding the other a scoop of ice cream. As I fill my mouth with a first icy spoonful, Kali leans in, his breath warm against my ear as he says, "You are beautiful. When I get you home, I'll show you how much I think so."

My face flushes pink under the pancake makeup.

I can't think about the gelato. Soon, Kali will drive us to his house and we'll have sex. Not sex with digitally purchased addons to correct our flaws, runtime scripts to make our movements porn-perfect, screenshots to save our intimate moments forever, or a log-out button if things get awkward. No, instead he'll take me to his bed, we'll take off our costumes, and have real human sex with my all-too-male-body pressed against his.

I suddenly wish there was another mall we could be humiliated at first.

◖ 21 ◗

Your Body

Kali leads me into an uninspired bedroom. Blank cream walls, brown comforter, white sheets, a pastel blue ceramic bulb lamp that was likely inherited rather than purchased, and nothing else. However, the adorable walleyed cheetah plushie he bought me stares at us from the night table and breathes a little fun into this otherwise boring room.

He walks backward, drawing me to the side of the bed by my fingertips. I've never been shy in the bedroom. In fact, throughout my life, I've often taken the lead. However, that's not how we play online. I realize we should have spent more time discussing how this moment should play out — what if he doesn't take the lead? What if he hasn't thought of how to make someone with my body feel like a woman? Or worse, what if he's comfortable with my body in a way I'm not?

What if he wants to suck my dick?

Kali pushes me onto his bed. I crawl back and rest my head on the pillow.

He motions toward the lamp. "On or off?"

"Definitely off."

He twists the switch, and with a *click* the room plunges into darkness, illuminated only by the crack at the base of the bathroom door. His shadow looms and the mattress compacts under his knee. He grasps my shoulder and lowers himself onto me. Having someone this large crushing me into the mattress is an unexpected new experience.

Even as he tries to kiss me, he's pressing my silicone bra inserts into my chest and I can't take a full breath. I have never considered in all my online encounters that I would have to breathe in a situation like this. I make a mental note to include that detail for the future.

What if there are other things I hadn't considered?

His hands are on my knees, and he spreads them apart. I'm not prepared for just how much I'll have to spread my legs to accommodate a bigger guy, and my hips ache in protest. I'm sure he believes that grinding and rubbing the unforgiving sandpaper denim fly of his jeans against my panties is sexy, but it only reminds me of how painful it is to have my penis tucked.

My enthusiasm for this fabled moment is quickly deflating, and I'm beginning to realize why some women might not enjoy having sex with men. As he presses me down and humps my lap, all I can think about is how uncomfortable I am in this itchy, hot wig. Part of me just wants this to be over so we can get to the affectionate after-sex cuddling — but the other part of me acknowledges that I'm not helping things by lying here like a dead fish. I wrap my leg around the back of his and he presses himself against me, cutting off my air. He kisses me, and his cheekbone shifts my mask.

Kali jerks away. "Ow! Your mask bit me."

I gasp some air.

I giggle breathlessly and untie the mask. "Mind if I take off this wig?"

"Whatever makes you comfortable."

I grit my teeth and pull the wig. The bobby pins tug at my real hair. I toss everything away from the bed as far as I can. Pins clack against the wall somewhere in the dark.

"Ready?" Kali asks.

"Yes," I lie.

He rests his weight back onto me, and though I can barely breathe, I do my best as he pushes my head into the pillow with his kisses.

Is Kali just bad at sex? I try to match his enthusiasm.

I turn my head, every so often sucking a breath of air out of alternating corners of my mouth like I'm a marathon swimmer. Then I get fed up and push back, and he relents, and I'm able to work out a rhythm as we exchange kisses. We maul each other like clumsy thirteen-year-olds trapped in a closet, though this is far from heaven. In his arms, I once again become a clumsy virgin instead of an adult with hundreds of Real Life sexual experiences.

Online, Kali and I have loved each other in more ways than I can count. And while this isn't *Second Life*, and his bed isn't pre-programmed with sexual positions integrated in its code, I'm still shocked at how little those hours spent together online prepared us for each other now. We kiss, tongues fiercely sparring, and saliva drips down my cheek. My tongue tires.

Though Kali mechanically kisses me and appropriately moans when I grab his ass, the fire I feel from him online isn't here. Where is that wild animal? The growls, the passion, the . . . hunger? I slide my hand around and massage the front of his jeans to discover his cock is soft.

Kali grabs a cup of my silicone cutlet–stuffed bra. While the visual is not uninteresting, the disconnect from sensation only reminds me how artificial my womanhood is. He's also likely trying to fool himself into believing I have them and to forget how disgusted he is with my body.

Determined to move this forward and give my tongue a rest, I say, "Your pants need to come off."

Perhaps neither of us will admit Real Life encounters can't hold up to the fantasies we've built.

Kali rolls off, and I use the opportunity to take a few deep breaths. My eyes have adjusted to the dark, and as I lay and watch his fingers at work on his fly, all I can smell is his spit on my face. He rolls back to wiggle down his jeans, and I help him tug them from his legs.

Kali says, "Now you."

It's exciting not knowing what men are planning for me online, and I typically enjoy the thrill of how excited they get when I fulfill their fantasies. However, in Real Life I often take control in the bedroom. It's not an expression of dominance, but rather an assurance I won't end up disappointed. I may have been so caught up in emulating my game character's personality that I wonder if maybe I need to assert myself more.

Before Kali can right himself, I crawl over him and straddle his hips. I grab his hands and push them into the mattress. Then I kiss him like I've kissed any girl I've dated and try to banish gender roles from my head. We only have a few days together, and I want to make the most of this.

His body tenses, but we exchange a few gentle kisses and then I open my mouth and our tongues meet. He melts under me and begins his previous lashing frenzy, but I maintain my lazy pace, and he slows to meet me. We find a relaxed, sexy rhythm and play. It doesn't take long before I feel that he's pushed out of his underwear, and when I massage him, I find him not only achingly hard, but shockingly large — way bigger than mine has ever been, even before hormones, and in a strange way that encourages my femininity.

As I push down his underwear and stroke him, I forget what I must look like to him, and just let my fingers play.

Kali breaks the kiss and in a throaty growl says, "Bad bunny likes to tease, hmm?"

There he is.

"Mmhmm," I say in falsetto.

Kali grabs my arms, and we wrestle. I let him win, and he pins me on my back. The next thing I know, he's crawling over my chest and pushing himself into my mouth. My jaw aches trying to accommodate him, and I'm terrified I'll scratch him with my teeth. Without time to breathe, I become lightheaded as he slides himself against my tongue. Overly eager, he thrusts himself against the back of my throat, and I gag. I now regret encouraging him by having my avatar deep-throat him all those times in the past. I dig fingernails into his sides, and he pulls out.

Gasping for air, I say, "Sorry, need a break."

"Want to try something else?" His cock bobs and shines in the dim light.

"I wish you could fuck me." While I ache for him, I regret reminding him of my deficiencies.

Kali says, "Maybe one day."

Not soon enough.

Kali fumbles in the nightstand and produces a bottle of lube and the jelly cock sleeve. "Want to try this?"

After all the cock sleeve and I have been through, I'm surprised I've forgotten it. Taking the toy and lubricant, I push the spout into the tube and squeeze until it drips out the end and onto my belly like an overstuffed cannoli.

I cradle the tube against my lap. "I'm ready."

Kali positions himself and pushes, but I've got lube on my hands, and I nearly drop the now slick silicone tube. When I grip it tighter, it seems to only make it more difficult for him to get started. But after a few jabs at the tube, the entrance seems to stretch, and he groans loudly as he slides in.

Kali moans, "Fuck, this feels great."

"Fuck me, Kitty."

Kali lunges forward, resting hands on either side of my head. He hunches over, and I realize that I may have made a tactical error. When he lowers his weight onto the back of my hands, his belly pins my arms, and I can't reposition the sleeve. And as he starts to really get into the act, lube is squelching out the back and onto my fingers, and my belly, and probably his bed too. With each thrust, I can feel the greased tube tugging and pushing out of my grasp more and more.

He seems to realize and lifts his belly and covers my hands with one of his to hold it in place. He thrusts again, but the tube pushes through my fingers. As it slides away, I fumble to catch it in the dark. It bounces off the bed and makes a wet *thuck* sound as it bounces and rolls away somewhere on the floor.

I reach. "If we can dry it first, we can —"

Kali takes my hand. "It's okay."

I relax, defeated. I wait for him to tell me we should give up, but he guides my hand to his cock and rests his forehead against mine. His breath puffs over my lips as he says, "Just touch me."

I stroke his now slick shaft as he kisses me, faster and hungrier than before. It doesn't take long before he grunts a warning and sits up, pushing my hands out of the way as he furiously jerks himself.

"Where do you want —" Kali groans. Wet strings rope onto my stomach as he grunts. A hot pool gathers in my navel. I stare down at myself, and the mess, unsure what to do now.

As Kali rolls off, the dim light coming from the bathroom makes my belly shine. I tug my dress down and mop up.

With a contented groan, Kali growls quietly into my ear, "That was fun."

Fun? That was a disaster.

Kali closes his eyes, sighing softly, and appears to be drifting off to sleep.

"I didn't get off yet," I say.

Kali props himself up on his elbow. "I thought it would upset you if I tried."

He has a valid point. What can he do? Blowing me would be too weird, and I'm glad he realizes that.

What if I played with myself? That would still be awkward in front of him.

After some negotiations, I'm sucking on him, and he's playing with me, but he's not allowed to look at his hand. It's not a reasonable solution, or even a sustainable one, but it feels like it's working for now. Kali lays back with his eyes closed, groaning as I tease him. I wonder if he's thinking about my avatar — he can't be thinking about me.

Soon my world explodes, and I whine and moan through my nose. I shiver and ride out the last waves of orgasm and then crawl up to cuddle beside him. I grab his arm and pull myself close to his larger body, basking in the warm afterglow of it all.

Maybe I can perform enough mental gymnastics to pull this thing off.

Kali sits up, his hand outstretched and glistening. He chuckles nervously and shows a handful of my cum. "What should I do with this?"

The warm glow is snuffed out like a wet matchstick.

"Get rid of it I guess?" I shout at him.

I want to die, to roll off the far side of the bed and hide under it — to grab my things and run out the door. This is not what I wanted, and possibly Kali doesn't understand at all. Maybe I'm overreacting, but everything suddenly feels so wrong.

Kali stares with wide eyes into what must be a look of utter panic. He says, "I'll wash it off."

He walks into the bathroom. When he closes the door, the room eclipses into merciful, utter darkness. The tap runs, and he washes for a very long time.

I pull off my sodden dress, drop it on the floor, and crawl under the covers. I curl into a ball, feeling sticky and foolish, still wearing the sweaty silicone-filled bra, and wondering if I will ever feel Real.

22

Love Me Now

2017 — Six years later

I find myself in a maze of twisty little passages, all alike.

How did I get here? At some point, I stopped making my own decisions and allowed myself to be guided by those who I believed knew better. Sometimes, when the road of life is bumpy, it's easier to hand the wheel to someone who says they know the way. But I've discovered that while doing so can make the trials of life easier, you can never discover your potential. And while I've lost myself this way many times, I always end up back here.

I find myself set before two paths. If I reach that crossroads when I'm strong and supported, I might choose a riskier path if I believe happiness lies at the end. However, if my choice happens during a time of poverty, desperation, or shame, I'll always take the safer route. But today I take the path crowded with brambles — the one where every step wounds. Though it sometimes feels like the entire world is telling me I'm insane, for once I have to trust myself.

It is down this darker path, the one I've never taken, that I come face to face with the Grue. With a hungry, sharp-toothed grin, she beckons me forward.

They say no one ever sees a grue — if you did, you'd be dead — and so against every survival instinct I've learned, I willingly step forward and embrace her.

She pulls me close, and true to the legend, I am undone.

Around me the maze breaks apart and falls away. The Grue and I become one, and as we merge, we float unified in a comforting, judgment-free void.

One with me now, the Grue battles my apprehensions and insecurities.

Together, we are alone.

Yet alone, I am strong.

Though dangers lie ahead on my path, I no longer fear the dark — because now I have claws.

"I think she's waking up," a woman says.

The outsider's voice dispels the blissful sanctuary. I want her to go away, to allow me to sink deeper and reach the moment of peace I've yearned for, but it melts away. The darkness abandons me, and I helplessly rise toward the light, and I emerge to a lungful of cool antiseptic hospital stink.

Weighted blankets pin me to a bed. The back of my hand hurts, and my eyelids are incredibly heavy. From somewhere far away, a woman with a pronounced southern drawl calls a "code orange." The clang of a metal tray triggers a zombie-like moan. I squeeze my eyes tighter, and my head pounds. Something gently massages my spread thighs beneath the covers.

I open my eyes, blurry and milky, and after several blinks the gooey membrane relents. What might be the face of an older woman leans over me.

"An early riser, I see," the woman says.

"Good morning," I mumble. While blurred, I note thick plastic rails on the side of my bed.

The nurse moves something toward my face. "You must want these." I reach for them, but the tubes tug at monitoring equipment and an IV pole. The nurse gently pushes my hands away. "Let me do this for you."

She slides glasses onto my face, and the room renders into crisp reality.

I'm lying in a recovery room, smaller and cleaner than any I've ever seen. Four women lie in recovery near me, and two of them are already sitting. One asks for lip balm in a croaking voice.

Then everything floods back.

Sarah and I took a Lyft to the hospital.

I remember the prep room where they put in my IV and gave me a puffy medical smock to wear.

How the nurses all laughed as I moaned in bliss as they pumped the smock full of warm, comforting air.

Trying to fill out last-minute paperwork looking like a marshmallow.

Kissing Sarah, and her encouraging smile as they wheeled me away to surgery.

When the nurse turns away from me, I nonchalantly slide my untangled hand under the covers, down my belly, past my mini-pouch, and over a padded diaper. I risk a little squeeze through the padding and there is nothing. No pain, no sensation at all, and no bulge.

"Your surgery went well," the nurse says.

"It's done?"

"I don't have any more details, but I hear that you have a recovery room waiting. Can I fetch you anything?"

I scratch a dry tongue inside my dry mouth. "Water and lip balm?"

The nurse smiles and walks away.

"Is Sarah around?" But the nurse doesn't seem to hear.

Something squeezes and rolls down my legs again. I lift the covers. Though the oxygen tube tugs my nose back and obscures the view, past my puffy taped diaper are long mechanical cushions gripping and massaging my legs.

What the hell is it for? Circulation?

Invisible fingers caress my brain. My body tingles and my eyelids grow heavy. The room spins. I succumb, let it envelop me, and I float away.

I wonder if it feels this good to die.

⠶

"Baby?"

I open my eyes to find Sarah holding my arm. Her face lights up as I smile. "They said you asked for me. They brought you here."

Warm California sunlight floods through a bay window into a private recovery suite, an included perk in the surgery cost, otherwise I could never afford something this exclusive. "This room is amazing."

"You've even got a menu." Sarah shows off a laminated card.

I take the menu, and the words twist and crawl on the page. Letters blur into each other and stretch into tiny worms and paisleys. My stomach turns. I shove it back into her hands. "I can't."

"Feeling sick?"

"Something is wrong with my eyes."

Sarah clasps my hand in both of hers. "You're on some heavy drugs. I spoke with Marci. She said your pussy is perfect."

My heart leaps, and I want to look, but I know it will probably be days before that. "She said that?"

"She actually said your pussy will be the pride of Canada."

I cackle, loud and dry and ending in a coughing fit that draws stares from people passing the room.

Marci Bowers knocks on the door and says, "Sounds like we are in excellent spirits. Mind if I come in?"

"Pride of Canada!" I shout at her, surprising myself with the volume.

"Of course, sweetheart," Marci says. She holds my bed rail and smiles. "How are you feeling?"

"These drugs are incredible, whatever they are."

"I'm glad you're comfortable."

I try to articulate words, but I end up slurring every time I try to say anything intelligent. I give up and settle for saying what's on my mind. "Marci, I wanna see my new pussy."

You just said pussy to a surgeon. Real classy, Paige.

Sarah says, "I think she's high."

Marci says, "We can have a peek now if you like?"

Faced with the possibility, I begin second guessing that desire. It hasn't even been a day, and I probably resemble freshly sliced meat. But I'm eager to feel better about myself, so I say, "I want to look."

Marci pulls down the sheets and exposes my frog-spread legs encased in robotic foam leg masseurs. She helps me free of them, takes the band of my hospital underwear, and pulls them down. I lift my hips so she can remove them, and Marci peels back the gauze covering my lap.

Sarah sucks on her teeth, cringing. She seems to realize her mistake and holds out a hand. "It's not bad. It's just raw. I actually didn't think it would be this nice already."

I try to look past my stomach, but other than a slight puffiness where my penis used to be, I can't see anything. Without thinking, I reach down, but Marci catches my arm in a firm grip.

"No touching," Marci says. "This is some of my best work. You might need a little tweak on one side, but we won't know until the swelling goes down."

Another wave of nausea forces me to lie back.

Sarah digs in her backpack and offers out a foundation compact.

I open it and lower it between my legs. It takes a moment for my drugged brain to negotiate the angle. I expected the worst, but in the mirror is a perfectly shaped vulva. A little puffy, a little Frankenstein's monster with ugly black stitches poking from my inner thighs and a catheter tube snaking out of my urethra. But for the first time in my life, I don't see testicles or a penis. As I stare, I start to doubt that this is reality.

Perhaps it's my drug-drenched brain, but I can't mentally connect the thing I'm looking at to my body. I have visualized this moment dozens of times, and in those fantasies, I'm performing mental cartwheels of euphoric joy. Instead, the only thing I feel is relief.

I want to believe that relief results from the affirmation of remedying a body part that should have always been there. That is what all the trans literature seems to suggest I should experience, but perhaps it's too early for joy. As I stare at my puffy, beautifully imperfect labia, the familiar dissonant dysphoric notes I normally feel when I look between my legs seem to quieten.

While this relief might not be joy, it could be closure. It's the end of a five-year battle with a rigid, ableist system that chooses only the fit to receive surgery. And it's realizing that this might be the first day I can start to learn how to love myself.

Part 5

Disconnect

◖ 23 ◗

Twilight

On the dance floor, I'm able to forget my insecurities and the lingering sting of being mocked by the two wrinkly lesbians at the gay bar across the street. The club twinkles with tinsel, and fairy lights in white, red, and green. Their bulbs gleam in expanding coronas and make me wonder just how much I have had to drink. I once again spot the trans man staring at me and dance up to him. He smiles and grinds against me, and as the bass drops and the chorus thumps, everyone throws their hands in the air, and we all leap in time with the beat.

He yells into my ear and says my accent is cute and asks me where I'm from, but then he's pulled away by a jealous girlfriend. I watch him be absorbed by the mass of writhing bodies and realize the building pressure in my bladder. I push through the crowd to the back of the club where everyone is lounging on the floor and making out.

No longer supported by the throng of dancers, I stumble and the world spins on its axis. I try to balance myself and wait for the world to align, but I notice how the neon red of a beer sign seems to smear and blur across the bar, like a watercolour painting left in a storm. The colours bleed across the wall, and the tiny fairy lights are now almost intolerably bright.

I'm not sure just how long I was standing there, but I vaguely acknowledge that Stuart, the guy from the gay bar across the street, is trying to get my attention. He looks concerned. He's about sixty, with grey hair and small, piggy eyes. He's been kind, though, and bought me two glasses of wine in the bar, and three times now he's had a glass waiting for me when I return from dancing. I've now even forgiven him for asking if I still have a dick. While this much wine isn't usually too much for me, tonight it feels as if I've polished off a barrel.

Stuart has a hand on my shoulder and asks, "Do you want to go home?"

"I'm fine," I shout above the music. "Gotta pee." I pull Stuart's hand off and stumble away. My leg doesn't respond, and I bump into a wall, but catch myself, hand slapping cold ceramic tile. That cute trans man pulls away from his girlfriend, and though I can't understand him, I think he asks if I'm okay. I nod and wave him off and sway into a blindingly bright bathroom.

I sit and pee and try to make the bathroom stop spinning. I silently swear off any more wine. When I reach the mirror, I'm shocked to see how badly my makeup has run. I sway into a stall, grab some toilet paper, and smear under my eyes, trying to clean myself up. Before I left the house, my stepmother, who I was instructed to call Mum, had curled my hair and helped me apply this makeup. And despite being drunk, I've managed not to spill anything on the new outfit my stepsister thoughtfully bought when I showed up in England with nothing but jeans and women's-cut t-shirts. After my dad left us to return to his birth home in England all those years ago, I never anticipated that meeting my new extended family across the pond could be so therapeutic. Maybe it's easier for them to accept me because they've only ever known Paige?

Outside the bathroom, everyone cheers as some pop number I've never heard before comes on, like a British version of Rihanna's "Umbrella." The entire club vocalizes the la-la-la in "Twilight."

While deceptively catchy, I don't feel like cheering or dancing. All I want is sleep.

The edges of my vision blur and darken, leaving a squirming, shadowy tunnel to the bathroom exit. Something is wrong. Somehow, I've lost control and drank too much. I swing open a bathroom stall and fall to my knees. Now there is a porcelain bowl in front of me and someone is holding my hair. I try to shove fingers down my throat, but I keep stabbing my cheek.

The next thing I know, I'm at the bar. I realize I've lost time and panic seizes me, cold and sobering. I realize that it's possible I might pass out in this club with little idea of where I am, in another country entirely, at risk of being robbed or worse. Some of the blurry edges of my world sharpen.

The bartender who earlier introduced himself as Ken is some extra-large guy wearing an extra-small tank top. He's cute with icy eyes like a husky. The side of his head is shaved. He leans over the bar and shouts. "You're cut off, I'm sorry."

I shake my head and try to reply, but the words I say don't make sense. It's as if my tongue is twice the size it should be.

Extra-large Ken asks, "What was that?"

I concentrate on slowly forming words. "Help me. Need a cab."

"Are you okay?"

I shrug.

"We're going to take care of you." He asks someone to take over at the bar. "Are you with anyone?"

I point across the dancefloor and wait until it clears enough so I can single out Stuart and say, "Him." Stuart is now sitting with the male sex worker he just introduced me to.

Ken says, "Don't go anywhere." He disappears.

Since I'm leaving, I figure it's only polite to say goodbye to the guy who bought me drinks all night. People seem to be more polite now and make way for me as I travel across the dance floor, and I nearly spill all the drinks on Stuart's table when I grab the edge.

"Sorry." I make a half-hearted attempt at mopping up some of the alcohol with a napkin. I say, "I'm going. Thanks for —" I forget the word for wine, so I just point at a glass, which has magically refilled again.

Stuart shouts against my ear, "It's not safe to go like this. Come with us. My hotel isn't far."

I kiss Stuart on the cheek. "Nope. Already called a cab."

When I stumble back, Stuart rises as if he's about to reach for me, but then stops as Ken catches me. He's about as strong as I expected. Ken shouts something and Stuart's face creases, and I can't figure out why he looks so furious. I'm led away, and next thing I know, I'm standing outside with Ken, and my arms are cold, and people are sucking on cigarettes.

Ken asks, "Did you bring a coat?"

"Don't remember."

"You don't sound like you're from around here."

"Nope, Canada."

"Do you know how to get home?"

"Aha!" I dig in my purse, thankful to still discover the phone my dad leant me. I hold my thumb on the button and it opens. I click on notes, and the address pops up. I shove the phone in Ken's face.

"Good. Do you have money?"

I nod.

Then I'm on a highway.

The driver is talking to me about Toronto. Then about how he wishes he could own a big truck like they drive in America. When we stop, he hands me back some money, but I make him keep a little more than he says he deserves. I stuff the rest in my purse.

The cabbie says, "I'll wait here to make sure you get in okay."

I waggle housekeys at the cab window and stagger to the gate and throw that open. The world darkens in my periphery, creating a tunnel that leads to the front door. I hold out the key and walk forward, aiming at the lock. I stab at the lock and manage to wiggle the key in. I turn and push and stagger inside. I close the door. The familiar scent of birds and old carpet. I lock the door. I drop the keys.

I stumble through the kitchen and into the living room, where Dad set up the inflatable mattress. I drop my purse and fall face first into my pillow.

I give in and allow the darkness to claim me.

▚▚▚

My headache wakes me just after noon. As I wait for the kettle to boil, I notice a letter on the table.

> *We hope you had a great night. We're down at the shops.*
> *Please don't leave things lying in the hall.*
> *— Love, Dad and Mum*

After a shower and having discovered something called Nurofen in the cabinet, the world makes sense again. The house is quiet, other than the occasional screech from one of Mum's birds. I sit on my bed and boot up my laptop. When I see that Kali's icon is green, I walk back the hours and discover that it must be six or seven in the morning for him, and it might be the earliest I've ever seen him awake.

```
You say: Hey early riser. What are you doing up?
Kali says: I was worried about you. How was the
bar?
You: It was a weird night. I think it was fun,
though.
```

Kali: Any hot guys try to pick you up?

I vaguely remember the cute trans guy, but decide against sharing my thoughts on him, or Stuart.

You: Lol! I came home alone, don't worry. Want to video chat?

Kali: Sure. Give me five minutes to sign off with my mom?

Kali calls me as I'm walking back with another cup of tea. I answer, and when his face leaps onto the screen with that familiar smile, my heart leaps.

"You look wet," Kali says.

"Let me send you some pics from last night." I go through my photos and send shots of me dolled up for the club. I make sure I send one with my shirt slightly open, so he can see a glimpse of my bra.

Kali whistles. "You look hot. Wow, you've got breasts now."

"Want to see 'em?"

"Uhm, yes!"

I wiggle away from the camera and drag up my top until the soft swells of my immature breasts appear over the flash of my white belly in the video frame. When I tug down my shirt and stretch out, resting on my elbows to talk to him, Kali is grinning devilishly. I say, "They've been growing."

"I can see that! Your nipples look bigger too."

"They are," I say. "I'm so glad we're talking again."

"Me too."

"I just needed some time to figure things out."

Wrinkles form on Kali's forehead as something chimes in his room. Kali picks up his phone, looks concerned, then taps at the screen. He glances up, seems to consider something, then puts the phone down. "Sorry, it's my mom. I'll message later. So, when are you coming back from England again?"

"In a week."

"Then you're coming to see me, right?"

"Or you could come to my place."

Another chime and Kali glances at his phone. "Sorry." He types out a long message, then makes a show of putting the phone face down. "I still need a passport. But maybe you could come here? I'll even pay for your ticket."

In the interest of rebuilding bridges, I resist the urge to remind him how many times I've asked him to get that passport. Instead, I say, "That sounds nice. I miss seeing you."

"I miss you too," Kali says, and excuses himself for the bathroom with his phone.

While he's away, I open Facebook and look up Kali's page. There's a new picture of him in an orange and yellow toque. Some girl named Ariel says that she's happy it fits, and that it looks great on him.

When Kali returns, I say, "I like your Jayne toque. I didn't know you liked *Firefly* so much."

"Oh, you saw that?"

I try to keep things light. "So, who's Ariel?"

"Just a friend."

"That knits you hats?"

Kali says, "I haven't slept yet. I need to lie down for a bit. My mom is picking me up in a couple of hours to spend Christmas together."

I let it go. "That sounds fun. Does she know about us yet?"

Kali looks sheepish and goes quiet.

"We've been together for four years," I say, "and you still haven't told her about me?"

"Well, she knows about you."

I ask, "She knows that I'm trans?"

"I promise I will tell her over Christmas. It'll be easier in person."

When we sign off, I return to Facebook. I pore through Kali's pictures and discover that Ariel has liked every single one. Though

Kali doesn't post a lot, Ariel has had something nice to say about them all. Under the picture with Kali in the pompom-topped hat, a new response appears.

Ariel says: I hope the hat keeps you warm when you come visit. <3

I slam the laptop shut.

◥ 24 ◣

How

Far from the safety of busy cities, away from the bloody slaughter of endless war fronts, at the edge of mapped civilization lies a
magical grove protected by snow-capped mountains. To reach this
sanctuary, one must face treacherous mountain passes and ancient
horrors, but should you survive, you'll emerge into a lush tropical
valley filled with tall, fragrant, flower-tufted grasses that sway lazily
with the perpetual warm breezes which blow through the vale.

Pale saucer-eyed lizards clamber up fruit trees untouched by
human hands. They feed on fat glow-bugs that struggle to stay
aloft on wings too small for their bulbous bodies.

Near the middle of the valley is a small lake cluttered with reeds
and iridescent water lilies, upon which rest fat, throatily croaking
bullfrogs. Half-sunken are the remains of a wooden dock where
I now sit, stringing my fishing rod and my thoughts. I cast my
line, and the bobber plunks into the placid surface. Rings cascade
outward, and bullfrogs bob upon their lily pads. I don't believe this

lake spawns any fishing locations, but just sitting here and doing nothing feels unproductive.

The rings calm, but bubbles rise to the surface, perhaps disturbed by some muck-dwelling fish interested in the twisting worm thrashing in the weeds. Even amongst this tranquility, I can't think of a way to tell him. They say love is enough, but is it? How can this be love if he's keeping me a secret?

A larger cluster of bubbles appear, then another, then the surface of the lake boils with them. I reach for my fire staff. The bubbles surge toward me, stringing across the surface of the water. A geyser of water explodes into the air, and from it leaps a shrieking werewolf.

Clinging to its tawny water-soaked body are large red crayfish pinched to its fur, dangling from its face, and some clinging to its flailing limbs and tail.

"Get them off!" the werewolf shouts. It flaps its arms, turns in circles as it grabs crayfish, rips them free, and tosses them into the water.

"Kali?" It's hard to believe anyone could find this place, let alone him.

Kali grabs the last crustacean, de-grips the pincer from his canine ear, and snarls at it. The crayfish snaps menacingly. Kali tosses it over his shoulder, and the wiggly legged mudbug plunks into the lake.

"Hey there, gorgeous," Kali says. He shakes his fur out, startling lizards into nearby trees. I cover my face and cringe, letting the spray drip from me. Now looking puffed, but dry, Kali strides forward, grinning and suave. "I had a hard time finding you."

I wring out my fishing hat and return to the dock only to find that Kali's explosive entrance must have washed my fishing supplies, my lunch, and the rod away. I stare across the lake, watching the water hurrying to return to tranquility. I sit and watch the tiny waves lap against the reedy shore.

Kali crouches beside me. "I've been worried about you." He plays with my hair, and I try not to pull away. He seems to note my lack of response and leans back on his hands. "You've been really hard to find since you've been back."

"Sorry."

Kali says, "You haven't been on *Second Life* in a month, and you haven't answered your Skype messages. Then I find you here, in a game that nobody even plays anymore. Did I do something wrong?"

I could have used that opportunity to confront him about all the warning signs I've ignored, but I've tried to fix this relationship too many times already. He always withdraws and goes quiet the moment I confront him, so I tried a heartfelt letter, which he avoided. Then there was the disaster argument we had about the girl on Facebook he visited, "as a friend," and, of course, the ex-girlfriend roommate he lives with. If I bring these up, I'll get nowhere, or worse, he'll call me hormonal and I'll feel unreasonable, and I'll never get around to saying the one thing I need to.

Instead, I say, "You haven't done anything wrong, I guess."

Kali rests his hand on my thigh. "You guess?" I push his hand off, and he recoils, cradling his paw as if I had pinched him with another crayfish.

I say, "I think we should break up." My heart races, but I feel like I can breathe again.

"Why would you want that?" The pain in his voice suggests surprise and proves he hasn't been paying attention to the things I've been saying during our last few fights. It eases the pain of elaborating.

I shuffle away from him and say, "I'll explain, but promise me you won't interrupt."

There is a long moment of silence. Accompanying the rustle of him eventually unmuting his mic, his voice has a slight hiccup. "Fine, but then you need to let me try to win you back."

"That's not how this works."

"At least promise me that." His words are slurred, as if spoken through clenched teeth.

I sigh. "I will let you have your say before I log off."

After another long pause Kali says, "Okay."

I wish I had time to gather my thoughts, but I try to recall some points from my letter. "You haven't had a job in over a year. If we hope to have the future you hint at, how can we if you —"

Kali interrupts, "I'm trying. I bought a truck to put out resumés."

"But Kali, you don't have ambitions. I'm going back to school and applying for jobs to pursue my writing. What are your dreams?"

Only Kali's increasingly agitated breath pants into my headphones for a disturbingly long time. He says, "Those things aren't important to me. My only dream is to be with you. I'll find a job. I'll get money, and we'll make it work. That's what people who love each other do."

His words sting. I realize he's trying to turn what I'm saying against me. I go on, "That might be enough if you were Canadian, but you live across a border and on the other side of the continent. If we ever hope to be together, we need a lot of money." I wonder if I'm being cold-hearted for focusing on our financial security.

Through my headphones, I hear the plodding steps of Kali pacing. "You don't have a job either."

"There's nothing holding you back from finding a job if you're not picky. I'm an awkward trans woman who's just started hormones, trying to figure out how to dress myself on a budget. I'm a mess and nobody will hire me."

"Baby, don't say that. You're beautiful."

"It's true. Every day someone laughs, or yells, or threatens me if I dare go outside. At least when I'm online, people accept my characters as women. You have no idea how difficult it is to just keep living when you're being humiliated and ridiculed every single day. Do you know what it's like trying to sit across from someone who can barely look at you in a job interview?"

"Yes, I do," Kali says indignantly, "because I'm here for you when you talk about it."

"But your words are not enough if you can't hold me."

We sit in silence.

I regret saying it.

Though I know those words for truth the moment I say them, it hurts to admit I need human contact. That admission also helps me to realize that online relationships aren't enough for me anymore.

All through my life, this window into a digital world was my salvation — so why does it now feel like a shackle? I hadn't realized how much I needed to be held until just now. But everything I said was accurate, and I hate myself for acknowledging that I am not enough.

Kali says, "Don't do this. We need each other. We'll figure out . . ."

I pull off my glasses, rub my eyes, and dislodge my headphones. There's nothing to figure out. Kali's voice continues to buzz the earphone speaker dangling by my neck. I stare at the screen, looking at the slender elven wizard and hunched werewolf sitting by the edge of the pond. Across the room, through the glass door of my balcony, a raven lands on the railing, its black wings shining iridescent blues and purples as it picks bugs out of my planter box.

Though I debate logging out, I note that Kali called my name. I resign myself to seeing this through. I replace my glasses and headset.

"Sorry," I say, "I needed tissue."

"I'm sorry, I had to say that."

While I'm curious about what he's said, something warns me not to ask. "Okay," I say. "Those things aside, the biggest problem is that I'm lonely because —"

"Is this your hormones? You say you want me to get a job, but then you want company?"

"It's difficult being on my own. My job laid me off, and my ex is threatening to sue me for wedding fees because, according to her, I deceived her and her family. Did I tell you she wants to annul the marriage?"

"No, but isn't that what you want?"

"I want a divorce, not to confirm that I tricked her into marrying a woman. I don't even know why she wants it, but I'm sure she has a motive."

Kali says, "I'm sorry, baby." I cringe, mostly at how much I still enjoy hearing him say that. He continues, "But you have your friend Kris there."

"Kris says I've changed. Maybe I have. He mostly hangs out with our friend Steve, doing 'guy things.'"

"I'm sorry, baby."

Baby again.

I say, "Listen, Jason."

"You used my real name." Kali sounds shocked.

"Is that okay?"

"It sounds weird."

We listen to each other breathe through our microphones. Neither of us volunteers to advance this doomed conversation.

It would hurt him more to know how I was unable to reconcile the discordance between our emotional connection and our physical incompatibility. No part of that trip fit the fictional relationship ideal we had envisioned. In retrospect, I should have recognized it sooner. You could see how awkward we were in every picture together, in our bedroom attempts, and even his refusal to hold my hand in public. Jason and Paige could never be Kali and Lydia, not until these too-slow hormones do their job, and not until I can, one day, afford the required surgery so we can *fit* the way we do online — the way I need us to. Until such a day, Kali and I are restricted by the limitations of our keyboards, and headphones, and when we reach out to touch each other, there's always a screen in the way. I can't allow myself to suffer being untouched in a digital daydream for another four years.

I say, "I need to find someone here."

"Can I speak now?" Kali asks.

"Yes."

"First, you said that you were okay with having an online relationship. You said that relationships in the game are better than Real Life because —"

"Things change," I interrupt. "My needs have changed. You live with your ex — you have friends and family you can talk to when you log out. I have nothing. When we log out, while you're living your life, I have nothing. An online relationship isn't enough."

"This is my turn," Kali says, "remember?"

"You're right. I'm sorry."

"Lyd . . . Paige, it won't always be like this. We love each other. Doesn't that mean anything?"

I say, "Everything we've shared has been magical. I'll never forget those moments, but I need more."

Something thumps and brushes loudly against Kali's mic. "You'll regret doing this."

Of course. I already do. And it hurts so much talking this through instead of going by my original plan to just tell him and log out. Tears sting my eyes, and I mute my mic until I'm confident I'm not going to start sobbing. I remove my glasses and clean a tear off the lens. I breathe a few times before I unmute.

"I might regret it," I say. Kali's character freezes, but through his mic I can hear him gasping every few seconds. Through the headset there is a crash followed by tinkling glass. "Kali?" I call into my mic.

Kali's mic rustles and thuds. Someone stomps away from the mic and mutters. Then the stomping thunders toward the mic, and after a deafening rustle, Kali says, "I need to clean something, and my hand is bleeding. Will you still be here after I take care of this?"

"Yes," I hurriedly say, "take care of yourself. I promise I'll stay."

"Thank you." The headset clatters and thuds again.

I sit by his idle character at the edge of the lake. The frogs harrumph to themselves, and the water has calmed to glass. High in the canopy, tropical birds cry for each other in the twilight. Of all the years I've known Kali, I've never seen him lose his temper. It goes to show how little I may truly know about him. How little we can know about anyone online.

One thing I've enjoyed most about online relationships is how easily I can pick what others know about me. But now I see there's also no place online to observe the unconscious nuances of your loved one's life — those little things that only someone close would know. I've never had an opportunity to see if his self-conscious lips purse when he concentrates, or the way he might run his fingers through his hair when he's worried, or apparently how he breaks things when he's frustrated and angry enough. I hadn't considered before that Kali might be capable of hurting me.

Kali shuffles back to the mic. "Hello? Are you still here?"

"Yes, I'm here."

He fiddles with the headset. "What if I drove up right now?"

The thought is preposterous. It would take more than a day to drive all the way here, and in that ridiculously huge pickup he bought, it would be prohibitively expensive. He can't afford to follow through with this.

I ask, "You're going to drive from Texas to Ontario right now?"

"Yes," he says. "Would that change anything?"

"Supposing you even had a passport, I don't know. Maybe? It's possible we might work things out, and we might have an enjoyable time while you're here, but the moment you leave the same problems would remain."

Another long silence.

He'd probably say anything to keep me. His desperation is breaking my heart, and I know that if I don't log out soon, I'm going to give in.

Kali says, "You've helped me learn so much about myself. No one will ever treat you as well as I can. Please, Paige, don't do this."

"I wish this were enough for me, that we were enough, but I need more. If you can't be here for me, I have to find someone who can."

"You will," Kali says, his voice filled with despair. "But I can do all that for you, just give me more time."

"I have to go," I say. "I'm sorry. I'll always love you and what we had, but I have to do this."

"How can you be so cold?"

My chest shakes as I struggle to contain my sobbing. I know I will be a mess in mere minutes. "I can't stay. I can't do this. Bye, Kali. I love you. I hope you find someone too."

A dialogue springs open.

Kali would like to initiate a hug. [Accept? YES / NO]

I move the pointer down, past the dialog box, to the corner of the screen and I click EXIT TO WINDOWS.

If you log out now, you will lose your saved progress. Leave anyway? [YES / NO]

I click yes.

The screen flashes white — the magical vale disappears, I disappear, and Kali disappears too. I don't bother shutting down properly, and instead jam my finger into the computer's power button, holding it down until it forces the system off. After several seconds, the music I was playing cuts abruptly, the speakers pop, the loud cooling fans whir and slow to silence, the screen fades to black, and my apartment is overwhelmingly, eerily silent.

Outside my balcony doors, cars whoosh by on the distant highway. Closer is the monotonous drone of someone mowing their lawn, and a bird is singing to another in a nearby tree.

Tears drip from my cheeks, and my chest heaves, but I allow myself to be drawn by the sounds of life. I step onto my balcony and am surrounded by the walls of greenery I've been growing. Flowers and fresh herbs spill from planter boxes. I hold the cool steel rail, the rough bite of curling paint flakes scratch my palms. Fragrant summer breezes caress my face. Far below me, some apartment kids have set up a banana-coloured Slip 'N Slide on the front lawn. I watch as they race each other, squealing as they tumble end over end.

I collapse into a wicker chair, my chest heaving. I bury my face in my hands and cry, snot dripping through my fingers, and I'm thankful to be surrounded by my privacy wall of plants.

My phone rings.

◖ 25 ◗

Somebody to Love

2013 — Three months later

A car slows down as it rounds the corner. It's the third time this orange Mustang has passed me, so I'm sure something is going on. Someone yells something that sounds like faggot out of the car, and when I look, I notice an arm drawing back. I jerk away from the road just in time as a fountain drink explodes on the sidewalk. Ice shatters into shards and a wave of Pepsi splashes up the wall next to where I stood just moments ago. The Mustang's engine roars, and two blocks down it turns a corner.

I run down a side street and hide behind a tree in case they come back for a fourth pass.

Generally, it's getting easier to ignore people like that, especially if they're going fast and I can't understand what they're saying. I can usually avoid comments altogether if I keep my head down and stare into my phone. I open Facebook and am greeted with a notification of a new response in the "Well-Known Secret Society" group. Natalie D is responding to Misandry J's post: "Being trans is playing life on expert mode."

The group has been chatting about this for days.

One thread splinters off, discussing how being trans is like rolling a D&D character. Vanessa S says she started her character at level twenty-five, but she's a natural rogue. Natalie D says she loves bards and will always invite them to her party, while Scarlet T says that someone once called her a bard and she doesn't speak to them anymore. Rani B wonders what's with all the bard hate and calls herself a bad bard bitch. Then the thread explodes. Everyone weighs in on what character class they most resemble.

Ellie D wonders if all trans women grew up as geeks in their youth with all this talk about role-playing and video games. Skye M responds that there are probably a lot of trans women who play games because they are an escape from the harshness of society. She also suggests that many trans women turn to drugs for the same reason. Then that thread splinters into a sub-thread with both confirming and conflicting stories from members discussing their addictions.

The rest of the threads branch into different aspects of video games. Isabela-Fay H suggests we get fifty Xbox achievement points the first time we're told we're brave. Megan K says she's got glitched code. Skye M says her game is broken. Aine Ni D announces that she just unlocked the Transsexual Menace achievement. I say I've recently re-rolled my character, but I'm having difficulty finding party members, and a few people offer to join my party. Jaye W calls us nerds.

A few people start a serious sub-thread about the therapeutic benefits of gaming. I bring up how *Second Life* has helped me, and others chime in with similar stories, but then goofy comments and furry criticism drown our thread. I give up pursuing the discussion.

I feel less alone since I joined the society, and I've made friends through it, but there's been a lot of infighting lately. People have been unfollowing, and there's talk about the group folding altogether, which is depressing.

Since it's been a while now since I've heard the Mustang, I get brave enough to continue walking home. When I turn onto my street, my Wi-Fi connects, and a notification appears on my phone, announcing that I have fifteen new email messages on OKCupid. I was initially optimistic about online dating, especially on a site that focuses on compatibility and shared interests, but now I see it more like buying scratch tickets. I invest in my profile, but mostly I end up disappointed. Still, I enjoy the anticipation, even if at least half of my messages end up being from men wanting me to peg them. I pocket my phone to enjoy the anticipation of reading them on my computer.

Inside, I light incense, pour a tea, and log in. I delete the aggressive payment reminder emails and open OKCupid.

I rip through all the chaser messages who call me princess and goddess, and those who think that unsolicited nudes might entice me. That leaves only three potential nibbles.

`Tye905 replies: Hey RabbitPaige, I know we've been talking, but I just saw you're trans. You're hella passable, but I'm not gay. Gimme a ring if you get the surgery.`

I delete the message and sip some tea.

`GrumpyGuts replies: That's awesome! I think we get along great too, but I have something to confess. I'm married, but my wife thinks you're cute. Think you might give a threesome a try?`

My heart sinks as I delete the message. I really liked him.

`SarahJaneK9 replies: You actually knew where my handle was from! You'd be surprised about what people think I'm into because of this name. My favourite Doctor is Tennant, but I have a soft spot for Tom Baker and his scarf. Who is yours?`

I reply that Tennant is also my favourite Doctor, and Sarah pops online. She responds immediately, and soon we're messaging back and forth. We move to Facebook, and I'm looking through her pictures. She comments on mine, and then I realize that we've been texting each other through dinner time.

We talk about our favourite video games, how she's gathered every achievement in *Assassin's Creed*, how she has a soft spot for Japanese thriller games, and then she shares a few pictures of her in her goth phase. Black lips and pouty. Her Lolita dress looks more expensive than my car. I forget to eat, and we talk about our favourite horror writers until almost midnight. On a whim, I ask if she would like to go on a date tomorrow. She says she's not busy and promises to buy me the new Joe Hill novel when we go out.

We reluctantly sign off, both saying how excited we are to meet each other. When I lie down to sleep, I feel like I'm floating — until I realize we were so distracted by each other that I forgot to confirm she knows I'm trans.

▗▄▖

The elevator opens, and I walk toward Sarah's door. My heart races. I wipe my palms on my jeans and knock. While I debated messaging Sarah on the way here to forewarn her, I couldn't think of an easy way to bring up that I'm trans, so I abandoned the idea.

But as footsteps thump toward the door, I wish I hadn't.

A woman opens the door. She says, "You must be Paige. Sarah is almost ready."

I follow her roommate into the living room, and I'm surrounded by anime DVD boxed sets, video game promotional posters, and crocheted Doctor Who monsters. While I'm waiting, I pick up a squishy white Adipose. I wonder how long it must have taken to crochet, and it helps distract me from worrying about what Sarah will think of me. I've mastered a skill of positioning cameras to only capture the most feminine aspects of my features, but there are no such MySpace angles in Real Life. Beads of sweat drip down my cleavage as I nervously wait for Sarah to be disgusted by the real me.

Sarah emerges from a room dressed in a puffy-sleeve blouse and shiny black shoes. Her hair is curled, with perfect laser-straight bangs, and her makeup is freshly applied. A porcelain doll stands before me, and in comparison I feel like I'm about to go chorin' in my jeans.

When she walks up to me, I notice she's shaking — vibrating, actually. She clasps her hands to steady them. She stops before me and just smiles, waiting.

"You look adorable," I say.

"You really think that?"

"Absolutely." The pictures she shared made her look a little skinnier than she is in person, but I'm no stranger to that form of deception. "If you still want to go, my car is outside."

Sarah says, "I definitely want to go."

We take the elevator, each of us sneaking glances. Soon we're driving down the highway. Though I'm sure she's guessed by now, I want to get the unicorn out of the room. I ask, "Did you notice my disclaimer at the bottom of my profile?"

"Disclaimer?"

"That I'm trans."

"Oh."

We drive past an exit. I move over a lane, just in case she wants me to use the next exit and take her home. I think about what I'll do with the rest of my day if she rejects me. While there are a lot of productive things I could do, I'll likely just look up Kali again and hate-scroll through all the cute things he's doing with his new girlfriend, Ariel, the one he was "only friends" with.

Sarah says, "I didn't know. I just thought you had a smoky deep voice. I don't care, though."

While it's hard to believe she didn't suspect it, I smile despite myself.

Sarah wrings her hands.

I ask, "Do I make you nervous?"

"No!" Sarah says. "I'm just worried that you won't like me."

I splutter and laugh before I can restrain myself. "Why wouldn't I like you? You're adorable."

"I haven't had much luck dating."

"I know what you mean."

Sarah says, "My last date was with a guy who turned me down at the door when he saw how fat I am. My roommate talked me out of cancelling our date today, actually."

The next exit is over two kilometres away.

I say, "I thought we were getting along . . ."

"We are. I just don't think I can handle someone as amazing as you doing something like that to me."

And then I get it.

The only thing more popular on television than mocking trans women are fat jokes. Society ridicules and blames us for our perceived poor life decisions, but the truth is, our appearance is often far from a choice. And truly, it is only society's perceived expectation of normalcy that dictates that we don't belong. Neither of us are flawed. Both of us are beautiful — just the way we are. While the world may one day better understand us, for now we find common ground as outcasts. As outsiders, we are sometimes both overwhelmed by societal pressure and try to integrate with surgery and body concealing garments. And when we are alone, we grieve our perceived social failings, and we do our best to forget the cruelties of the world by escaping any way we can.

I hold out my hand to Sarah, whose eyes have pooled with tears. She hesitantly laces her fingers in mine, and I squeeze her smaller hand reassuringly.

I say, "You never have to worry about that with me."

Connected by Love

**2018 - Five years later,
in a rental house in the Hammer**

Deep breaths and try to relax, that's what the nurse said.

I hold a green plastic dilator, its tip curved to make insertion easier, but unnaturally chilled from being stored in a room with drafty windows. Outside, late January snow is falling. Fat flakes gather into little drifts in our window frames. It's beautiful to watch, but those flakes accumulate swiftly, and that means I'll have to waddle outside to shovel again soon. However, I dread shovelling less than pushing this dilator into my swollen, post-surgical pussy. The task is painful, but essential, and while I have my doubts, they say if I don't do this several times a day, I'll heal and lose depth, and I'll regret my cowardice for the rest of my life.

"Baby," I ask, "pass the lube?"

Cuddled up in blankets next to me on a pull-out couch, Sarah watches *Sense8* on the television near our feet. She sorts through a basket full of medical ointments, estrogen patches, and colostomy supplies, and pulls out a squeeze bottle of water-based medical lubricant I bought on the cheap from my colostomy supply store.

Sarah asks, "Didn't you just do this?"

I take the bottle and squelch a Hershey's Kiss of glistening lube onto the tip of the dilator. "Only two more times today, after this."

"Did you want me to hold your hand?"

"No, I need both hands."

In slow, gelatinous globs, lube sneaks down the shaft. While I've always known this would be my aftercare, I fantasized that fucking myself with a dildo would be sexier. I envisioned openly complaining about the chore of stretching myself with a piece of plastic several times a day but secretly craving the task. I only hope that as my nerve endings heal, and sensation returns, I'll feel something other than pain.

I coax the lube down the shaft with my fingertips, careful not to smear too much away from the tip. I lube up one finger and spread my knees and slicken my entrance, working a finger in. I'm already a little wet, but tight, even with a single finger, and so this starter dilator is more intimidating than it should be.

Marci gave me a full set of dilators, each increasing in girth. Tomorrow, I graduate to the second, and in another week or two, the third. The last dilator, which I call The Violator, is a thick orange beast that waits ominously for me in its velvet sleeve.

I nose the dilator between swollen labia and take deep breaths to relax my inner muscles. I push in. Not an inch inside, and my muscles clamp onto the intruder and refuse to budge. Pushing harder only spikes the sharp pain, and sweat beads on my forehead. I try rotating, rocking back and forth, but that just makes it squeak inside. I pull out slightly, then I coax some back in and make headway.

I pause, and whine, and sob pathetically for myself.

Sarah pets my arm as we watch Nomi, enviably, fucking her girlfriend with a rainbow strap-on. After almost twenty minutes of coaxing, I finally sink the dilator all the way in to the third marker on its shaft. Only four inches, though it feels like twice that. My pussy throbs around the intruder, inner muscles flexing, trying to push it out. Since the surgery used a lot of my existing "material," as Marci called it, I thought, surely this would feel like someone stroking my shaft, but it doesn't — it's entirely new.

I'm surprised how fast my brain rewired to recognize that I now, somehow, have a vagina. A healing, painful, wounded vagina, perhaps — and though it hurts, and this process is frightening, there's something sexy about how unique and natural it feels when I finally have this inserted in my body. It's a sensation I've never experienced, even in dreams, as if my brain has been eager to surprise me.

I breathe out slowly as sweat drips down my nose. "Okay, I'm in."

Sarah taps the box of wine beside the bed and pours two glasses. "How long again?"

"Fifteen minutes." I take the glass and angle it carefully to my mouth before slurping its contents down in three big gulps and handing it back. I rest both hands on the end of the dilator, gripping firmly so it doesn't push out again. It doesn't take long for the alcohol to go to my head, and everything goes numb and spins — no doubt boosted from the cocktail of meds with labels that warn against this behaviour.

Sarah uses her phone to set an alarm.

I close my eyes and try to be somewhere else. On the television, Sun kicks the ass of someone who sorely deserves it. I want to be like her, to be strong, to stand before insurmountable odds and emerge confident and victorious on the other side. I want to show my family, my friends, and my haters how strong I am, and that I don't need their permission to feel this way. But it would all be for show — I don't feel strong at all.

Maybe it's because my lap is covered in ugly black stitches, and my pussy only feels pain as it recovers, but I feel like a compromised freak. I don't miss my penis. I doubt I ever will. But as I lay in this bed, weak and in pain, I can't help but wonder if life was so horrible with one. On one hand, I want to triumphantly shout that I've won, that on the other side of this pain I'll explode out of bed like a blazing phoenix to conquer my dreams — but as I lay in agony, with my pussy throbbing around a silicone dick substitute, I wonder if I've made a mistake.

I'm a forty-something trans woman who barely passes in public, with a colostomy, and now this? A four- or five-inch-deep pussy that I can't enjoy. Sarah's already told me she's happy no matter what my body looks like. But if I weren't dating Sarah, what would the chance be that any guy would want to be with a destitute, barely passing trans woman with a colostomy bag?

I hate being trans, and I hate everyone who hates trans people. I hate all the people who call us men, call us deceivers and worse. I especially hate all the people who think we transition because it's cool. As if anyone would ever choose to be trans and go through what we do.

With a musical chime, a phone wakes on the table and buzzes.

Sarah says, "That's time." Sarah hugs herself to my side, and I lean into her and sob. Soon my chest is heaving, and I'm crying into her shirt. I make the mistake of crying hard enough that I cough and my inner muscles contract hard around the dilator and it punches against and through my fingers, slides across the covers and clatters to the floor.

"Fuck!" I shout and double over in pain as I grip my swollen, lube-slicked pussy.

"Oh, no!" Sarah cups her mouth, mostly to avoid laughing at me.

I imagine the dildo firing out of me, and I can't help but laugh too, and soon we're both laughing so hard we're crying.

"Did you see?" I ask. I thumb the inside of my cheek to make a loud popping sound, and I point at the wall. "Like a rocket!"

Sarah hugs me, and we laugh together. My pussy aches, but the warmth of laughter is more healing than any of the drugs I'm on. Sarah fetches the now-cat-hair-coated dilator. She says, "Still hating everything when you're dilating?"

She knows me so well. As soon as the dilation is over, colour returns to the room, and my optimism comes flooding back. I say, "It's getting better."

"I'm sorry this is so hard. You're on a lot of opioids, and I think that you're going through post-surgical depression."

"That's a thing?" I ask, scrunching my nose to reposition my glasses as I clean up.

She rests her cheek on my shoulder. "Yeah, it might be anaesthesia withdrawal, or upset digestive bacteria from antibiotics, or because your body is in shock from the intense physical trauma. Just be easy on yourself. You're not thinking clearly."

I laugh despite myself. "You're so smart."

"I enjoy learning about the body." She holds up the dilator, her nose wrinkling in disgust as she inspects its hair- and grime-covered length. "I'll wash this for you and make lunch."

"Thank you, baby," I call after her. I power up my laptop and relax into the pillows as cooling fans whir to life. Maybe she's right. What if this is all in my head? The pain will lessen, the numbness will subside, and someday I'll be able to feel pleasure again — I'm sure of that.

As is typical, once I start on a self-loathing spiral, I search through horrific pre-transition pictures of myself. The wounded but healing *after* me reflecting on the badly lit before pictures of my life.

I open a picture of Kali and me, cuddled next to each other at the entrance of the Houston Zoo. My corporate office worker hair and facial stubble. How did he ever love me like that? He seemed to know I wouldn't always be the guy in this photo. I wonder if he ever imagined I'd turn out like this.

Back then, we fantasized about our future — after my transition and surgery. Kali would get a job, and I would work part time in a book shop, writing books on the side. We even talked about adopting a kid one day.

Maybe our timing was off. Maybe we weren't supposed to meet until after I had transitioned. Or maybe I just wasn't cut out to be the wife and mother I thought I was. So few of us know what we want to be until we're properly grown. Maybe some of us need to grow up more than once?

When it comes down to it, sometimes people destroy relationships because they are too close to understand how beautiful they are together. However, once something precious is shattered, it can never be properly reassembled. Sometimes the best thing you can do is pick up the shards worth keeping and share them with other people.

Another photo, this one from *Second Life*. A lithe and very naked cheetah cradles his arm around a curvy bunny girl. I took this screenshot moments after I told him about myself. I was vulnerable, and he was kind. We shared our names and pictures. While I didn't know it then, this moment was the first step in my transition — the first time I had ever openly told anyone, even myself, that I was a woman. I think I surprised myself more than him.

Exploring deeper in the computer, I find a hidden file section where I secreted away the *Second Life* program launcher. Through two computer transfers, the program remains. I click the icon and a progress bar slides across the screen as it reinstalls and updates. Moments later, the login screen loads. I panic and nearly kill the program, fearful that Sarah will return and not understand my sentimental need to explore this. That I needed, at least once more, to plug into that perfectly imperfect virtual world and escape.

Something is frying in the kitchen, so I probably have more time.

I surprise myself that I remember my login information; muscle memory perhaps. A cog wheel spins, and there is a bright flash of light. I slip on my headset, and the welcome sound jingles through the earphones.

The soft static of white noise digitizes into the rolling crash of nearby waves. I stand on a path under a large willow tree in front of a cottage. A comforting breeze hisses through thin willow leaves and carries with it the scent of the ocean. Far away a seagull jeers.

I'm overwhelmed that our place still stands. Kali and I once dreamed our future lives together on the other side of this red door. I remember Kali building our porch, how he bent me over the kitchen counter. The rent on this land surely should have run out by now, and all of this should have been derezzed, but I'm thankful to see it one last time.

I let myself in and wander through the house. As I walk toward the bedroom, an orange shadow slides past the back window.

"Kali?" I burst out the back door.

A chilled glass of lemonade rests on the arm of a lounge chair, and standing there in alarm is Kali. He's updated his appearance with a high poly avatar and now sports some distinguished greys in his orange fur. He looks good — fantastic even.

"Lydia?" Kali asks, "What are you doing here?"

I scan the area, worried I may have intruded on him introducing his wife to our previous life. I say, "I've been having a rough time. I wanted to remember something happy."

Kali says, "It's good to see you."

"Same. You look . . . hot, actually."

Kali pats the lounge chair beside him. "Thank you. I can't stay long, but we can chat a little?" Heartbeat pounding in my chest, I sit by Kali. He rests his hand on my knee and continues. "I saw on Facebook that you finally got the surgery you wanted."

I gather his hand, holding it in both of mine. "It's been a couple of weeks. I wish you could have been there to hold my hand."

Kali gazes over the water as he grips my hand tighter. "I wish that too. You're so beautiful, you know that? Not just Lyds, but the real you — Paige."

"You said that before I even transitioned."

"You were, but now everyone can see what I saw . . . I wish we could enjoy this new you, together."

"You're going to make me cry," I say. "But I think that time has passed."

Kali squeezes my hand knowingly and pulls his chair closer.

I say, "I'm sorry I hurt you. I was hurting too. I was scared and selfish, and some of those emotions might have been heightened by hormones. I think I threw us away."

Kali smiles and rubs my hand. We sit and watch the waves and listen to each other breathe.

Eventually, Kali says, "Don't be so hard on yourself. I'm not angry anymore, but I also wasn't entirely innocent back then. I wish I could be there and take care of you like I said I would. I'd bring you food, rub your feet, tuck you in, and . . ." Before I can stop him, Kali straddles my lap and presses his lips against mine.

I fumble to return the kiss, my mouth opening against his, our tongues sparring like no time had ever passed between us. Kali pulls away, stares into my eyes and says, "You will always be my bunny, no matter what."

"Oh, Kitty . . ." I say. "This might sound crazy, but wouldn't it be fun if someday we —" but I cut myself off as a baby's cry pierces through Kali's mic and freezes my heart. A second baby joins in chorus.

"Shit, wait a second," Kali says. He squeezes my hand, and his avatar freezes.

An invisible hand grabs my heart. "What am I doing?"

I pull a headphone away from my ear and listen to Sarah singing to Depeche Mode from the kitchen. The scent of veggie burgers is much stronger now. I stare at the screen and the waves lapping at the nearby shore, and how our avatars are wrapped around each other. Away from the headphones, somewhere far away in his apartment, Kali soothingly sings "Earth Angel."

The babies' cries soften.

Choking on the lump in my throat, I open the in-game mail client.

You mail to Kali: It was a nice surprise to see
you. Thank you for saying those kind things, and
I'm sorry I had to leave.

Do you remember the Christmas card you sent
years ago? You wrote, "If only in my dreams . . ."?
I still think about that sometimes. It's comforting
to know that a part of us was, and will forever be,
together in this place.

I hope that life is kind to you, and you've
found happiness. Goodbye. <3

I drag the pointer to the corner, open the system menu, and
shut down the program. I uninstall the client, and then push
myself to delete the entire hidden file folder. It feels like I'm
carving something out of my chest as I follow through and
empty the trash bin of every photo of Kali and Jason. Though I
fight back tears, and my chest heaves with the emotional effort
of purging Kali, I somehow resist crying.

But when I double-check that I have deleted everything, I'm
distracted by a familiar title in the program list:

Zork — The Great Underground Empire (DOS Emulator)

I forgot that I had bought the game to finally complete it after
all these years.

As I fight back tears, my throat is so tight I feel as if I'm going
to choke, I know that there is no better time to allow myself to be
swept away into a beautiful world of adventure. *Zork*, I'm coming
home. I double-click the icon, and my heart quickens in anticipation. I ready myself to be swallowed into a world of the grandest
of adventures.

West of House

You are standing in an open field west of a white
house, with a boarded front door.

There is a small mailbox here.

I could have sworn that it said something about tall grasses and
spooky forests . . . Where are the birds and the ivy on the house?

Certainly, there was more to this. A quick Google search confirms it's my memory at fault.

Reasoning that perhaps I just need to get further into the game, and that the magic of immersive nostalgia probably lies deeper, I press on. What am I supposed to do again? I'm west of the house, so I must have to go east.

I type:

```
east
The door is boarded and you can't remove the
boards.
```

I don't remember this being so complicated.

```
go around house
North of House
You are facing the north side of a white house.
There is no door here, and all the windows are
boarded up. To the north a narrow path winds through
the trees.
```

I lean back and stare at the glowing text.

I feel nothing.

Whatever spark of magic and thrill of adventure this game once held has faded with time. Have modern graphics spoiled me? Has instant gratification ruined my imagination? Or is it something else?

"It's lunchtime," Sarah sings. She hands me a burger on a plate. "What are you playing?"

"It's this old game I used to play when I was a kid — *Zork*."

Sarah hands me a paper towel. "Is it any good?"

I glance at the glowing words on the screen one last time, then I close my laptop.

"It used to be the world to me."

Notes

Introduction

The quote from the *Oxford English Dictionary* (OED) is paraphrased from the 3rd edition (2010).

The quote from Mihaly Robert Csikszentmihalyi is from his book *Flow: The Psychology of Optimal Experience* (1990).

Chapter 0

The lines of quoted game narrative are from *Zork I* (release date: 1980).

Chapter 5

The game referenced is *Warhammer Online: Age of Reckoning* (release date: 2008).

Chapter 6

The game referenced is *Second Life* (release date: 2003).

Chapter 7

The messaging and social platform quoted is Tapestries MUCK (release date: 1991).

Chapter 10

The quoted lines of dialogue are from the animated television series *Beetlejuice* (1989–1991).

Chapter 26

The lines of quoted game narrative are from *Zork I* (release date: 1980).

Acknowledgements

I would like to first thank my loving partner, Sarah Jane Forbes, who found it difficult to digest sections of this memoir, yet relentlessly supported me anyhow. Also, much love to the rest of my family, with special thanks to my siblings Lana Irwin, Jay Maylott, and Scott Stronghill, for graciously accepting that you weren't included in this book (until now).

Thank you to my initial readers, but especially August Dexter, Jessica St-Pierre, and Madison Bird. I owe you a debt for being my star readers, my first cheerleaders, and my voice of reason. You read (and reread) this memoir in its rawest form, and I hope the finished product lives up to your expectations.

Kris Lafavor, my best friend of many years has my thanks for allowing me to remember him the way I wanted in these pages, even if he would rather forget, along with all the others who allowed me to use their names and likenesses without pseudonyms — you're very brave.

To Chelene Knight, my agent and the best partner I could have hoped for to launch a book into the world. Thank you for taking a chance on me, for providing emotional and editing support, and for employing your many considerable talents to prepare and comfort me in my journey through this crazy publishing industry. As you say, more great things are on the horizon. Thank you also to Amanda Orozco, for accepting the passed torch and helping to see this book across the finish line. I look forward to our next adventure. And much thanks to the others behind the scenes at Transatlantic.

This book could not have been realized without the enthusiastic vision of my editor, Jen Sookfong Lee, who I swear can read my mind. Thank you also to Rachel Ironstone who copy-edited this book, your warmth and wit made this last edit a breeze. You have both contributed so much to this project, protected me from myself, and worked tirelessly to make me look good. My appreciation also to the rest of the ECW Press team, especially Shannon Parr, Michela Prefontaine, Victoria Cozza, and Jessica Albert.

Thank you once more to Marci Bowers, for doing the "impossible."

And last, thank you to all my online friends and lovers who have helped shape the woman behind this memoir. This book is proof you have remained with me long after I logged out.

About the Author

Paige Maylott is a Hamilton-based writer, gamer, and explorer of virtual worlds. She is a 2021 Hamilton Arts & Letters Award winner for Creative Non-Fiction, and a recipient of the 2022 Canada Council for the Arts grant.

This book is also available as a Global Certified Accessible™ (GCA) ebook. ECW Press's ebooks are screen reader friendly and are built to meet the needs of those who are unable to read standard print due to blindness, low vision, dyslexia, or a physical disability.

Get the ebook free!*
*proof of purchase required

At ECW Press, we want you to enjoy our books in whatever format you like. If you've bought a print copy just send an email to ebook@ecwpress.com and include:

- the book title
- the name of the store where you purchased it
- a screenshot or picture of your order/receipt number and your name
- your preference of file type: PDF (for desktop reading), ePub (for a phone/tablet, Kobo, or Nook), mobi (for Kindle)

A real person will respond to your email with your ebook attached. Please note this offer is only for copies bought for personal use and does not apply to school or library copies.

Thank you for supporting an independently owned Canadian publisher with your purchase!